Medals and Ribbons of The United States Air Force
A Complete Guide

Dedicated to our Air Force veterans who served loyally and with valor in the Aeronautical Division of the Army Signal Corps, the Army Air Service, the Army Air Corps, the Army Air Force and

The United States Air Force
and to their marvelous families who supported them.

By
Colonel Frank C. Foster
USA (Ret.)
First Edition

Library of Congress Catalog Card Number - 2013904144
Hardcover Edition ISBN - 978-1-884452-60-4
Softcover Edition ISBN - 978-1-884452-55-0

Copyright 2016 by MOA Press

All rights reserved. No part of this publication may be reproduced, stored in retrieval systems or transmitted by any means, electronic, mechanical or by photocopying, recording or by any information storage and retrieval system without permission from the publishers, except for the inclusion of brief quotations in a review.

Press

Published by:
MOA Press (Medals of America Press)
114 Southchase Blvd.
Fountain Inn, SC 29644-9019
Telephone: (800) 308-0849
WWW.MOAPRESS.COM

2015.01.06

About The Author

Col. Frank C. Foster (USA, Ret.), grew up in Greenville, South Carolina and earned his BS from The Citadel, MBA from the University of Georgia and is a graduate of the Army's Command and General Staff College and Army War College. He saw service as a Battery Commander in Germany and served in Vietnam with U.S. Army Republic of Vietnam (USARV) General Staff and with the 173rd Airborne Brigade. In the Adjutant General's Corps, he served as the Adjutant General of the Central Army Group, the 4th Infantry Division and was the Commandant and Chief of the Army's Adjutant General's Corps from 1986 to 1990 during which time he activated the Adjutant General Corps Regiment. His military service provided him a first hand understanding of the Armed Forces Awards System. He currently operates Medals of America Press and is the author of *United States Army Medals, Badges and Insignia*, co-author of *The Military Medals of the United States* and *The Decorations and Medals of the Republic of Vietnam*. He and his wife Linda, who was decorated with the Army Commander's Medal for service to the Army, live in Greenville, South Carolina.

Colonel Frank Foster

Acknowledgements

Authors, Consultants and Reviewers without which this book would not have been written:

Mr. Lawrence H. Borts for splendid editing and suggestions. Much of this work is attributed to his years of research which earned him the title; "Dean of American Ribbons". Co-author, *Military Medals of the United States*.

Mr. Peter Morgan for loans of anything I needed and reviewing the text. **Mr. Jim Thompson** for blazing the way with his two outstanding books on Marine Corps and Navy military awards and insignia.

Lieut. Colonel Anthony "Tony" Aldebol, USAF Ret. for his leadership and vision in writing *Decorations, Medals, Ribbons, Badges and Insignia of the United States Air Force* as the first real book on Air Force awards.

Institute of Heraldry, United States Army: This talented staff have provided material on awards over the past years: **Colonel Charles V. Mugno** - Director, The Institute of Heraldry, who is always there to help.

Ms. Denise Harris - U.S. Air Force Awards Branch.

Mr. John Sylvester - Co-author of *The Decorations and Medals of the Republic of Vietnam*.

Medals of America, Inc. For their willingness to provide any help requested: Mrs. Linda Foster; Lee Foster, Ms. Buz Buswell and Mrs. Lois Owens.

Joint Staff/Pentagon Cdr. Jerry Mahar, (Retired), DOD Awards.

Design and format : Mr. Kirk Stotzer, Art Director, Medals of America, especially for the Cover design.

Mr. Augusto Meneses for his fine design and graphic work in laying out the book.

Dr. Steve Hines for advice and guidance. **Mrs. Terri Hines** for her techinical assistance in getting the the book on all the different productions platforms.

Mr. Steve Russ for much of the beautiful medal photography.

Mr. Carl E. Bailey, UASF Organizational History Branch, AFHRA/RSO, Maxwell AFB, AL.

Table of Contents

Introduction iv

History of United States Air Force Military Medals 1
Types of Military Medals, Ribbons and Devices 26
How to Determine a Veteran's Military Medals, Ribbons and Devices 28
Displays of Air Force Veteran's Medals, World War II to Present 32
Issue of U.S. Medals to Veterans, Retirees, and Their Families 40
Wear of Decorations, Medals and Insignia by Active Duty, National Guard and Reserve Personnel 42
Wear of Medals and the Uniform by Veterans, Retirees and Former Service Members 50

Visual History of AAF and USAF Ribbon Awards, Order of Precedence and Attachments 53
Current USAF Ribbons, Order of Precedence and Devices 57

Air Force Decorations, Medals, Ribbons and Unit Awards in Order of Precedence since 1914 ... 68
Foreign Decorations often awarded to Air Force Personnel 162
United Nations Medals authorized Air Force (USAF) Personnel 171
NATO Medals authorized Air Force (USAF) Personnel 174
Foreign Campaign Medals Commonly Awarded 176

Commemorative Medals 182
Bibliography 184
Institute of Heraldry 190

Introduction

The first memory I have of military awards was wearing my father's World War II ribbons to kindergarten. I was so proud to do this in front of all the other little boys and girls.

In the early 70s I decided to try and obtain all of my father's World War II medals and present them to him in a framed case for Christmas. I was taken back by how difficult it was to obtain the information and the actual medals. I then began to understand and learn that none of the World War II veterans received their service medals at the end of the conflict. During the war only the higher decorations and Purple Hearts were made due to brass being reserved for munitions. Returning veterans were issued ribbon bars to represent their service medals. In fact a number of service and campaign medals were not struck or even designed until after the war. In the years following the war the government did make medals available if veterans requested them but it was a bureaucratic, difficult and time-consuming process that veterans busy building a career and families had little time to pursue. That is why displays of World War II or Korean veteran's military medals were seldom seen.

As I worked my way through the laborious process of acquiring my father's medals, the one bright spot was the French government. A simple request to the French military for a French Croix de Guerre awarded my father received a rapid response complete with a page-long handwritten letter from a French general thanking my father and all of his fellow servicemen for what they had done for France. It was a very touching letter and it began to impress upon me the significance and meaning of military medals to veterans.

After almost a year, I was finally able to identify, acquire and mount my father's medals in a display case. It was the best Christmas present that I ever gave him. When he opened it there was a very quiet moment and then he stood up and walked over to the most prominent picture in the den, took it down, and hung up his medals.

Throughout the holiday festivities all of his World War II friends who came to visit spent time looking at his medals and then came to me requesting that I get their medals for them and mount them for display.

On the long ride back home my wife and I began to discuss the emotional impact and the significance of seeing dad's fellow veterans all express a real desire to have the medals they had earned so many years ago. That led me into a lifelong study of United States military awards, their criteria, their symbolism and how they should be displayed to honor the veteran who earned them and the families who supported them during their service.

So let's start at the beginning and follow the history of the United States Air Force medals and ribbons. While the real history of military awards begin in Rome our Air Force awards history begin with the Army Air Service support of the Mexican Border Campaign in 1916 and continues on to fulfilling its worldwide missions in the 21st century. Of the millions of American citizens who have served in the Air Force, this book tells the story of the honors they earned, the skills they developed and the military symbols that honored them.

The book is not only for veterans of World War II, Korea, Vietnam, the Gulf War, Kosovo, the Liberation of Iraq, Afghanistan and dozens of other skirmishes and expeditions, but also for veterans' families. It is probably more important for an Airman's family to have this book and gain an appreciation for the dedication and skill that goes into earning these awards.

Finally, as hard as we try, we know there will be mistakes in this book. We therefore invite all readers to send their comments, suggestions and corrections in care of the publisher. Thank you for using this book; in doing so you honor the memory of those great Americans, our veterans.

Frank Foster,
Greenville, South Carolina

Air Force Military Awards

Roman Centurion with Eagle Standard

The History of Military Awards can be traced back to the ancient Egyptians and the Greeks. But the Roman Legions were the first to have an organized award system honoring soldiers for bravery and service. Once recognized the Roman soldiers wore these decorations in battle, in parades and displayed them in their homes after their military service. If an entire Roman legion was cited for valor a decoration was added to the Legion's eagle standard.

More than 2,000 years ago the Greek historian Polybius wrote: "If there was any fight, and some soldiers distinguish themselves by bravery, the legion commander would bring his troops together and call forward those to be decorated. The Roman commander would call out the merits, deeds and heroic actions for which the Roman soldier was to be decorated and present the legionnaire with a necklace, armbands or set of disks. During the ceremony the commander would often tie the item to Legionnaires armor." (Just as today's commander pins a military medal on the chest of a soldier.)

Torques

Armillae

Phalerae

During the time of the Roman Empire, the Roman army established a series of decorations for military bravery. The most common decoration for bravery was a golden circle necklet called a Torques. Torques were worn around the necks of Celtic Warriors, and their award originally represented the defeat of an enemy in single combat. Over time the Torques became an award for bravery. A second type of valor award for all ranks were embossed or plain armbands called Armillae. Another highly coveted award was an embossed disc called a Phalerae which were sometimes awarded in sets and worn on a leather harness over the legionnaire's armor. These discs were presented in bronze, silver and gold and there was no limit to the number a soldier could be awarded.

Above these three awards were various crowns such as the Corona Aurea (Golden Crown) presented to Centurions for victorious personal combat and the Corona Vallaris (Fortification) crown awarded to the first legionaries or centurion over the walls of an enemy fortification. A very high honor was the Corona Civia, a crown of Oak leaves for saving the life of a fellow Roman citizen during battle. Eventually, the Corona Civia allowed recipients to serve as Senators in the Roman Senate. The one distinction between Roman army awards and today is the Romans only decorated living soldiers. There were no posthumous honors for the fallen.

The symbols from the Roman standard pictured can be seen in the decorations and awards of Napoleon, United States Army insignia as early as 1812 and the Third Reich to name a few. So as we begin the history of United States decorations and awards it is clear our early designs of the eagle, lightning, victory wreaths of laurel and oak came from ancient Roman Legions.

After the Roman Empire the first major medal that was not an order of chivalry but a recognition of merit for all was established in 1802 when Napoleon Bonaparte created the Legion of Honor (Légion d'Honneur). Napoleon awarded it on the basis of bravery or merit to both soldiers and civilians of any rank or profession.

Knight medal of the French Legion of Honour

The Beginnings of our awards system:
Revolutionary War 1775-1782.

"Few inventions could be more happily calculated to diffuse the knowledge and preserve the memory of illustrious characters and splendid events, than medals."
Colonel David Humphreys, Mount Vernon, Nov. 1787

These words written in 1787 expressed the Continental Congress feelings in March 1776 when they established the tradition of awarding medals as the highest distinction of national appreciation for our military heroes.

George Washington's success in driving the British from Boston in 1776, General Horatio Gates's victory at Saratoga in 1777, the storming of the British Forts at Stony Point and Paulus Hook in 1779, and General Greene's Southern victories in 1781 all led to the final British surrender at Yorktown in 1781. These were great milestones in the United States' War of Independence. The American people and Congress were proud of their heroes and wished to bestow a sign of national recognition especially upon the leaders who distinguished themselves in battle.

As a result, Congress voted to award gold medals to outstanding military leaders. The first medal honored General Washington and similar medals were bestowed upon other victors such as General Gates and Captain John Paul Jones for his naval victory over the *H.M.S. Serapis* in 1779.

Benjamin Franklin, the U.S. Ambassador to France at the time, had access to the best of the French Royal engravers. It was only natural for America to turn to France for help in the production of our first military medals. Under Franklin's leadership the Chief Engraver of the Paris

General Horatio Gates wearing his medal.

Mint produced the first medal in 1781. However, following Franklin's departure from France, the development of the other medals was extremely slow until Col. David Humphreys and, later, Thomas Jefferson became involved. It was not until March 1790, that President Washington received his gold and silver medals approved by Congress more than 10 years earlier.

Unlike present practice, these large table top presentation medals were not designed to be worn on the military uniform. Evidently many thought otherwise since General Gates' portrait shows his medal hanging from a neck ribbon. It is interesting to note that Thomas Jefferson wanted to see that these medals, of which he was very proud, were known and preserved throughout the world. He intended to present sets of these medals to heads of state, foreign dignitaries and every college in the United States. Jefferson saw medals as the best way to preserve the memory, valor and distinction of America's soldiers and sailors (many of these early commemorative medallions are still being struck and offered for sale by the U.S. Mint).

Gold medal struck to honor George Washington for his service in driving the British from Boston in 1776.

Medals of America 3

The "Andre" medal broke the custom of restricting the award of medals to successful senior officers and is doubly unique in that it was designed to wear around the neck. The medal was presented by Congress in 1780 to the three enlisted men who captured British Major John Andre with the plans of the West Point fortifications in his boot. Patriots John Paulding, Isaac Van Wart and David Williams were the recipients of the Andre medal and as time passed were additionally authorized a lifetime pension. Major Andre, the captured British officer, was hung as a spy.

In August 1782, George Washington established the Badge of Military Merit, the first U.S. decoration which had general application to all enlisted men and one that he hoped would inaugurate a permanent awards system. At the same time, he expressed his fundamental awards philosophy when he issued an order from his headquarters at Newburgh, New York:

"Andre" Medal

Patriots John Paulding, Isaac Van Wart and David Williams were the recipients of the Andre medal

"The General, ever desirous to cherish a virtuous ambition in his soldiers, as well as to foster and encourage every species of military merit, directs that, whenever any singularly meritorious action is performed, the author of it shall be permitted to wear on his facings, over his left breast, the figure of a heart in purple cloth or silk, edged with narrow lace or binding. Not only instances of unusual gallantry, but also of extraordinary fidelity, and essential service in any way, shall meet with a due reward...the road to glory in a patriot army and a free country is thus opened to all. This order is also to have retrospect to the earliest days of the war, and to be considered a permanent one." No decoration had been established which honored the private soldier with a reward for special merit. The wording of the order is worth careful study. The object was "to cherish a virtuous ambition" and "to foster and encourage every species of military merit." Note also that Washington appreciated that every kind of service was important by proposing to reward, "not only instances of unusual gallantry, but also of extraordinary fidelity and essential service in any way." And finally, the wonderfully democratic sentence, "the road to glory in a patriotic army and free country is thus opened to all."

Coming as it did, almost a year after Cornwallis' surrender at Yorktown, the message was never given widespread distribution and, as a result, there were only three known recipients of this badge, Sergeants Elijah Churchill, William Brown and Daniel Bissell. Unfortunately, after the Revolution the award fell into disuse and disappeared for 150 years.

Badge of Military Merit

Sergeants Elijah Churchill, William Brown and Daniel Bissell are the only known recipients.

However, it did not die, primarily due to the efforts of the Army's then Chief of Staff, General Douglas MacArthur, (and, by no accident, one of its first recipients). On the 200th anniversary of Washington's birth, February 22, 1932, the War Department announced that:

"By order of the President of the United States, the Purple Heart, established by Gen. George Washington at Newburgh, New York ....is hereby revived out of respect to his memory and military achievements."

1932 Purple Heart

Washington's "figure of a heart in purple" was retained as the medal's central theme and embellished with Washington's likeness and his coat of arms. The words "For Military Merit" appear on the reverse as a respectful reference to its worthy predecessor.

Toward the end of the war or immediately after, General Washington also authorized a stripe to be sewn on the sleeve of outstanding noncommissioned officers to honor three years of exemplary service or those with six years wore two stripes. These exemplary service or good conduct stripes disappeared after the Revolutionary War along with the original Badge of Military Merit.

While Congress would not approve medals for the Revolutionary soldiers, the Continental Army officers banded together with their French counterparts and created the Order of the Cincinnati with a very distinctive medal to wear. In the years after the revolution, membership grew and members served in all the major offices of the United States Government as well as many state and local governments. Some, including Thomas Jefferson, were alarmed at the apparent creation of an elite order that excluded enlisted men and in most cases militia officers. However over time, the order has evolved into a patriotic society and its first members set the tone by establishing commemorative decorations or medals when none were authorized by Congress.

During this first thirty-plus years of our new nation, regular and volunteer Army and Navy Commanders were honored for their service with large medallions authorized by Congress as described earlier or with special commemorative swords often paid for by public subscription from a patriotic and grateful community. Enlisted soldiers and sailors were rewarded in various monetary ways with naval prize money or land grants for soldiers in the newly acquired territories.

Order of the Cincinnati

Peter Gansevoort was a Colonel in the Continental Army during the American Revolutionary War. Shown here wearing his Society of Cincinnati medal.

The Mexican War (1844-1848)

During the Mexican War (1844 – 1848) the Federal Government still showed a great reluctance to provide military medals for soldiers and sailors. The individual states, however, showed no such reluctance. For example, South Carolina struck 1000 sterling silver medal for members of the Palmetto Regiment who served during the Mexican War. Each large silver medal was engraved with the name of the soldier and individually presented. Some individual cities such as Charleston commissioned special gold medals for the local company that served in the Mexican war. The state medal such as the South Carolina example shown was designed to display on bookshelves or tabletops. Most veterans actually wore them as watch fobs or drilled a small hole in the medal so they could hang it from their coat lapel.

After the Mexican War regular Army officers established the Aztec Club of 1847 and commissioned a distinctive medal for their military uniform. Their influence was such that the Congress later authorized the officers to wear the Aztec Club medal on their uniforms. This began a tradition of officers forming military societies that commission special medals for overseas combat service such as the China Relief campaign and the Philippine Insurrection. Congress later approved these society medals for wear on the uniform.

The Army did establish a certificate of merit in 1847 for soldiers who distinguished themselves in combat during the Mexican war. However, this was not translated into a medal until 1905. With the exception of Congressionally awarded medals, Congress rejected the use of military decorations, orders and medals as being in the image of royalty and aristocracy. It was an attitude that was to last more than 50 years until the Army and Navy began to reflect the Republic's rise as a world power at the beginning of the 20th century. The development of America's pyramid of military honors reflects the nation's ascendancy as a world power beginning with the the Spanish-American War, through its significant role in World War I and finally emerging as leader of the Free World in World War II.

Col. Charles C. Warren wearing the Aztex Club and other Society Medals.

Aztec Club of 1847, the Aztec Club medal and insignia are copyrighted by the Aztec Club of 1847.

South Carolina struck 1000 sterling silver medals for members of the Palmetto Regiment who served during the Mexican War.

Both sides uses ballons for observation in the Civil War.

Civil War (1861-1865)

The Civil War saw the first United States military decorations. The Navy Medal of Honor arose from a public resolution signed into law by President Lincoln on December 21, 1861. It authorized the preparation of 200 Medals of Honor to promote the efficiency of the Navy. It was followed by a joint resolution of Congress on the same day that approved the design and defined the requirement eligibility of the potential recipients. The Army Medal of Honor was established by a joint resolution of Congress on July 12, 1862 with an effective date of April 15, 1861. The Medal of Honor was originally only to be presented to enlisted men for heroic service in the United States Army. However, as the war continued the awarding of a Medal of Honor was extended to include Army officers.

Union Officers began creating unit medals as early as 1862 when the officers of General Kearny's division ordered a gold medal after the General's death to commemorate serving under his command. The next Division commander ordered a bronze cross for award to enlisted men of the division. Other private medals were the Gilmore Medal struck by General Gilmore for his troops around Charleston, South Carolina and the Butler Medal for colored troops in the Battle of Newmarket Heights in 1864. Most of these were paid for by the commanders and had limited use.

Gilmore Medal

Civil War Medals of Honor

Butler Medal for Newmarket Heights

Following the Civil War, there was an absolute explosion of veterans commemorative medals, reunion medals and badges. The Grand Army of the Republic reunion medals began to so closely resemble the Medal of Honor that Congress was eventually forced to change the Medal of Honor and to patent its new design.

Grand Army of the Republic Reunion Medal.

In 1905, President Theodore Roosevelt authorized campaign medals retroactive to the Civil War. The Civil War Campaign Medal (Army) was issued for any federal army service between April 15, 1861 and April 9, 1865 (with extended service in the state of Texas through August 20, 1866). The Navy and Marine Corps were also authorized Civil War Campaign Medals, with each service having a different design on the reverse of the medal. The original Army campaign medal had a red, white and blue ribbon which was changed in 1913 to match the blue-and-gray ribbon design of the Navy and Marine Corps Civil War Medal.

Army Civil War Medal

Military Society Medals (1865-1913)

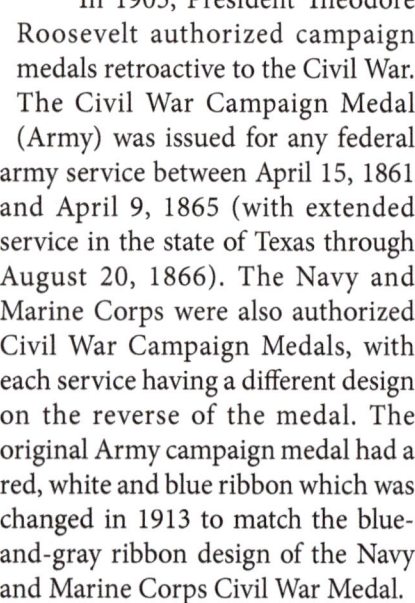

"Military Order of the Dragon"

Up until the Spanish American War no Army or Navy in the world was so little decorated as the United States. The simplicity of uniforms were set off by no medals or ribbons. After the Civil War, Congress under pressure from veteran's organizations permitted officers and enlisted men to wear their Corps and Division badge. For nearly twenty years, the Medal of Honor remained the sole American military award of any kind. Although the Navy had authorized the first Good Conduct Badge in 1869, clearly the officers and enlisted personnel of the Army and Navy wanted to have medals like their counterparts around the world. Their solution was to have Congress approve the wearing of the military society medals such as The Aztec Club which consisted of officers who served in Mexico in 1847; the Grand Army of the Republic; the Loyal Legion; Army and Navy Union of the United States of America; and the Imperial Order of the Dragon, commemorating the China Relief Expedition were just a few of them. The professional officer corps wanted an awards system to recognize service, and if the government was not going to create one, they would. The post civil war Congress contained a large number of veterans so approval to wear these society medals on uniforms was not difficult. The demand for a national military awards system was present and support slowly gained ground. The election of President Theodore Roosevelt opened the flood gates.

Spanish American War (1898 -1899)

It was not until the turn of the 20th Century that a host of medals were authorized to commemorate the events surrounding the Spanish-American War. This was future President Theodore Roosevelt's "Bully Little War" that produced seven distinct medals for only four months of military action. Supply had finally caught up with demand.

Manila Bay ("Dewey") Medal

The first of these was the medal to commemorate the victory of the naval forces under the command of Commodore Dewey over the Spanish fleet at Manila Bay. This award was notable as it was the first such medal in U.S. history to be awarded to all officers and enlisted personnel present during a specific military expedition. It is also one of the handsomest American medals ever designed.

When Roosevelt, an ardent supporter of the military, ultimately reached the White House, he took it upon himself to legislate for the creation of medals to honor all those who had served in America's previous conflicts. Thus, by 1908 the U.S. had authorized campaign medals, some retroactive, for the Civil War, Indian Wars, War with Spain, Philippine Insurrection and China Relief Expedition of 1900-01. While the Army, Navy and Marines used the same ribbons, different medals were struck. Concurrently the custom of wearing service ribbons on the tunic was adopted (using different orders of precedence for each service). Thus, the Armed Services managed to establish a certain principle of independence in the creation and wearing of awards that is virtually unchanged today.

Lieutenant Thomas E. Selfridge, America's first military pilot died in 1908 crash of a Wright Flyer III.

The modern-day Air Force was created in August 1907 when the Aeronautical Division was formed within the U.S. Army Signal Corps. The Wright brothers had only made their first flight in 1903 so the initial focus of the Aeronautical Division was on balloons and dirigibles. Both the Union and Confederate armies used balloons for observation during the Civil War. The Army continued to use balloons with mixed success during the Spanish-American War. But the focus on balloons changed when Wright brothers delivered the young Aeronautical Division's first airplane in 1909 and a handful of Army airmen began testing different aircraft and formed the first Aero Squadron as an operational unit in late 1913. Lieutenant Thomas E. Selfridge became America's first military pilot but was unfortunately killed in an aircraft crash a few months later at Fort Meyers, Virginia.

By 1914, as a result of congressional prodding, the Army expanded its aviation efforts by establishing an Aviation Section in the Signal Corps. Within two years the 1st Aero Squadron became the first American operational unit flying in support of General Pershing Mexican border Campaign against Pancho Villa.

The Mexican Expedition (1916 - 1917) took place just prior to World War I. Once again, civil disobedience, this time in the form of large-scale military activities by well-armed revolutionaries, caused the United States to mount a Punitive Expedition into Mexico to bring peace to the region. In the aftermath of the conflict, the Army Mexican Service Medal was awarded to approximately 15,000 soldiers. For those Army members who had been cited for gallantry in combat, the Citation Star was retroactively authorized in 1918 as a device to the Mexican Service Medal. Early versions of the Campaign medals of this period were issued with serial numbers stamped on the bottom rim of the medal or engraved on the reverse side with the date of service. This practice was discontinued on

Lt. C.G. Chapman preparing for scouting mission at Casas Grandes, 1916.

Medals of America 9

Lt. Luke, American ace with his French Spad

World War I (1917-1918)

World War I brought on a major expansion of military aviation. When the United States entered the war in April 1917 European aircraft were far superior to anything developed by the American aviation industry and available to the Army Air Service.

The United States could not match the technological progress of the European aircraft. In a major effort to enhance and strengthen the nation's aviation effort, President Woodrow Wilson ordered the establishment of the Army Air Service and assigned it directly under the War Department in May 1918. By the end of World War I the Army Air Service had expanded to almost 20,000 officers and 180,000 enlisted men. At home the American aircraft industry had gone into overdrive and produced almost 12,000 aircraft with nearly all being trainers. When the war ended most air service personnel were released and airplanes sold as surplus.

During combat in World War I the majority of American pilots flew French-built aircraft, and their initial service was often in French units. But by 1918, the Army Air Service was a major part of the American Expeditionary Forces (AEF). Under the leadership of Brigadier General Billy Mitchell the AEF aero squadrons and fighter groups developed into a highly competent force. While World War I was basically a ground and sea war, it was clear to future-thinking leaders that the air service was going to become extremely important in both offensive and defensive operations.

At the time of the U.S. entry into World War I in the spring of 1917, the Medal of Honor, Certificate of Merit and Navy/Marine Corps Good Conduct Medals still represented America's entire inventory of personal decorations. This presented the dangers that the Medal of Honor might be cheapened by being awarded too often and that other deeds of valor might go unrecognized. By 1918, popular sentiment forced the authorization of two new awards, the Army's Distinguished Service Cross and Distinguished Service Medal, created by Executive Order in 1918. In the same year, the traditional U.S. refusal to permit the armed forces to accept foreign decorations was rescinded, allowing military personnel to receive awards from grateful Allied governments.

Certificate of Merit Medal

Captain Eddie Rickenbacker with fellow pilots

The issuance of the World War I Victory Medal established another precedent: wearing clasps with the names of individual battles on the suspension ribbon of a general campaign medal. This was an ongoing practice since the 19th Century in many countries, most notably Britain and France. When the ribbon bar alone was worn, each clasp was represented by a small (3/16" diameter) bronze star. Fourteen such clasps were adopted along with five clasps to denote service in specific countries. However, the latter were issued only if no campaign clasp was earned. Only one service clasp could be issued to any individual and they were not represented by a small bronze star on the ribbon bar.

During this period, the Army introduced the Citation Star which was established by Congress on July 9, 1918. This award, a 3/16" diameter silver star device, was originally authorized to be worn on the World War I Victory Medal to denote those who had been cited for extreme heroism or valor. The device, which evolved into the Silver Star Medal in 1932, was soon made retroactive as an attachment to the Army service medals for the Civil War, Indian, Spanish, China and Mexican campaigns. The Citation Star was strictly a U.S. Army device. Bronze oak leaf clusters were also introduced to indicate a second award of the Medal of Honor or other decoration in lieu of a second medal.

World War I Commemorative Medals

Upon the return of troops to the United States after World War I, many county, state and federal organizations rushed to produce Commemorative medals to honor their local sons. The quality of medal design and strike was quite good, and the local commemorative medals were highly prized by veterans and their families. Almost a thousand different WWI Commemorative Medals were presented to their returning veterans by city, county, state and fraternal organizations A handsome example is South Carolina's Greenville County medal shown below.

South Carolina's Greenville County WWII Commemorative Medal

World War I Victory Medal with Campaign Clasps

With Silver Citation Star

After the war the Army reorganization act of 1920 made the Air Service a combat arm of the Army. The Air Service was renamed the Air Corps in July 1926. During the period of the 1920s and 30s the Army Air Corps remained a small organization due to the limited funding.

Brig. Gen. Billy Mitchell wearing U.S. and foreign medals authorized in WW I, note Victory Medal with multiple clasp.

Lt. Erickson, Army Air Force recieves the Distinguished Flying Cross

World War II

On September 8, 1939, in response to the growing threat of involvement in World War II, President Franklin Roosevelt proclaimed a National Emergency in order to increase the size of U.S. military forces. For the first time, a peacetime service award, the American Defense Service Medal, was authorized for wear by those personnel who served during this period of National Emergency prior to the attack on Pearl Harbor on December 7, 1941.

With the beginning of World War II in Europe, the Army Air Corps began to expand from a base of less than 2,000 aircraft. By the summer of 1941 the War Department established the Army Air Force and made it the co-equal of the Army Ground Forces. The Air Corps retained its designation as a combat arm of the Army along with its sister combat arms; the infantry, artillery, armor and combat engineers. From the very small base at the beginning of World War II, the Army Air Force expanded to nearly 80,000 aircraft and almost 2 1/2 million soldiers. Army Air Force units covered the wide range of training, transportation, fighter and attack aircraft, reconnaissance aircraft and light, medium and heavy bombers. Army Air Force units conducted air operations from the shores of the United States to the Southwest Pacific, North Africa and Europe.

Flight students Jim Leach (left) and Jack Hoover beside a BT-13 basic trainer. (U.S. Air Force photo)

12 Decorations, Medals, and Ribbons of the United States Air Force

World War II Campaign Areas

American Defense Service Medal | Women's Army Corps Service Medal | American Campaign Medal | Asiatic Pacific Campaign Medal | European African Middle Eastern Campaign Medal | WW II Victory Medal

With America's participation in World War II, there was a significant increase in both personal decorations and campaign medals. Since U.S. forces were serving all over the world, a campaign medal was designed for each major (and carefully defined) area. The three medals for the American, Asiatic-Pacific and European-African-Middle Eastern Campaigns encompassed the globe. However, the World War I practice of using campaign bars was discarded in favor of 3/16" bronze stars that could denote each designated military campaign from a major invasion to a submarine war patrol.

World War II also introduced the first (and only!) service medal unique to female military personnel. Known as the Women's Army Corps Service Medal, it was authorized for service in both the WACs and its predecessor, the Women's Army Auxiliary Corps which was formed in 1943. There were over 40,000 WACs in the AAF during WW II. In 1942 the Army also started a flight program to qualify women pilots for the delivery of aircraft from production facilities to Army Air Force airfields. These female pilots of the Army were originally designated Women Auxiliary Ferrying Squadron or (WAFS) but by 1943 women's auxiliary were designated Women's Air Force Service Pilots (WASP). The units were disbanded in 1944 and were considered civilians until designated veteran status by Congress in 1978.

The war also saw the large scale award of foreign medals and decorations to American servicemen. The Philippine Government, for one, authorized awards to commemorate the Defense and Liberation of their island country. The first foreign award designed strictly for units, the Philippine Presidential Unit Citation, patterned after a similar American award, was also approved for wear by American forces. In the European Theater, France and Belgium made many presentations of their War Crosses (Croix de Guerre) to U.S. military personnel.

The end of World War II saw the introduction of two counterparts of previous World War I awards, the Victory and Occupation Medals. This time, no bars or clasps were authorized for the Victory Medal, but bars were issued with the Occupation Medal to denote the recipient's area of service.

During World War II generally only decorations such as the Distinguished Service Cross, Silver Star, Distinguished Flying Cross and Purple Heart were manufactured. Brass was restricted to the manufacture of munitions so campaign medals were mainly issued as ribbon bars. In fact most of the campaign medals were unavailable to veterans until several years after the war. By then many service personnel had been discharged from the Armed Forces and returned to civilian life. Unless the veteran went through the process of writing the government and asked for their medals, many World War II veterans never received their actual campaign medals. In fact a number World War II awards were not approved until several years after the war.

Army and Navy Occupation Medal

The World War II Occupation Medals were not approved until mid-1946 by which time many of the personnel authorized such awards had left the Armed Forces. The Prisoner of War Medal and the Philippine Independence Medal are other examples of medals approved after the war.

By 1945 the sheer number and flying abilities of the Army Air Force units controlled the skies over both Germany and Japan. While the Army Air Force did not win the war by itself, its aggressive combat role resulted in levels of casualties among airmen only exceeded by the Army infantry. The delivery of the atomic bombs on Hiroshima and Nagasaki in August 1945 in all probability saved tens of thousands of American casualties that would have occurred with the invasion of the Japanese homeland.

Philippine Defense Medal   Philippine Liberation Medal

While this book is about the decorations and awards earned by the men and women of the U.S. Air Force very few readers have a feel for the enormous effort our country and airmen put into achieving the great victories of World War II. To have even a small appreciation of the symbolism of World War II medals and the sacrifice it took to earn them we need to look at the magnitude of United States air campaigns.

During World War II more than 276,000 aircraft were manufactured in the U.S. This was not only for Army Air Force, Navy and Marine Corps, but also for allies as such as Britain, Australia, China and Russia. Production numbers for some aircraft were; 15,875 North American P-51 Mustangs, 13,738 Curtiss P-40 Warhawks, 12,731 Boeing B-17 Flying Fortresses (a B-17 carried 2,500 gallons of high octane fuel and a crew of 10 airmen), 10,037 Lockheed P-38 Lightnings, 9,984 North American B-25 Mitchells, 9,584 Bell P-39 Aircobras, and 18,482 Consolidated B-24 Liberators.

Out of over a quarter of a million aircraft, 43,581 aircraft were lost overseas including 22,948 on combat missions (18,418 in Europe) and 20,633 due to non-combat causes overseas. In a single 376 plane raid in August 1943, 60 B-17s were shot down. That was a 16 percent loss rate and in 1942-43, it was statistically impossible for bomber crews to complete the intended 25-mission tour in Europe. Over 40,000 airmen were killed in combat and another 18,000 wounded. From Germany's invasion of Poland in 1939 until Victory over Japan in September 1945 (a period of 2,433 days) America lost an average of 170 planes a day.

In the continental U.S. 14,000 aircraft were lost in training or accidents. There were 52,651 aircraft accidents (6,039 involving fatalities) in 45 months. The U.S. lost 14,903 pilots, aircrew and support personnel plus 13,873 airplanes inside the continental United States and almost 1,000 planes disappeared en route from the U.S. to foreign lands.

Army Air Force Pacific theatre losses were less owing to smaller forces committed and the huge Navy and Marine air effort. But on one B-29 mission against Tokyo in May 1945, 26 Super fortresses, 5.6 percent of the 464 dispatched from the Marianas were shot down.

Training and demand for fighter planes resulted in some pilots entering combat during the early part of the war with less than 3 or 4 hours of stick time in their new fighter planes. The famed 4th Fighter Group commander, Col. Donald Blakeslee, said, "You can learn to fly 51s on the way to the target", when the unit converted from P-47s to P-51s in February 1944.

By 1944, the USAAF had 2.6 million people and nearly 80,000 aircraft of all types operating around the globe. Today the U.S. Air Force employs 327,000 active personnel (plus 170,000 civilians) with 5,500+ manned and perhaps 200 unmanned aircraft or about 12% of the manpower and 7% of the airplanes of the World War II peak. It staggers one today to envision the size, scope, and personal bravery of the airmen who flew 1,000-plane formations and fought major battles five miles above the ground. While the Army Air Force was generous with its Air Medals let there be no doubt they were earned with real blood, sweat and tears.

The B17 Memphis Belle, the first AAF bomber to complete 25 missions in Europe.

Post World War II

The Army Air Force as well as the Army and Navy underwent enormous reductions in size after World War II. Based on the lessons learned about the size and scope of airpower during World War II, the U.S. Army Air Force was redesignated a separate branch of the Armed Forces and renamed the United States Air Force in September 1947. For the first few years the Air Force continued to use Army awards and insignia. In 1950 the Air Force formally adopted its new blue uniform with silver buttons.

President Eisenhower signed a bill an April 1954 establishing the United States Air Force Academy and the first class began in July 1955. The first significant and unique Air Force medal was created in 1958 with the authorization of the Air Force Commendation Medal. In the 1960s the Air Force medal system was authorized and established: the Air Force Cross, the Air Force Distinguished Service Medal, the Airman's Medal, the Combat Readiness Medal, the Air Force Good Conduct Medal and the Air Reserve Forces Meritorious Service Medal.

The Cold War

As the Iron Curtain descended over Europe and the Cold War became a major geographical and political threat, the United States Air Force undertook drastic new roles. One of the most demanding was it's demonstration of major airlift capacity in 1948 to break the Berlin blockade. Concurrently, the establishment and importance of long-range bombers carrying atomic weapons served as a big deterrent to Soviet aggression.

Beginning in 1946, the Cold War lasted more than 40 years with tension and intense competition between the West under the leadership of the United States, and the East led by the Soviet Union and its satellites. From the mid-1940s to the early 1990s, both sides tried to gain advantage using weapons development, military coalitions, espionage, invasions, propaganda and competitive technology, including the famous space race. The Cold War produced massive defense spending on conventional forces and nuclear arms and multiple proxy wars but no actual combat between the USA and USSR. Millions of Americans served in the Armed Forces often in tense and dangerous situations during this period.

In 1998, Congress authorized the Secretary of Defense to award a Cold War Victory Medal to all veterans of the Cold War. However, to date the Secretary of Defense has only authorized a Cold War Recognition Certificate to all members of the armed forces and qualified federal government civilian personnel who served during the Cold War, September 2,1945 to December 26, 1991 .

The Department of Defense has stated that it will not create a Cold War Service Medal nor authorize any commemorative medals made by private vendors for wear on the military uniform. The DOD position is that manufacturing the medal would be too expensive.

Air Force Commendation Medal

Cold War Recognition Certificate

This is a surprising position, since processing and mailing the certificate cost about the same as supplying a medal. However, Commercial Cold War Victory Commemorative Medals are perhaps one of the most popular and frequently purchased military medals today. They are not official nor can they be worn on active duty uniforms but they continue the tradition going back to the Revolution of veterans filling their own needs.

The Army runs the Cold War Recognition Certificate program and Cold War veterans can write to the address below for a certificate. Response can take more than a month. Write:

U.S. Army Human Resources Cmd
Cold War Recognition Program
ATTN: AHRC-PDP-A Dept 480
1600 Spearhead Division Ave.
Fort Knox, Ky 40122-540

Korea (1950-1954)

The North Korean invasion of South Korea in June 1950 saw deployment of the U.S. Air Force as a major deterrent using new jet fighters and long-range bombers to counter the Communist aggression during the bitter three-year fight to reestablish the independence of South Korea. The Korean Conflict, fought under the United Nations banner, saw the creation of two new medals for service. The first was the Korean Service Medal, which continued the practice of using 3/16" bronze stars on the ribbon to denote major campaigns. The second, the National Defense Service

Cold War Victory Commemorative Medal

National Defense Service Medal

Korean Service Medal

UN Korean Service Medal

Medal, was established to recognize the contribution of all military personnel to national defense during a period of armed hostility. Some outstanding units were also awarded the Republic of Korea Presidential Unit Citation and all participants were awarded the United Nations Service Medal.

In the 1950s, the Republic of Korea (ROK) asked the United States Government for approval to present the Korean War Service Medal to the U.S. troops who served in the Korean conflict, but the award was turned down by the U.S. Government. However as the 50th Anniversary of the Korean War approached, veterans groups placed more pressure on their congressional representatives and in 1999 the medal was approved for Korean War veterans. The late approval results in the Korean War Service Medal's order of precedence being after the Kuwait Liberation Medal instead of the normal chronological order for foreign awards.

The Korea Defense Service Medal (KDSM) was instituted in 2003 and made retroactive to 1954. The medal is awarded to members of the Armed Forces who have served in the Republic of Korea or adjacent waters since the Korean War to uphold the armistice between South and North Korea. A service member must have at least thirty consecutive days service in the Korean theater to qualify for the KDSM. The medal is also granted for 60 non-consecutive days of service for reservists on annual training in Korea. All Korean War veterans who served 30 days in Korea after 27 July 1954 are eligible for the Korea Defense Service Medal. The Korea Defense Service Medal is retroactive to the end of the Korean War and is granted for any service performed after July 28, 1954.

Korean Presidential Unit Citation

ROK War Service Medal

Korean Defense Service Medal

In addition to campaign and service medals normally awarded to a veteran of the Korean War, most Services approved the award of the Good Conduct Medal for a period of one year when service was in Korea. During the Korean War, the Air Force, a separate service since 1947, still used many Army awards. As a result, Air Force veterans who earned the Good Conduct Medal during the conflict were awarded the Army Good Conduct Medal.

The period of the Korean War saw the standardization of service ribbons for the Navy and Marine Corps to a smaller size of 3/8 inch high by 1 3/8 inch wide. This had long been the service ribbons size used by the Army and the Air Force. Prior to the standardization the Navy and Marine Corps used ribbons 1/2 inch high by 1 3/8 inches wide.

By the 1960s the Air Force's Strategic Air Command (SAC) had become the major force of the United States defense strategy. The combination of long-range B-52 bombers coupled with the development of intercontinental ballistic missiles such as the Titan and Minuteman were the country's major defensive shield during the Cold War.

Long before the United States sent the 173rd Airborne Brigade to aid the South Vietnamese in 1964, the Air Force had been providing clandestine aircraft support to French forces during their fight in Indochina. By 1965 the Air Force expanded military operations such as Rolling Thunder against selected targets in North Vietnam. While operating under political constraints and an unfriendly liberal press in the United States, the Air Force application of airpower against the North Vietnamese facilities and forces was a major reason the Communists signed a peace treaty in January 1973.

Vietnam (1961-1973)

The first American advisors in the Republic of South Vietnam were awarded the new Armed Forces Expeditionary Medal which was created in 1961 to cover campaigns for which no specific medal was instituted. However, as the U.S. involvement in the Vietnamese conflict grew, a unique award, the Vietnam Service Medal was authorized, thus giving previous Air Force recipients of the Expeditionary Medal the option of which medal to accept. The Government also authorized the acceptance of the Republic of Vietnam Campaign Medal for six months service in-country, or in the surrounding waters or the air after 1960. Towards the end of the war a blanket general order authorized the RVN Gallantry Cross Unit Citation for all military personnel who served in Vietnam.

The most notable change in medal policy occurred during the Vietnam War when the Department of Defense authorized the large scale acceptance of South Vietnamese awards. The South Vietnamese Armed Forces had a comprehensive awards system built to reflect their past as a former French colony. Since a large number of American military advisors and special forces worked with the South Vietnamese Armed Forces for more than 15 years, (many serving multiple tours) numerous medals for valor and service were presented to U.S. personnel. Some of the most awarded were the Vietnamese Cross of Gallantry (for valor), the Civil Actions Medal and the Armed Forces Honor Medal (meritorious service). The last two medals are unusual since they were in two different degrees; first class for officers and second class for enlisted personnel.

National Defense Service Medal | Armed Forces Expeditionary Medal | Vietnam Service Medal | RVN Campaign Medal

All foreign medals awarded to members of the U.S. Armed Forces were either furnished by the foreign government or purchased by the recipient since the United States government does not provide foreign medals to members of the Armed Forces.

The termination of the Vietnamese war and the drawdown of the United States Armed Forces saw the Air Force put a major focus on modernization and worldwide capabilities. Major airlift operations to support Israel during the 1973 Arab-Israeli war demonstrated America's enormous airlift capabilities and commitment to her allies. During the Reagan era with the American defense buildup, the Air Force expanded its structure and training. The USAF supported such special operations as Operation Urgent Fury in Grenada, operation El Dorado Canyon raid on Libya in 1986 and Operation Just Cause, the invasion of Panama in 1989. The amazing abilities of the U.S. Air Force to go anywhere at any time was one of the significate contributors to the collapse of the Soviet Union and the end of the Cold War.

After Vietnam, many new decorations, medals and ribbons came into being as the Department of Defense and the individual Services developed a complete awards structure to reward performance from the newest enlistee to the most senior Joint Staff officer. Some of the awards, such as the Air Force Training Ribbon have no medal but reward the young recruits for successfully completing their transition from civilian to a ready member of the Air Force. Achievement and Commendation Medals provide a powerful means for Air Force commanders to recognize younger individuals for outstanding performance.

Vietnamese Cross of Gallantry (for valor)

Armed Forces Honor Medal

Civil Actions Medal (Foreign Decoration)

RVN Gallantry Cross Unit Citation

Medals of America

USAF Commendation and Achievement Medals

Oman, Bahrain, Qatar and United Arab Emirates. Between January 17, 1991 and November 30, 1995, service members who performed duty "in support of" the Persian Gulf War are eligible to receive the Southwest Asia Service Medal if duty was performed in either Israel, Egypt, Turkey, Syria or Jordan.

The Department of Defense also approved the wear of the Saudi Arabian Medal for the Liberation of Kuwait and later the Department of Defense also authorized the Kuwait Medal for the Liberation of Kuwait.

Liberation Of Kuwait

The end of the Cold War did not mean the end of the Air Force mission of worldwide deterrent. Operation Desert Storm in early 1991 saw the amazing ability of the Air Force to fly halfway around the world and smash the invading forces of Saddam Hussein. The awesome effect of US Air Force air power allowed the rapid liberation of Kuwait and struck awe and shock into the enemies of our country.

The conflict in the Persian Gulf saw the reinstitution of the National Defense Service Medal (this time it also covered the Reserves) and the creation of the Southwest Asia Service Medal for the personnel in Iraq, Kuwait, Saudi Arabia,

Operation Desert Storm

22 Decorations, Medals, and Ribbons of the United States Air Force

National Defense Service Medal

Southwest Asia Service Medal

Saudi Arabian Medal for the Liberation of Kuwait

Kuwait Medal for the Liberation of Kuwait.

With the collapse of the Soviet Union and the ending of the Cold War, the Air Force underwent a complete reorganization in the 1990s to streamline and consolidate its major commands. By 1996, the USAF downsized from more than 600,000 officers and men to 400,000. Although smaller by one third, the Air Force saw its mission stay at a high operational level to meet contingency operations. Units have been maintained in the Persian Gulf area, Turkey and places like Somalia. Special missions to Somalia, Rwanda (Support Hope), Haiti (Uphold Democracy) and the Balkans (Provide Promise) have helped maintain stability and peace. Air Force units made precision strikes to help end a terrible civil war in Bosnia in 1995.

NATO Medals (1998 to Present)

In 1998 the North Atlantic Treaty Organization began authorizing military medals for NATO specific service. The NATO Kosovo Campaign Medal was issued to United States armed forces personnel for participation in the Kosovo operations. For U.S. Forces, the Non-Article 5 Medal for Balkan Service replaced the NATO Kosovo Medal effective 1 January 2003. NATO also created an Article 5 Medal, a Non-Article 5 Medal and a NATO Meritorious Service Medal.

The idea is somewhat similar to the U.S. Joint Service awards which are used to reward joint staff service outside of a service member's normal branch of service (i.e. Army, Navy, Air Force, Marines or Coast Guard). U.S. Forces use service stars to indicate additional awards of the NATO Medal.

For U.S. Forces, the NATO medals authorized for wear include the NATO Medal for Former Yugoslavia, the NATO Medal for Kosovo Service, both of the Article 5 Medals, the Non-Article 5 medals for the Balkans and Afghanistan International Security and Assistance Force (ISAF), The NATO Meritorious Service Medal, the Macedonia NATO Medal and the Non-Article 5 Medal for service in the Global War on Terror. There are now currently ten versions of the NATO Medal.

Former Yugoslavia

Kosovo

NATO Non Article 5 Medal

NATO Article 5 Medal

NATO ISAF Medal

24 Decorations, Medals, and Ribbons of the United States Air Force

National Defense Service Medal | Afghanistan Campaign Medal | Iraq Campaign Medal | Global War on Terrorism Expeditionary Medal | Global War on Terrorism Service Medal

❖ The Global War on Terrorism, The Liberation of Afghanistan and Iraq
Global War on Terror

Beginning in 2001 the Air Force was deployed from Diego Garcia against Taliban positions inside of Afghanistan. In 2003 the Air Force deployed to support the invasion of Iraq and after the defeat of Saddam Hussein's forces established a base at Baghdad International Airport. The Air Force continued operations to support coalition and Iraqi forces in major operations to eliminate insurgents in both the north and west of Iraq. During operations in Iraq and Afghanistan, the Air Force led the way in the development of unmanned air vehicles (drones) as critical air surveillance elements.

The cruel and cowardly terrorist hijacking and attack on the World Trade Center led to a vigorous series of counter attacks on terrorists and their supporters. To recognize these efforts, the National Defense Service Medal was reauthorized in 2001 and two new awards, the Global War on Terrorism Expeditionary and Service Medals were created. A White House spokesman said the medals recognize the "sacrifices and contributions" military members make in the global war on terror.

Following the liberation of Afghanistan, an Afghanistan Campaign Medal was created on November 29, 2004 retroactive to October 24, 2001 to acknowledge service there. A similar medal, known as the Iraq Campaign Medal was authorized for service during the same period within the borders of Iraq and it is retroactive to March 19, 2003. These medals replace the Global War on Terrorism Expeditionary Medal for service in Afghanistan and Iraq and military personnel cannot receive both for the same period of service.

Today the United States Air Force is the most technologically advanced and modern Air Force in the world with almost 6,000 military aircraft. In addition there are about 450 intercontinental ballistic missiles remaining as a deterrent against any worldwide aggression. The Air Force has approximately 320,000 personnel on active duty, 104,000 in the Air National Guard and about 75,000 in the select individual ready reserves. These forces are supported by almost 170,000 civilian personnel in the United States and overseas.

All Air Force decorations, service medals and ribbons provide a unique and handsome way for our nation to honor veterans for valor and faithful service but also have another important purpose. Their wear on a uniform can tell a commander, fellow members of the Armed Forces and veterans the level of experience and performance of the wearer. When a commander reviews his officers, noncommissioned officers and airmen; it takes only a minute to recognize their backgrounds and performance based on their ribbons. From the individual service members viewpoint, military awards recognize devotion to duty, performance, valor and service in a way no other manner can accomplish. The medals and ribbons of the Air Force reflect how our country recognizes hundreds of years of unbroken dedicated service and valor by members of our Armed Forces going back to the birth of the Republic.

Types of Military Medals, Ribbons and Devices

Decoration   Service Medal

The two general categories of military medals awarded by the United States are (1) decorations which are presented for valor and merit and (2) service medals.

Decorations. Since the establishment of our first awards, decorations for valorous or meritorious actions have traditionally been in the shape of a star, cross, hexagon or similar heraldic configuration. However, a small number of decorations are round, (e.g., Navy Distinguished Service Medal, Airman's Medal, Coast Guard Achievement Medal, etc. are circular).

Service Medals. The circular shape has been used almost exclusively for service medals. These can be awarded for good conduct, participation in a particular campaign, expedition or service on foreign soil. Generally full size medals are restricted for wear on full dress uniforms, the miniature medals for wear on mess dress or evening dress uniforms and ribbon bars for everyday service uniforms. On civilian clothing, wearing miniature medals or an enameled lapel pin, in the colors of a specific ribbon, has been in vogue since the early part of the 20th Century. Additionally, since World War II, the enamel hat pin in the form of the appropriate medal has found favor with veterans' organizations for unofficial wear on their organizational hats.

Enameled Lapel Pins

Ribbon Only Awards. Ribbon only awards may be personal decorations (such as the Navy Marine Corps Combat Action Ribbon), unit awards or individual service awards. The use of ribbon only awards began during World War II. Some ribbon only awards have later been converted to full-size medals. Today all five of the military Services use ribbon only awards especially as individual service awards.

Air Force Overseas Service Ribbon (Short Tour)   Air Force Small Arms Expert Marksmanship Ribbon

Unit Citations. The use of unit citations to recognize outstanding performance by a military unit or ship really came into play during World War II. The War Department decided the best way to recognize individual members of a unit or squadron for outstanding performance in combat or support should be a ribbon only award. The Air Force Presidential Unit Citation is the organizational equivalent of an individual award of The Air Force Distinguished Service Cross. Since the establishment of the Presidential Unit Citation, a number of additional unit citations as well as foreign unit citations have appeared. Some U.S. Air Force unit citations are unique in that they are mounted within a gold frame whereas others may or may not have a gold frame.

Air Force Presidential Unit Citation   Air Force Gallant Unit Citation

Attachments or Appurtenances. Small metal devices are worn on the ribbon bar or the medal's suspension ribbon to denote additional awards, campaigns, additional honors or subsequent service. These attachments come in the form of stars, oak leaf clusters, numerals, arrowheads, etc. and are another means to indicate the level and extent of the medal holder's service to his country. The attachments and the manner of their placement are shown in detail in subsequent pages.

Ribbon and Medal Devices/Attachments

❖ Military Medal Variations

Bronze — Anodized or Gold-Plated
Full Size Medals

Bronze — Anodized or Gold-Plated
Miniature Medals

Regulation Ribbon Bars

Enamel Hat Pins (unofficial)

Mini Ribbons (unofficial)

Enamel Lapel Pins (unofficial)

Silver Star Certificate,

Boxed Bronze Star in Presentation Case

Decorations are announced in official military orders. The orders are filed in an individual's military record jacket and retired to a records holding area when the individual is discharged or retired. A decoration usually comes with a citation, certificate and boxed medal with ribbon and lapel pin.

Authorization for service medals are noted in an individual's official military records. They are generally issued in a small cardboard box. Ribbon-only awards and unit citations are sometimes issued but generally the individual has to purchase them. Foreign medals, such as the Republic of Vietnam Campaign Medal are generally required to be purchased by individual service members.

1966 Airman's Medal Certificate and Citation

Medals of America 27

How to Determine a Veteran's Military Medals

Many veterans and their families are unsure of which military medals they were awarded and often for good reasons. Twenty-five, 30, even 50 years after military service, it is often difficult to remember or clearly identify the awards a veteran may have earned the right to wear or display. Thousands of veterans have been heard to say "I don't want any awards I'm not authorized, but I want everything I am authorized." So the question is, "What are the medals authorized the veteran for his military service during each conflict?"

There are a number of reasons besides the passage of time that veterans are not always sure of their military awards. At the end of World War II many campaign medals had not yet been struck and were only issued as ribbons due to the restriction on brass and other metals for the war effort. Many unit awards had not yet been authorized and on the whole, most soldiers, sailors, marines and airmen were more interested in going home than they were in their military records. Other changes such as Congress' decision in 1947 to authorize a Bronze Star Medal for meritorious service to all recipients of the Combat Infantryman and Combat Medical Badge was not well known. Many veterans never realized that they had earned a Bronze Star Medal. Perhaps the most striking example is the recently-approved Republic of Korea War Service Medal. The Republic of Korea offered the medal to all U.S. Korean War veterans but it was not accepted by our government until 1999. In other cases, veterans came home and stuffed their medals and awards into a cigar box which usually found its way into the hands of children and these magnificent symbols of valor and service from a grateful nation simply disappeared over time.

Today there is a wonderfully renewed interest in wearing and displaying United States military medals, both to honor veterans' patriotic service and to display a family's pride in military service. World War II, Korea and Vietnam veterans now wear their medals at formal social and patriotic events and a display of military medals and insignia is often in the family home place of honor.

As mentioned earlier, military medals are divided into two categories: Decorations awarded for valor or meritorious service and Campaign and Service medals awarded for a particular service or event. Additionally there are Unit Awards that are for unit valor and meritorious service and ribbon-only awards presented for completing special training or recognizing certain service.

Decorations are individual awards are of such singular significance that most veterans and their family will remember when such awards have been presented. Decorations are noted on a veteran's official discharge papers (called a DD Form 214) as well as published in official unit orders. However there are exceptions, such as the Bronze Star Medal issued for meritorious service after World War II and in some cases Purple Heart medals that were never officially presented. Someone who is unsure if they received a decoration can request the National Records Center in St. Louis or other veterans records holding areas to check their records. Home of Heroes at www.homeofheroes.com list all Medal of Honor, Service Crosses and most Silver Star awardees. Bronze Star, Air Medal, Purple Heart, Commendation and Achievement medals are announced in unit orders which are normally found in the individual's military service record.

Campaign and service medals, unit awards and ribbon-only awards are more clearly identifiable. The Air Force for example, has a campaign register that provides a clear indication of which campaign medals, unit awards, campaign stars and foreign unit awards are authorized a particular unit during certain periods of time. To aid in identifying the campaign medals authorized veterans of different conflicts and to show how they can be displayed, United States and Allied campaign medals authorized since World War II are summarized on the next page. Exact criteria for each medal and the campaigns associated with it are shown in detail later in the book.

Commemorative medals have long been an American tradition going back to the Revolution. World War I saw the greatest use of Commemoratives with thousands being struck by almost every major city, county and society to honor their veterans. Today veterans, especially Cold War veterans, use Military Commemoratives to help tell the story of their service not reflected by medals of the Armed Forces.

Medals of America 29

World War II Medals

World War II saw Good Conduct Medals available to all four services. The Navy, Marine Corps and Coast Guard had already established Good Conduct Medals while the Army (which included the Army Air Force) established a Good Conduct Medal in 1941.

The American Defense Service Medal was authorized for the period of national emergency prior to 7 December 1941. After America declared war, the conflict was divided into (1) the American theater, (2) the European, African, Middle Eastern theater, and the (3) Asiatic Pacific Theater. Examples of the medals awarded are shown below.

❖ World War II Campaign Medals

- ★ American Defense was awarded for service between 1939 and 7 Dec. 1941.
- ★ American Campaign was for service in the American Theater, outside the US for 30 days or in the US for a year. Most veterans qualified for this medal.
- ★ All WW II veterans qualified for the Victory Medal.
- ★ WW II veterans who served 30 days in an occupied country qualify for an Occupation Medal.
- ★ Philippine Defense and Liberation Medals for service in the Philippines.

Good Conduct Medals (Army as example) — American Defense Service Medal — American Campaign Medal — Europe-African-Middle Eastern Campaign — Asiatic Pacific Campaign

Women's Army Corps — WW II Victory — WW II Occupation Medal, Army — WW II Occupation Medal, Navy — Philippine Defense Medal — Philippine Liberation Medal

❖ Korea Campaign Medals

The Armed Forces approved acceptance of the ROK War Service Medal in Oct. 1999 for all Korean War Veterans. The Korea Defense Service Medal for 30 days service in Korea after 27 July 1954 was approved in 2003. Air Force used the Army Good Conduct Medal in Korean War.

Good Conduct Medals (Army as example) — National Defense Service — US - Korean Service — US - Korea Defense — UN - Korean Service — ROK War Service

30 Decorations, Medals, and Ribbons of the United States Air Force

❖ Vietnam Campaign Medals

Air Force established its own Good Conduct Medal in 1963.

❖ Southwest Asia, Bosnia/Kosovo, Afghanistan & Iraq Campaign Medals

The Display Case tells the Story of a Veteran's Service to Our Country

What branch and unit, ship or squadron, what awards and campaigns, what skills and rank, where and when.

 5th Air Force Patch shows unit, the branch of service and serves as a focal point.

 Distinguished Flying Cross shows his exemplary service and achievement.

 Republic of Korea Presidential Unit Citation

Gold Oak leaf shows rank of Major.

Korean War Display

Each display case will be different just as each veteran's service was different and each service will have different insignia. Each case will show the honors a grateful nation has bestowed on her veterans.

32 Decorations, Medals, and Ribbons of the United States Air Force

The most appropriate use of military medals after active service is to mount the medals for permanent display in home or office. This reflects the individual's patriotism and the military service rendered to the United States.

Decorations are usually awarded in a presentation set which normally consists of a medal, ribbon bar and lapel pin, all contained in a special case. During World War II, the name of the decoration was stamped in gold on the front of the case. However, as budget considerations assumed greater importance, this practice was gradually phased out and replaced by a standard case with "United States of America" emblazoned on the front. At the present time, the more common decorations, (e.g., Achievement and Commendation Medals), come in small plastic cases suitable only for initial presentation and storage of the medal.

The most effective method of protecting awards involves the use of a shadow box or glass front display case with at least 1/2 inch between the medals and the glass. This provides a three dimensional view and protects the medal display in a dust-free environment.

Any physical alteration destroys the integrity of the medal and the use of glue ruins the back of the ribbon and medal. The best way to mount medals is in a display case specially designed for that purpose.

The mounting board is absolutely critical. Acid-free Gator board at least 1/4 inch thick covered with a high quality velour-type material to which Velcro™ will adhere will allow the medals to be mounted using Velcro™ tape which locks the medal firmly into place without damage. The added advantage is the medals and insignia can be moved without damage.

- Framed photograph adds special touch to display.
- Wings identify him as a pilot.
- Korean Service Medal with 2 campaign stars.
- United Nations medal shows he served in the largest UN operation in the world.
- Commemorative Medals honor special events and qualifications.
- Engraved brass plate tells who, what, when, where.

  MAJOR JOHN COOTER
  5th AIR FORCE
  KOREA
  1952-1953

Cold War Veterans Display

Medals of America 33

U.S. Army Air Force Display Examples World War II

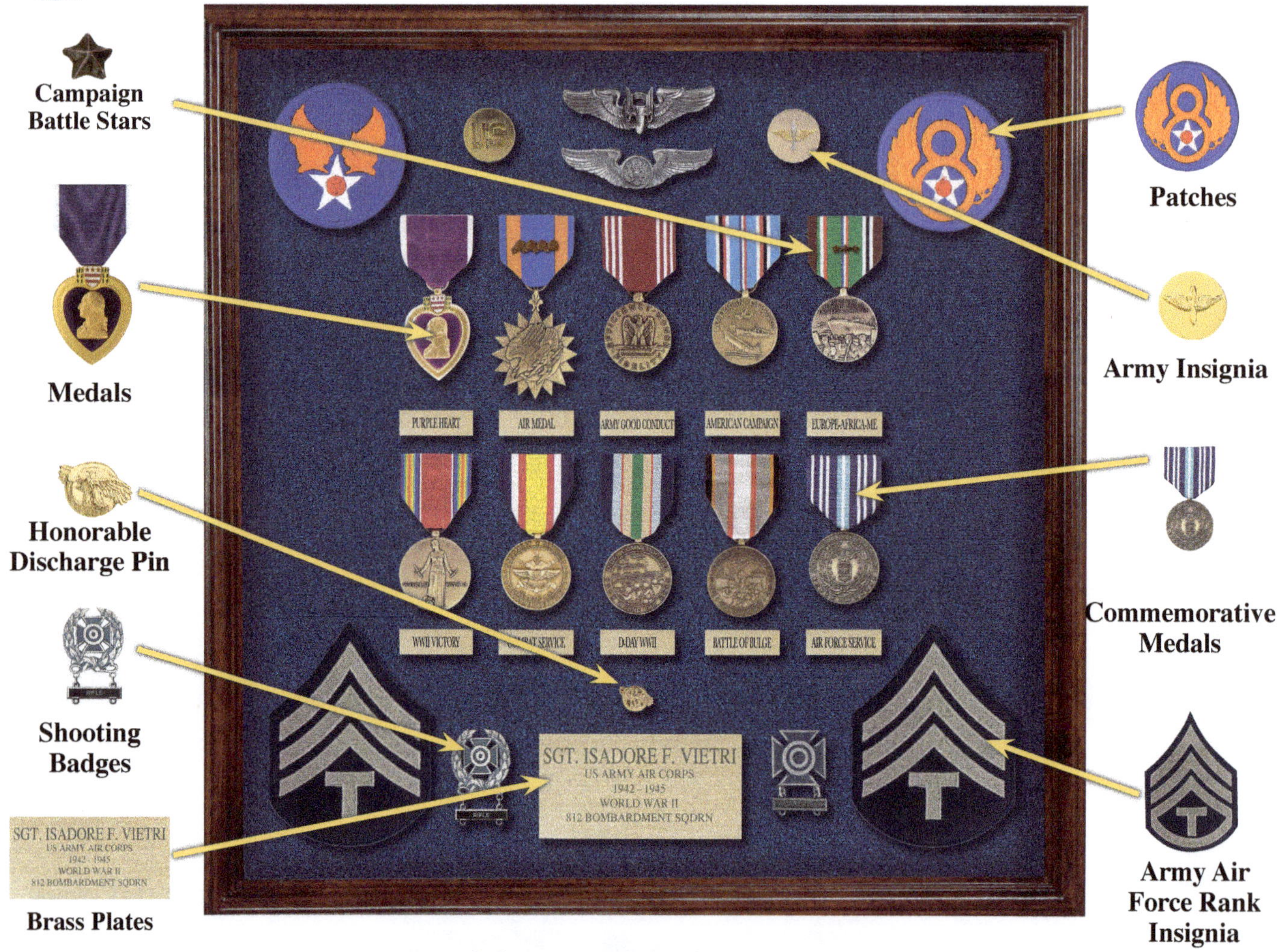

Campaign Battle Stars

Medals

Honorable Discharge Pin

Shooting Badges

Brass Plates

Patches

Army Insignia

Commemorative Medals

Army Air Force Rank Insignia

World War II, 8th Air Force
Display Cases

US Army Air Force

The Army Air Force, fighting on 3 fronts, swept the sky clear of all foes but not without sacrifice. At times, their losses were second only to the Infantry. Fighters, bombers & transports flew from Berlin to Burma and back. No country, no Air Force had ever met such a challenge as World War II and no other deserved the awards more than the Army Air Corps. From the beginning at Pearl Harbor to the finish of the Japanese Empire with the Atomic bombs, America's airmen were patriots.

These two cases are good examples of adding personal items to a veteran's award display that make them truly unique. The 9th Air Force veteran to the left is one of the lucky ones. An aerial gunner shot down over Europe, he has his caterpillar pin, a handmade parachute badge and his German issued Stalag POW ID tag. You will note his POW Medal just after his Air Medal. This a good example of how the addition of personal items can enhance the story of a veteran's military service.

The case to the right features a pilot who served in China. He has added his Nationalist Chinese pilot wings and his dog tag. The next to last medal is the WW II Nationalist China Memorial Medal followed by the Air Combat Commemorative medal.

Medals of America 35

U.S. Air Force Display Examples 1947 to Present

U.S. Air Force Korea The U.S. Air Force became a separate service from the Army in 1947. The USAF continued to use many Army medals until after the Korean War (the Army Good Conduct Medal was used until 1963).

In Korea the new USAF gained control of the sky using a combination of prop and jet aircraft. The new F86 soundly defeated the Russian built MIG 15, allowing the bombers to pound the enemy in front and in the rear. Airmen suffered in boiling summer heat and freezing winter snows to keep air superiority over the communist Chinese and North Koreans. In recent years, 2 new medals recognize that service: the new Korea Defense Service Medal and ROK War Service Medal.

Korean War

This Airman's case has the new Korean Defense Service, ROK War Service, and ROK Presidential Unit and UN Commemorative medal.

Vietnam

This Pilot has added a Vietnamese Cross of Gallentry Commemorative Medal in honor of his RVN Cross of Gallantry Unit Citation.

36 Decorations, Medals, and Ribbons of the United States Air Force

U.S. Air Force Vietnam. Vietnam saw the Air Force carrying the battle to the enemy stronghold through a barrage of SAM missiles and enemy Migs. In the south they flew close air support, built airfields and flew B52 raids from as far away as Guam. Their courage and ability deserves real recognition.

Vietnam

This Airman uses challenge coins, his lapel insignia and an Air Force Crest across the top. His Air Force Commendation Medal has the place of honor and two commemorative medals representing combat service and the RVN Unit Cross Of Gallantry are at the end of his medal display. His unit award and a brass identification plates flanked by metal rank insignia personalize his award display case.

Cold War - The Cold War was kept cold by the enormous deterrent of SAC and our world wide airmen. Cold War Veterans number in the millions, serving in 70 different countries under very difficult and often dangerous circumstances with little reward or acknowledgment. Their service needs to be recognized since it was key to bringing down the USSR and its satellites. Cold War Veterans selfless duty deserves to be rewarded.

This Airman's display is topped by the Air Force Shield and displays his ribbons above his medals which is an excellent way to show Unit and ribbon only awards. He has two decorations for Meritorious service and the Good Conduct Medal. Below those medals are the National Defense Service Medal, The Humanitarian Service Medal and the Air Force Service Commemorative Medal. His metal rank insignia flank his brass name plate.

Medals of America 37

Liberation of Kuwait

A dazzling 100 hour war reflected the long preparation in the blistering desert heat and the high degree of spirit and professionalism of the Airmen of the 90s. Honors well earned and applauded by our country.

Liberation of Kuwait and Global War on Terrorism

The Lieutenant Colonel's case on the right displays a Command Pilot's wings and awards for service in both the Liberation of Kuwait and Iraq as well as the Global War on Terrorism. Ribbon only awards are displayed below his medals. Note the multiple awards of the Air Medal are arranged vertically in the Air Force as opposed to the Army and Army Air Corps who mounted them horizontally.

The Master Sergeant's case below displays a full set of ribbons representing all of his military awards with the ribbons of the Commemorative medals he has added to his display, since these ribbons are not being worn on an official uniform that was his personal option. The Armed Forces Reserve Medal with Mobilization device indicate he was called to active duty from the reserves for service in Southwest Asia. His brass plate spells this out. It is fact of life that major combat operations generally require mobilization of critical Air Force Reserve talent.

38 Decorations, Medals, and Ribbons of the United States Air Force

Global War on Terror

The brilliant liberation of Afghanistan and Iraq reflect great credit on the airman of today - strong, victorious and compassionate. Their military honors are justly won and displayed.

The Staff Sergeant's case above and to the right give an idea of the many different ways an individual's awards can be presented. The case above uses standard bronze medals with individual medal identification plates and includes dog tags. The case to the right uses ribbons over gold plated (anodized) medals such as worn by USAF Honor Guards.

Not all displays have to be multiply medals, some can show just a single medal while others can be hand polished and mounted in 8x10 display frames.

Medals of America 39

❖ Issue of U.S. Medals to Veterans, Retirees and Their Families

The Air Force normally issues decorations and service medals as they are awarded or earned. The Services do not issue or replace any foreign awards, only United States awards.

Veterans of any United States military service may request medals never issued or replacement of medals which have been lost, stolen, destroyed or rendered unfit through no fault of their own. Requests may also be filed for awards that were earned but, for any reason, were never issued to the service member. A good example of this type of medal is the Korea Defense Service Medal which was approved in 2003 and back dated to cover everyone who served in Korea after 1954. More than 2 million former service personnel are now authorized this medal. *The next-of-kin of deceased veterans may also make the same request for the medals of their veteran family member.*

The National Personnel Records Center, Military Personnel Records (NPRC-MPR) is the repository of millions of military personnel, health, and medical records of discharged and deceased veterans of all services during the 20th century. Information from the records is made available upon written request (with signature and date) to the extent allowed by law.

There are two ways for those seeking information regarding military personnel records stored at NPRC (MPR). If you are a veteran or next-of-kin of a deceased veteran, you may now use *vetrecs.archives.gov* to order a copy of your military records. For all others, your request is best made using a Standard Form 180. It includes complete instructions for preparing and submitting requests.

Military Awards and Decorations

When you request issuance or replacement of Air Force (including Army Air Corps) military service medals, decorations, and awards, the National Personnel Records Center will verify the awards and forward the request with the verification to the appropriate Air Force service department for issuance of the medals.

The Standard Form (SF 180), Request Pertaining to Military Records, is recommended for requesting medals and awards. Provide as much information as possible and send the form to the appropriate address shown on the next page.

1. **How to Obtain Standard Form 180 (SF-180), Request Pertaining to Military Records**

There are several ways to obtain an SF-180. You can:

A. Download and print a copy of the SF-180 in PDF format by going to: ***http://www.archives.gov/facilities/mo/st_louis/military_personnel_records standard_form_180.html#sf.***

B. Order the form to be faxed to you from the National Archives and Records Administration's Fax-on-Demand System

- Call the Fax-on-Demand System at (301) 837-0990 from a fax machine, using the handset.
- Follow the voice instructions and request document number 2255.
- There is no charge for this service except for any long distance telephone charges you may incur.

C. Write to The National Personnel Records Center

9700 Page Avenue, St. Louis, Missouri 63132.

The SF 180 may be photocopied as needed but you must submit a separate SF 180 for each individual whose records are being requested.

2. **Write a Letter to Request Records**

If you are not able to obtain SF-180, you may still submit a request for military records by letter. The letter should indicate if the request is for a specific medal(s), or for all medals earned. It is also helpful to include copies of any military service documents that indicate eligibility for medals, such as military orders or the veteran's report of separation (DD Form 214 or its earlier equivalent). Federal law [5 USC 552a(b)] requires that all requests for information from official military personnel files be submitted in writing. Each request must be signed (in cursive) by the veteran or his next-of-kin indicating the relationship to the deceased and dated (within the last year). For this reason, no requests are accepted over the internet.

Requests must contain enough information to identify the record among the more than 70 million on file at NPRC (MPR). Certain basic information is needed to locate military service records. This information includes:

- The veteran's complete name used while in service, Service number or social security number
- Branch of service
- Dates of service
- Date and place of birth may also be helpful, especially if the service number is not known

If the request pertains to a record that may have been involved in the 1973 fire, also include:

- Place of discharge
- Last unit of assignment
- Place of entry into the service, if known

Please submit a separate request (either SF 180 or letter) for each individual whose records are being requested. Response times for records requested from the National Personnel Records Center (NPRC) vary greatly depending on the nature of the request. For example, the NPRC Military Records Facility currently has a backlog of 180,000 requests and receives approximately 5,000 requests per day. The Center may have a difficult time locating records since millions of records were lost in a fire at the National Personnel Records Center in 1973. The fire destroyed 80 percent of the Army's discharge records between November 1912 and December 1959. World War II Army Air Force records were in this group. Seventy-five percent of Air Force discharge records before 1964 and whose last names that fall alphabetically between Hubbard (James E.) and Z were also burned. Only four million records from this period were saved. Although the requested medals can often be issued on the basis of alternate records, the documents sent in with the request are sometimes the only means of determining proper eligibility.

Finally, you should exercise extreme patience. It may take several months or, in some cases, a year to determine eligibility and dispatch the appropriate medals. The Center asks that you not send a follow-up request for 90 days. Because of these delays, many veterans simply purchase their medals from a supplier such as Medals of America.

Generally, there is no charge from the Air Force for medal or award replacements. The length of time to receive a response or your medals and awards varies depending upon the work load.

The Air Force processes requests for medals through the National Personnel Records Center, which determines eligibility through the information in the veteran's records. Once verified, a notification of entitlement is forwarded to Randolph Air Force Base, Texas, from which the medals are mailed to the requester. To request medals earned while in the Air Force or its predecessors, the Army Air Corps or Army Air Force veterans or their next-of-kin should write to:

National Personnel Records Center
Air Force Reference Branch (NRPMF)
9700 Page Avenue
St. Louis, MO 63132-5100

In case of a problem or an appeal write to:

Headquarters Air Force Personnel Ctr
AFPC/DPPPR
550 C Street West, Suite 12
Randolph AFB, TX 78150-4714

Cold War Recognition Certificate

In accordance with section 1084 of the Fiscal Year 1998 National Defense Authorization Act, the Secretary of Defense approved awarding Cold War Recognition Certificates to all members of the armed forces and qualified federal government civilian personnel who faithfully served the United States during the Cold War era, from Sept. 2, 1945 to Dec. 26, 1991. A quick search on the internet for Cold War certificate will provide the latest process for obtaining one.

A Cold War medal has been approved but the Department of Defense has no plans to strike one.

Veterans have the option of purchasing an unofficial Cold War Commemorative Medal for their service during the Cold War.

Cold War Recognition Certificate

Cold War Victory Commemorative Medal

❖ Wearing USAF awards, Order of Precedence and Attachments

(USAF photo)

The Air Force awards system has evolved into a highly structured program often called the "Pyramid of Honor." The system is designed to reward services ranging from heroism on the battlefield to superior performance of non combat duties and even includes the completion of entry level airman training.

Since World War II the Air Force has generally embraced Napoleon's concept of liberally awarding medals and ribbons to enhance morale and esprit de corps. The large number of Air Medal awarded in World War II is an example of this policy. Air Force losses were second only to the infantry and the leadership wanted an immediate way to recognize the extraordinary service of the air crews. Over the years an expanded and specifically-tailored awards program became generally very popular in the all-volunteer Air Force and has played a significant part in improving morale, job performance, recruitment and reenlistments among junior officers and enlisted personnel.

The various ways of wearing decorations and awards by active duty, reserve and veterans are shown on the following pages. These awards paint a wonderful portrait of the Air Force men and women whose dedication to the ideals of freedom represent the rich United States Air Force military heritage.

Wearing military ribbons, miniature medals and full size medals on uniforms.

This section shows examples of wearing awards starting from World War II to today along with a brief description of Air Force regulations governing current wear.

Ribbon Chart Showing the Complete History of U.S. Air Force Awards

This one of a kind chart on pages 54-55, reads left to right and shows the ribbon for every Air Force award since 1916 with many of the variations used. The chart is a colorful walk through U.S. Air Force Military awards history and was originally developed by Lonny Borts, America's expert on military ribbons.

USAF Order of Precedence Ribbon Chart

On page 57 the current correct order of precedence for Air Force ribbons is shown going back to World War II. Authorized attachments for each ribbon are displayed below the ribbon and a reference bar on the right side of the page provides guides to a detailed device graphic.

Next is the USAF Order of Precedence Chart for Multi service awards. Veterans who have service in multiple branches of the Armed Forces can determine their military ribbon order of precedence beginning on page 58.

Air Force Ribbon Devices (Appurtenances) start on page 62 and all Air Force ribbon devices are shown as correctly mounted to ribbons and medals. All Air Force ribbon devices are shown in alphabetical order starting with the Gold Airplane. For those who desire even more detail charts for proper placement of Air Forces Ribbon Devices (Appurtenances) are on pages 64 and 65.

Full Size Variations of a United States Military Medal

❖ Wearing of Ribbons, Miniatures and Medals

Mr. Johnny Schlund photo

World War II Army Air Corps
Officer uniform with ribbons.

World War II Army Air Corps
Enlisted uniform with ribbons.

One of the best ways possible to understand military ribbons is to study actual examples. Mr. Johnny Schlund was kind enough to provide these examples from his extensive collection of senior Air Force officers uniforms spanning the last 75 years. Each example gives you a very interesting opportunity to read and interpret the ribbons on the chest of an Air Force uniform whether it is World War I or II, Korea, Vietnam, the Liberation of Kuwait, Iraq or Afghanistan or in several of the cases shown, combinations of service in multiple wars.

The first example shows a long abandoned practice of putting a clear plastic film over the ribbons to protect them from getting dirty. *On the uniform display above the bottom 2 ribbon rows are mounted upside down and backwards.* If you the use ribbon chart on pages 54,55 you will note that all of the service was in the Army Air Force and began in World War I, followed by service in all three theaters of World War II, participation in the Liberation of the Philippines (note the battle star) and final service in the occupation forces.

The second example just above shows the Army Distinguished Service Cross and the Air Force Distinguished Service Medal. This is also an example of so many awards of the Air Medal that two ribbons are required to display all of the devices.

Korean War Enlisted uniform with ribbons. National Defense Service Medal Ribbon is missing and the Air Force is still used the Army Good Conduct Medal for the Korean War.

Current USAF uniform with ribbons.

In the second dispay note there is both an Air Force Commendation medal and an Army Commendation Medal. Following the ribbons you can see the recipient served in World War II, Korea and Vietnam. The display also shows the French Cross of War and the Belgium Cross of War both obviously awarded during World War II.

Third display, above, is interesting and that it has the Army Good Conduct Medal which means that the recipient began his military service as a private in the U.S. Army. This display has several unusual awards to include service in the Antarctica and the Republic of Vietnam Air Service

Medal. By reading the ribbons you can read the history of service.

The final display is again unusual in several ways. It shows three awards of the Air Force Distinguished Service Medal and three awards of the Legion of Merit. That many awards is extremely rare and indicates service of very high responsibility very well done. While this book does not carry a detailed review of all of the Republic of Vietnam awards this veteran had received two; the first one with a set of wings is the Air Gallantry Cross and the second one is the National Order of Vietnam. Unfortunately this general's aide has the correct order of these two medals reversed since the National Order of the Republic of Vietnam is the highest decoration the Republic had. The Vietnam Campaign medal with three bronze stars should be after the National Defense ribbon.

Medals of America 45

❖ United States Air Force Uniform Regulations

Officer Blue Uniform with Service Ribbons

Wear of Service Ribbons on Officer's Shirt

Felmale Officer Blue Uniform, note rows of 4 ribbons.

Wear of Service Ribbons — Ribbons may be worn on service dress and blue shirt. Ribbons are normally worn in rows of three with the bottom bar centered and resting on the top edge of the pocket. Ribbons may be worn four-in-a-row with the left edge of the ribbons aligned with the left edge of the pocket to keep the lapel from covering ribbons. There is no space between rows of ribbons. Current regulations stipulate that members may wear all or no ribbons and devices. USAF personnel do not have the option to choose which ribbons to wear.

All USAF Photos

NCO's Blue Uniform with Service Ribbons

Wear of Service Ribbons on NCOs Shirt

Female NCO's Blue Uniform with Ribbons

Wear of Ribbons on Female Enlisted Shirt

Identification Badges
Name plate
Rank insignia

U.S. Lapel Insignia
Air Force Specialty Badge
Military Service Ribbons

USAF Photos

Wear of Miniature medals on Enlisted Male Mess Dress.

Wear of Miniature medals on Enlisted Female Mess Dress.

Miniature Medals — Miniature medals are worn on the blue mess dress or on formal dress. The miniatures are centered between lapel and arm seam and midway between top shoulder seam and top button of jacket. If more than four miniatures, the wearer has the option of mounting up to seven by overlapping or going to a second bar. Seven is the maximum on one bar, however, many in the Air Force prefer only a maximum of four to a bar.

Wear of Miniature medals on Male Officer Mess Dress uniform.

Wear of Miniature medals on Female Officer Mess Dress uniform.

Full Size Medals — Normally worn three to a row, but may be overlapped up to five medals on a 2-3/4 inch holding bar. No medal should be overlapped more than 50 percent and the medal nearest the lapel should be fully exposed. Six medals should be displayed in two rows, three over three. Regular size medals are worn on the service dress and ceremonial dress uniforms with the medal portion of the bottom row immediately above the top of the pocket button.

USAF Photos

Full Size Anodized Medals are only authorized for wear by the USAF Honor Guard and Arlington National Cemetery Chaplains (AFI 36-2903)

Full Size Medals in brass

Miniature Medals anodized (Gold Plated)

Medals of America 49

❖ How Medals are Worn and Displayed by Veterans

Introduction

One of the first lessons taught to new airmen is proper wear of the uniform and insignia. The same rules apply to veterans and retirees wearing military awards on their former uniform or civilian dress. There are many occasions today when tradition, patriotism, ceremonies and social occasions call for the wear of military awards.

Civilian Dress

The most common manner of wearing a decoration or medal is as a lapel pin in the left lapel of a civilian suit jacket. The small enameled lapel pin represents a decoration or medal an individual has received (usually the highest award or one having special meaning to the wearer). Many veterans always wear a lapel pin. Lapel pins are available for all awards and ribbons such as the Air Force Commenation Medal or Unit Citations.

Honorably discharged and retired Air Force members may wear full-size or miniature medals on civilian suits for appropriate occasions such as Memorial Day and Armed Forces Day. Female members may wear full-size or miniature medals on equivalent dress. It is not considered appropriate to wear skill or qualification badges on civilian attire.

Formal Civilian Wear

For more formal occasions, it is correct and encouraged to wear miniature decorations and medals. For a black or white tie occasion, the rule is quite simple: if the lapel is wide enough wear the miniatures on the left lapel or, in the case of a shawl lapel on a tuxedo, the miniature medals are worn over the left breast pocket. The center of the holding bar of the bottom row of medals should be parallel to the ground immediately above the pocket. Do not wear a pocket handkerchief. Miniature medals really do make a handsome statement of patriotic service at weddings and other social events.

Miniature medals can also be worn on a civilian suit at veterans' functions, memorial events, formal occasions of ceremony and social functions of a military nature.

50 Decorations, Medals, and Ribbons of the United States Air Force

Wear of the Uniform

On certain occasions, retired Air Force personnel may wear either the uniform prescribed at the date of retirement or any of the current active duty authorized uniforms. Retirees should adhere to the same grooming standards as Air Force active duty personnel when wearing the uniform (for example, a beard is inappropriate while in uniform). Whenever the uniform is worn, it must be done in such a manner as to reflect credit upon the individual and the Air Force. (Do not mix uniform items.)

The occasions for uniform wear by retirees are

Military ceremonies, funerals, weddings, memorial services and inaugurals.
Patriotic parades on national holidays.
Military parades in which active or reserve units are participating.
Educational institutions when engaged in giving military instruction. Social or other functions when the invitation has obviously been influenced by the member's earlier active service.

Honorably separated wartime veterans may wear the uniform authorized at the time of their service for:

Military funerals, memorial services, and inaugurals.
Patriotic parades on national holidays.
Any occasion authorized by law.
Military parades in which active or reserve units are participating.

Non-wartime Air Force personnel separated (other than retired, Air National Guard and Reserve) are not authorized to wear the uniform but may wear the medals.

Mini ribbons and Hat pins (Unofficial)

WW II Honorable Discharge Lapel Pin

Former WW II Women's AirForce Service Pilots (WASP) Madge Moore is shown in her uniform when recieving the Daedalian Fighter Flight Congressional Gold Medal for her service in World War II. (Photo by Jkotto)

Neck ties.

A Visual walk through the History of the Army Air Force and U.S. Air Force Military Ribbons and Attachments

In order to provide a complete and historical overview of United States Air Force military awards the ribbon charts on the next facing pages display all Air Force awards from 1914 to the present. Starting with the Medal of Honor in the upper left-hand corner of page 54, all decorations, service medals, unit awards and service ribbons are shown in the correct order of precedence. The chart provides an easy reference guide to identify any Air Force military ribbon. The chart also provides a complete historical overview of U.S. Air Force awards along with authorized United Nations and NATO awards. Detailed illustrations and descriptions of all awards are presented following this section on military ribbons.

The ribbon chart on page 57 displays current USAF awards in the correct order of precedence and authorized ribbon attachments for Air Force personnel from World War II, Korea, Vietnam, Liberation of Kuwait, Global War on Terror, Iraq and Afghanistan. They include the newly authorized Nuclear Deterrence Operations Service Medal and Air Force Special Duty ribbon.

The third chart, on pages 58-61 is our very best effort to show the correct order of precedence for when multi-service U.S. military and foreign ribbons are worn with United States Air Force ribbons. The placement of foreign decorations is not shown in the first chart (page 54) since it is a historical overview of the United States Air Force awards and approved foreign service medals since 1914.

Medals of America 53

History of United States Air Force Decorations, Unit Awards & Service Ribbons 1914-2016

Medal of Honor	Distinguished Service Cross	Air Force Cross	Defense Distinguished Service Medal	Army Distinguished Service Medal	Air Force Distinguished Service Medal	Silver Star	Defense Superior Service Medal

Legion of Merit (Legionnaire)	Distinguished Flying Cross	Soldier's Medal	Airman's Medal	Bronze Star Medal	Purple Heart	Defense Meritorious Service Medal	Meritorious Service Medal

Air Medal	Aerial Achievement Medal	Joint Service Commendation Medal	Army Commendation Medal	Air Force Commendation Medal	Joint Service Achievement Medal	Air Force Achievement Medal	Air Force Combat Action Medal

Army Presidential Unit Citation	Air Force Presidential Unit Citation	Joint Meritorious Unit Award	Air Force Gallant Unit Citation	Air Force Meritorious Unit Award	Air Force Outstanding Unit Award	Air Force Organizational Excellence Award	Prisoner of War Medal
	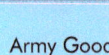						
Air Force Combat Readiness Medal	Army Good Conduct Medal	Air Force Good Conduct Medal	Air Reserve Forces Meritor's Service Medal	Outstanding Airman of the Year Ribbon	Air Force Recognition Ribbon	Mexican Service Medal (1914-17)	Mexican Border Service Medal (1916-17)

World War I Victory Medal (1917 - 18)	Occupation of Germany (1918-23)	Amer. Defense Service Medal (1939-41)	Women's Army Corps Service Medal	American Campaign Medal (1941-46)	Asiatic-Pacific Camp'n Medal (1941-46)	Europe-African-Mid East Camp'gn (1941-46)	World War II Victory Medal (1941 - 46)

World War II Occupat'n Medal (1945-57)	Medal for Humane Action (1948-49)	Nat'l Defense Service Medal (1950, 61, 90, 01)	Korean Service Medal (1950-54)	Antarctica Service Medal	Armed Forces Expeditionary Medal	Vietnam Service Medal (1965-73)	Southwest Asia Service Medal (1991-95)
						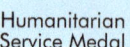	
Kosovo Campaign Medal (1999-2013)	Afghanistan Campaign Medal (2001-)	Iraq Campaign Medal (2003 - 11)	War on Terrorism Expeditionary Medal (2001-)	War on Terrorism Service Medal (2001-)	Korea Defense Service Medal (1954-)	Armed Forces Service Medal	Humanitarian Service Medal

54 Decorations, Medals, and Ribbons of the United States Air Force

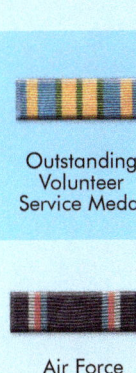 Outstanding Volunteer Service Medal	Air Force Air & Space Campaign Medal	USAF Nuclear Deterrence Opn Svs Medal	Air Force Overseas Ribbon (Short Tour)	Air Force Overseas Ribbon (Long Tour)	Air Force Expeditionary Service Ribbon	Air Force Longevity Service Award Ribbon	Air Force Special Duty Ribbon
Air Force Military Training Instructor Rib'n	Air Force Recruiter Ribbon	Armed Forces Reserve Medal	Air Force NCO Prof. Military Education Grad.	Air Force Basic Military Training Honor Graduate	Air Force Small Arms Expert Marksman	Air Force Training Ribbon	Philippine Presidential Unit Citation
Korean Presidential Unit Citation	Vietnam Presidential Unit Citation	Vietnam Gallantry Cross Unit Citation	Vietnam Civil Actions Unit Citation	Philippine Defense Ribbon	Philippine Liberation Ribbon (1944 - 45)	Philippine Independence Ribbon (1946)	United Nations Korean Service Medal
UN Palestine Mission (UNTSO)	UN India/ Pakistan Mission (UNMOGIP)	UN New Guinea Mission (UNTEA)	UN Iraq/ Kuwait Mission (UNIKOM)	UN Western Sahara Mission (MINURSO)	UN Cambodia Mission 1 (UNAMIC)	UN Yugoslavia Mission (UNPROFOR)	UN Cambodia Mission 2 (UNTAC)
UN Somalia Mission (UNOSOM)	UN Haiti Mission (UNMIH)	ONUMOZ Mozambique	UNOMIG Georgia	UNPREDEP Macedonia	UNTAES E. Slavonia, Baranja	MINUGUA Guatemala	UNMIK Kosovo
UNTAET East Timor	MONUC Congo	UNMEE Ethiopia, Eritrea	UNMISET East Timor	UNMIL Liberia	UNAMID Darfur	MINURCAT Cent. Afr. Rep, Chad	MONUSCO Congo
UNAMI UN Assistance Mission in Iraq	UN Special Service Medal (UNSSM)	NATO Meritorious Svs Medal	NATO Medal for Bosnia	NATO Medal for Kosovo	NATO Medal for Operation Eagle Assist	NATO Medal for Operation Active Endeavor	NATO Medal for Balkan Operations
NATO Medal for Afghanistan, Sudan, Iraq	Multinational Force & Observers Medal	Inter-American Defense Board Medal	Republic of Vietnam Campaign Medal	Kuwait Liberation Medal (Saudi Arabia)	Kuwait Liberation Medal (Kuwait)	Republic of Korea War Service Medal	

Copyright Medals of America Press 2015

USAF Photos

The Ribbons

One of the attributes the Air Force expects of its officers, noncommissioned officers and airmen is to properly wear and display their military awards on their uniform. This can be especially challenging when as you can see by the chart to the right there are over 80 military ribbons that can be awarded and earned by Air Force personnel.

The senior noncommissioned officer ribbon chest above reflects his service and level of performance. By identifying his ribbons using the chart to the right you can see that he has had multiple decorations for meritorious service in both the Air Force and on the Joint Staff of the Defense Department. Understanding the meaning of the various attachments show he has earned eight awards of the Air Force Good Conduct Medal so you can reasonably assume he has over 20 years service in the Air Force. His campaign medals shows service in Afghanistan and Iraq. While other ribbon show he served both short and long tours of duty overseas. The final ribbon in the bottom right-hand corner of his ribbon chest is a NATO award (foreign award) for service in the former Republic of Yugoslavia or Kosovo.

The ribbon chart on the next page shows the United States Air Force ribbons from WW II to today in the correct order of precedence (reading left to right, top to bottom) with their appropriate devices. The right-hand side of the chart shows all of the authorized Air Force attachments for ribbons. Using the reference number under the attachment you can locate how the devices are worn on the ribbon and their meaning in the Air Force ribbon device chart on pages 62 and 63.

56 Decorations, Medals, and Ribbons of the United States Air Force

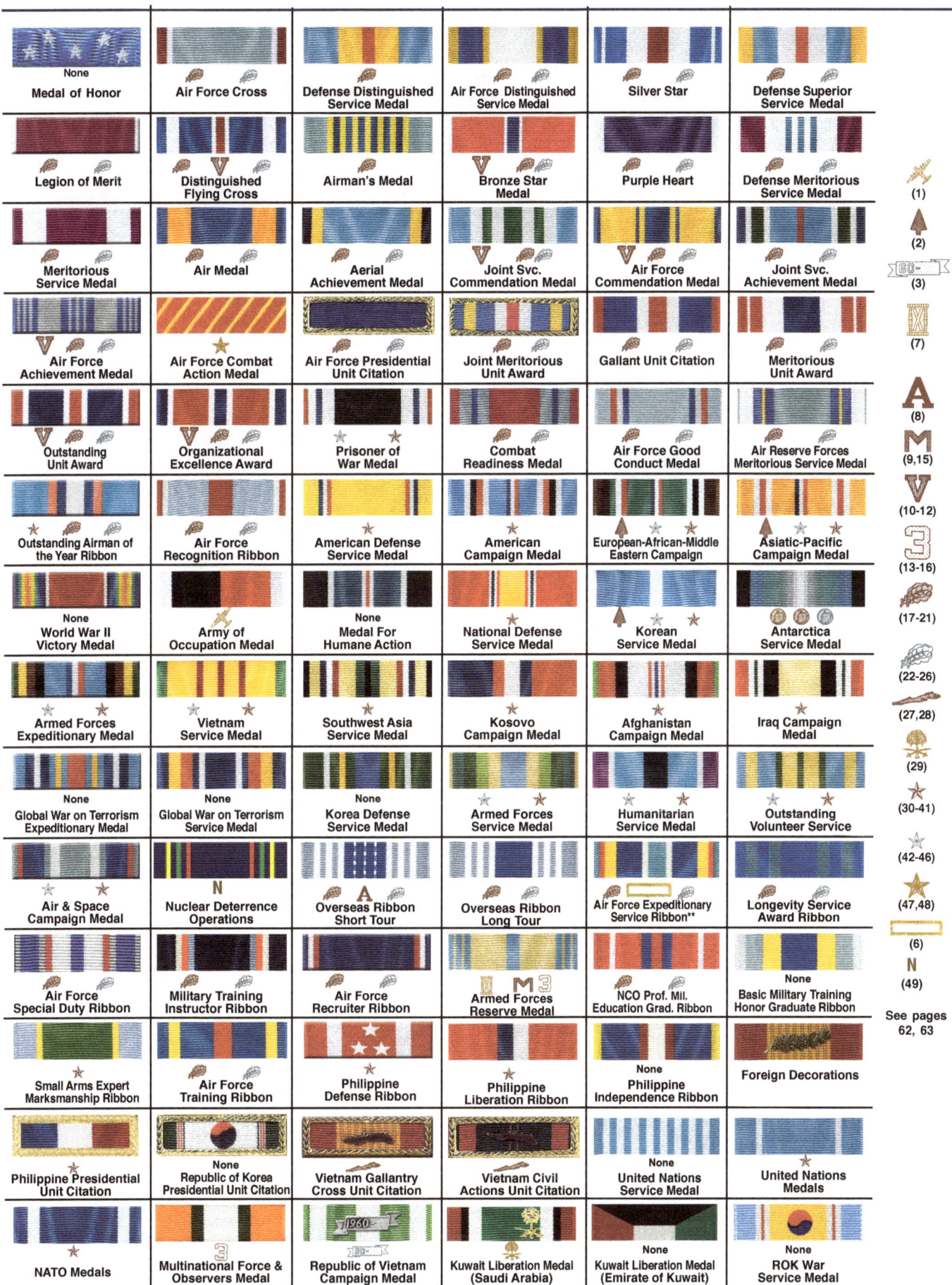

United States Air Force Current Multi-Service Order of Precedence

Air Force and Navy Service

Air Force and Army Service

Air Force and Marine Service

In todays Armed Forces it is not unusual for a member of the Air Force to have served in another branch of the Armed Forces before joining the Air Force. The examples above show ribbons of previous service in the Navy, Army and Marine Corps before joining the Air Force. The chart below and extenting to the next pages lays out the correct order of precedence to the best of our knowledge for members of the Air Force to wear their ribbons from previous service. There are no specific restrictions for wearing other service awards on the Air Force uniform. However only one UN ribbon maybe worn with additional awards incdicated by bronze stars.

58 Decorations, Medals, and Ribbons of the United States Air Force

|  Air Medal |  Aerial Achievement Medal |  Joint Service Commendation Medal |  Air Force Commendation Medal |  Army Commendation Medal |  Navy & Marine Corps Commendation Medal |  Coast Guard Commendation Medal | Transportation 9-11 Medal (Coast Guard) |

|  Joint Service Achievement Medal | Air Force Achievement Medal | Army Achievement Medal |  Navy & USMC Achievement Medal | Coast Guard Achievement Medal | USCG Commandant's Letter of Commendation |  Air Force Combat Action Medal |  Navy & Marine Corps Combat Action Ribbon |

| Coast Guard Combat Action Ribbon |  Air Force Presidential Unit Citation | Army Presidential Unit Citation | Navy Presidential Unit Citation | Coast Guard Presidential Unit Citation | Joint Meritorious Unit Award | Air Force Gallant Unit Citation | 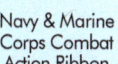 Air Force Meritorious Unit Award |

| 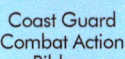 Air Force Outstanding Unit Award |  Air Force Organizational Excellence Award |  Army Valorous Unit Award | Navy Unit Commendation | D.O.T. Secy's Outstanding Unit Award |  Coast Guard Unit Commendation |  Army Meritorious Unit Commendation | 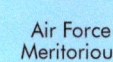 Navy Meritorious Unit Commendation |

| Coast Guard Meritorious Unit Commendation |  Coast Guard Meritorious Team Comndatn |  Army Superior Unit Award |  Navy "E" Ribbon |  Coast Guard "E" Ribbon | Coast Guard Bicentenniel Unit Commendation |  Gold Lifesaving Medal |  Silver Lifesaving Medal |

| Prisoner of War Medal | 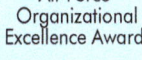 Air Force Combat Readiness Medal | 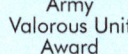 Air Force Good Conduct Medal | Army Good Conduct Medal | Reserve Special Commendation Ribbon | Navy Good Conduct Medal | Marine Corps Good Conduct Medal | Coast Guard Good Conduct Medal |

|  Air Reserve Forces Meritor's Service Medal |  Army Reserve Components Achvm't Medal |  Naval Reserve Meritorious Service Medal |  Selected Marine Corps Reserve Medal |  Coast Guard Reserve Good Conduct Medal |  Coast Guard Enlisted Person of the Year |  Navy Fleet Marine Force Ribbon |  Outstanding Airman of the Year Ribbon |

Air Force Recognition Ribbon

Copyright Medals of America 2015

United States Air Force Current Multi-Service Order of Precedence Continued

Navy Expeditionary Medal	Marine Corps Expeditionary Medal	China Service Medal (1937, 1945)	Amer. Defense Service Medal (1939-41)	Women's Army Corps Service Medal	American Campaign Medal (1941-46)	Asiatic-Pacific Camp'n Medal (1941-46)	Europe-Afri-can-Mid East Camp'gn (1941-46)

World War II Victory Medal (1941 - 46)	U.S. Antarctic Expedit'n Medal (1939-41)	World War II Occupat'n Medal (1945-57)	Medal for Humane Action (1948-49)	Nat'l Defense Service Medal (1950, 61, 90, 01)	Korean Service Medal (1950-54)	Antarctica Service Medal	Coast Guard Arctic Service Medal

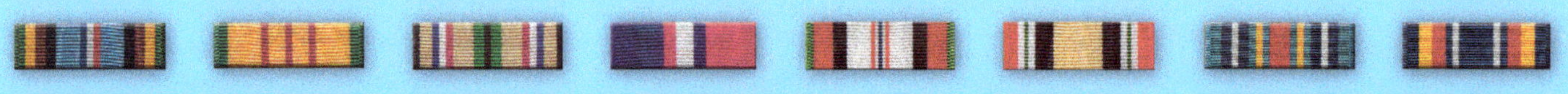

Armed Forces Expeditionary Medal	Vietnam Service Medal (1965-73)	Southwest Asia Service Medal (1991-95)	Kosovo Campaign Medal (1999-2013)	Afghanistan Campaign Medal (2001 -)	Iraq Campaign Medal (2003 - 11)	War on Terrorism Service Medal (2001-)	War on Terrorism Expeditionary Medal (2001-)

Korea Defense Service Medal (1954-)	Armed Forces Service Medal	Humanitarian Service Medal	Outstanding Volunteer Service Medal	Air Force Air & Space Campaign Medal	Nuclear Deterrence Operations	Air Force Overseas Ribbon (Short Tour)	Air Force Overseas Ribbon (Long Tour)

Air Force Expeditionary Service Ribbon	Army Overseas Service Ribbon	Army Reserve Comp. Overseas Training Ribbon	Navy Sea Service Deploy-ment Ribbon	Navy Arctic Service Ribbon	Naval Reserve Sea Service Ribbon	Navy & Marine Corps Overseas Service Ribbon	Navy Recruiting Service Ribbon

Navy Recruit Training Service Ribbon	Navy Ceremonial Guard Ribbon	Marine Corps Recruiting Ribbon	Marine Corps Drill Instructor Ribbon	Marine Security Guard Ribbon	Marine Combat Instructor ribbon	Coast Guard Special Oper'ns Service Ribbon	Coast Guard Sea Service Ribbon

Coast Guard Restricted Duty Ribbon	Coast Guard Overseas Service Ribbon	Air Force Longevity Service Award Ribbon	Air Force Special Duty Ribbon	Air Force Military Training Instructor Rib'n **(Obsolete)**	Air Force Recruiter Ribbon **(Obsolete)**	Army Sea Duty Ribbon	Armed Forces Reserve Medal

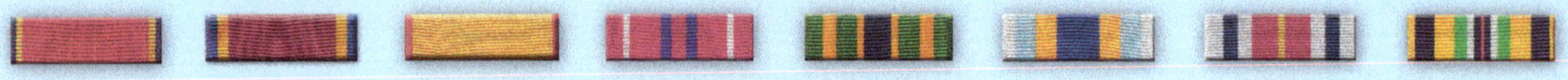

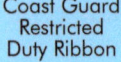

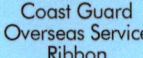

Naval Reserve Medal **(Obsolete)**	Naval Reserve Medal (1st Ribbon)	Marine Corps Reserve Ribbon **(Obsolete)**	Air Force NCO Prof. Military Ed-ucation Grad.	Army NCO Prof. Development Ribbon	Air Force Basic Military Training Honor Graduate	Coast Guard Basic Training Honor Graduate Ribbon	Coast Guard Recruiting Service Ribbon

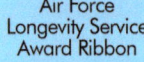

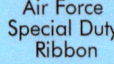

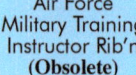

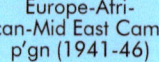

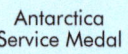

| 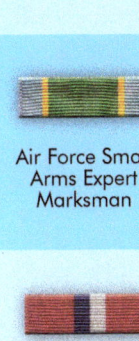 Air Force Small Arms Expert Marksman | 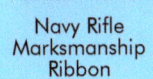 Navy Rifle Marksmanship Ribbon |  Navy Pistol Marksmanship Ribbon | Coast Guard Rifle Marksmanship Ribbon | Coast Guard Pistol Marksmanship Ribbon |  Air Force Training Ribbon |  Army Service Ribbon |  Philippine Defense Ribbon |

|  Philippine Liberation Ribbon (1944 - 45) | 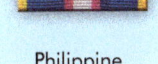 Philippine Independence Ribbon (1946) |  Foreign Decoration 1* | Foreign Decoration 2* | Foreign Decoration 3* |  Foreign Decoration 4* |  Philippine Presidential Unit Citation |  Korean Presidential Unit Citation |

|  Vietnam Presidential Unit Citation |  Vietnam Gallantry Cross Unit Citation | 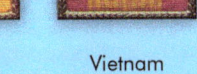 Vietnam Civil Actions Unit Citation |  United Nations Korean Service Medal** | UN Palestine Mission (UNTSO) | UN India/ Pakistan Mission (UNMOGIP) | UN New Guinea Mission (UNTEA) |  UN Iraq/ Kuwait Mission (UNIKOM) |

| 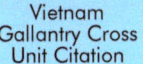 UN Western Sahara Mission (MINURSO) |  UN Cambodia Mission 1 (UNAMIC) | 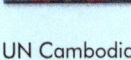 UN Yugoslavia Mission (UNPROFOR) |  UN Cambodia Mission 2 (UNTAC) |  UN Somalia Mission (UNOSOM) |  UN Haiti Mission (UNMIH) | 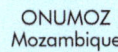 ONUMOZ Mozambique |  UNOMIG Georgia |

| 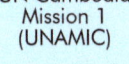 UNPREDEP Macedonia |  UNTAES E. Slavonia, Baranja |  MINUGUA Guatemala | UNMIK Kosovo |  UNTAET East Timor |  MONUC Congo |  UNMEE Ethiopia, Eritrea |  UNMISET East Timor |

|  UNMIL Liberia |  MINUSTAH Haiti |  UNAMID Darfur |  MINURCAT Cent. Afr. Rep, Chad |  MONUSCO Congo |  UNAMI UN Assistance Mission in Iraq |  UN Special Service Medal (UNSSM) |  NATO Meritorious Svs Medal |

|  NATO Medal for Bosnia** |  NATO Medal for Kosovo |  NATO Medal for Operation Eagle Assist | NATO Medal for Operation Active Endeavor | 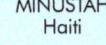 NATO Medal for Balkan Operations | NATO Medal for Afghanistan, Sudan, Iraq | 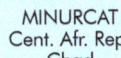 Multinational Force & Observers Medal |  Inter-American Defense Board Medal |

|  Republic of Vietnam Campaign Medal |  Kuwait Liberation Medal (Saudi Arabia) |  Kuwait Liberation Medal (Kuwait) |  Republic of Korea War Service Medal | | | | |

* The examples of foreign awards are displayed in the foreign order of precedence.

** Only one United Nations and one NATO ribbon can be worn regardless of the number awarded.

Copyright Medals of America 2015

Air Force Medal and Ribbon Devices Listed Alphabetically

1. Airplane, C-54, Gold

Services: All
Worn on: World War II Occupation Medals
Denotes: Service during Berlin Airlift (1948-49)

2. Arrowhead, Bronze

Services: Army, Air Force
Worn on: Campaign awards since World War II
Denotes: Combat assault or invasion

3. Bar, Date, Silver

Services: All
Worn on: Republic of Vietnam Campaign Medal
Denotes: Worn upon initial issue; has no significance

4a. Bar, Knotted, Bronze

Services: Army
Worn on: Army Good Conduct Medal
Denotes: Additional periods of service (awards 2 through 5)

4b. Bar, Knotted, Silver

Services: Army
Worn on: Army Good Conduct Medal
Denotes: Additional periods of service (awards 6 through 10)

4c. Bar, Knotted, Gold

Services: Army
Worn on: Army Good Conduct Medal
Denotes: Additional periods of service (awards 11 through 15)

5. Frame, Gold

Services: Air Force
Worn on: Expeditionary Service Ribbon
Denotes: Satisfactory participation in combat operations

6a. Hourglass, Bronze

Services: All
Worn on: Armed Forces Reserve Medal
Denotes: 10 Years of service in the Reserve Forces

6b. Hourglass, Silver

Services: All
Worn on: Armed Forces Reserve Medal
Denotes: 20 Years of service in the Reserve Forces

6c. Hourglass, Gold

Services: All
Worn on: Armed Forces Reserve Medal
Denotes: 30 Years of service in the Reserve Forces

7. Letter "A", Serif, Bronze

Services: Air Force
Worn on: Overseas Service Ribbon (Short Tour)
Denotes: Service at bases above the Arctic Circle

8. Letter "M", Block, Bronze

Services: All
Worn on: Armed Forces Reserve Medal
Denotes: Mobilization for active military service

9. "New "Letter N ,Gold
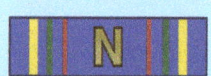
Services: Air Force
Worn on: Nuclear Deterrence Opn Award
Denotes: Direct support of ICBM operations

10. Letter "V", Serif, Bronze

Services: All (Except Marine Corps)
Worn on: Personal decorations
Denotes: Valorous actions in combat

11. Letter "V", Serif, Bronze

Services: All
Worn on: Joint Service Commendation Medal
Denotes: Valorous actions in combat

12. Numeral, Block, Bronze

Services: Army
Worn on: Air Medal
Denotes: Total number of awards

13. Numeral, Block, Bronze

Services: All (Except Coast Guard)
Worn on: Humanitarian Service Medal
Denotes: Number of additional awards (Obsolete)

14. Numeral, Block, Bronze

Services: All
Worn on: Armed Forces Reserve Medal
Denotes: Number of times mobilized for active duty

15. Numeral, Block, Bronze

Services: All
Worn on: Multinational Force & Observers Medal
Denotes: Total number of awards

16. Oak Leaf Cluster, Bronze

Services: Army, Air Force
Worn on: Personal Decorations
Denotes: One (1) additional award

17. Oak Leaf Cluster, Bronze

Services: Army, Air Force
Worn on: Unit Awards
Denotes: One (1) additional award

18. Oak Leaf Cluster, Bronze

Services: Air Force
Worn on: Service and Reserve Awards
Denotes: One (1) additional award

19. Oak Leaf Cluster, Bronze

Services: All
Worn on: Joint Service Decorations and Joint Meritorious Unit Award
Denotes: One (1) additional award

20. Oak Leaf Cluster, Bronze

Services: Air Force
Worn on: Recognition Awards
Denotes: One (1) additional award

21. Oak Leaf Cluster, Silver

Services: Army, Air Force
Worn on: Personal Decorations
Denotes: Five (5) additional awards

22. Oak Leaf Cluster, Silver

Services: Army, Air Force
Worn on: Unit Awards
Denotes: Five (5) additional awards

23. Oak Leaf Cluster, Silver

Services: Air Force
Worn on: Service and Reserve Awards
Denotes: Five (5) additional awards

24. Oak Leaf Cluster, Silver

Services: All
Worn on: Joint Service decorations and Joint Meritorious Unit Award
Denotes: Five (5) additional awards

25. Oak Leaf Cluster, Silver

Services: Air Force
Worn on: Recognition Awards
Denotes: Five (5) additional awards

26. Palm, Bronze

Service: Air Force
Worn on: Vietnam Gallantry Cross Unit Citation
Denotes: No significance, worn upon initial issue

Chart designed by Mr. Lonny Borts, America's Master Military Ribbon Expert

27. Palm, Bronze
Services: All
Worn on: Vietnam Civil Actions Unit Citation
Denotes: No significance, worn upon initial issue

28. Palm & Swords Device, Gold
Services: All
Worn on: Kuwait Liberation Medal (Saudi Arabia)
Denotes: No significance, worn upon initial issue

29. Star 3/16" dia., Bronze
Services: All
Worn on: Campaign awards since World War II
Denotes: Battle participation (one star per major engagement)

30. Star 3/16" dia., Bronze
Services: All
Worn on: Expeditionary Medals
Denotes: Additional service (one star per designated expedition)

31. Star 3/16" dia., Bronze
Services: All
Worn on: Prisoner of War and Humanitarian Service Medals
Denotes: One (1) additional award

32. Star 3/16" dia., Bronze
Services: All
Worn on: Service Awards
Denotes: One (1) star per each additional award

33. Star 3/16" dia., Bronze
Services: Air Force
Worn on: Outstanding Airman of the Year Award
Denotes: "One of 12" competition finalist

34. Star 3/16" dia., Bronze
Services: Air Force
Worn on: Small Arms Expert Marksmanship Ribbon
Denotes: Additional weapon qualification

35. Star 3/16" dia., Bronze
Services: All
Worn on: World War I Victory Medal
Denotes: One (1) star for each campaign clasp earned

36. Star 3/16" dia., Bronze
Services: All
Worn on: American Defense Service Medal
Denotes: Overseas service prior to World War II

37. Star 3/16" dia., Bronze
Services: All
Worn on: National Defense Service Medal
Denotes: Additional awards (one star per designated period)

38. Star 3/16" dia., Bronze
Services: All
Worn on: Philippine Defense and Liberation Ribbons
Denotes: Additional battle honors

39. Star 3/16" dia., Bronze
Services: All (Except Army)
Worn on: Philippine Presidential Unit Citation
Denotes: Additional award

40. Star 3/16" dia., Bronze
Services: All
Worn on: United Nations and NATO mission medals
Denotes: One (1) star for each additional mission

41. Star 3/16" dia., Silver
Services: All
Worn on: Campaign awards since World War II
Denotes: Battle participation in five (5) major engagements

42. Star 3/16" dia., Silver
Services: All
Worn on: Expeditionary Medals
Denotes: Five (5) additional expeditions

43. Star 3/16" dia., Silver
Services: All
Worn on: Prisoner of War and Humanitarian Service Medals
Denotes: Five (5) additional awards

44. Star 3/16" dia., Silver
Services: All
Worn on: Service Awards
Denotes: Five (5) additional Awards

45. Star 3/16" dia., Silver
Services: Army
Worn on: Campaign medals up to World War I
Denotes: Citation for Gallantry

46. Star 5/16" dia., Gold
Services: Air Force
Worn on: Combat Action Medal
Denotes: One (1) additional award

47. Star 5/16" dia., Gold
Services: All
Worn on: Inter-American Defense Board Medal
Denotes: One (1) additional award

Obsolete Letter "V", Serif, Bronze
Services: Air Force
Was Worn on: Outstanding Unit Award and Organizational Excellence Award
Denotes: Valorous actions by unit in combat

Copyright Medals of America 2015

Examples of Air Force Ribbons and Devices

❖ Placement of the Bronze Letter "V" on the Ribbon and Medal

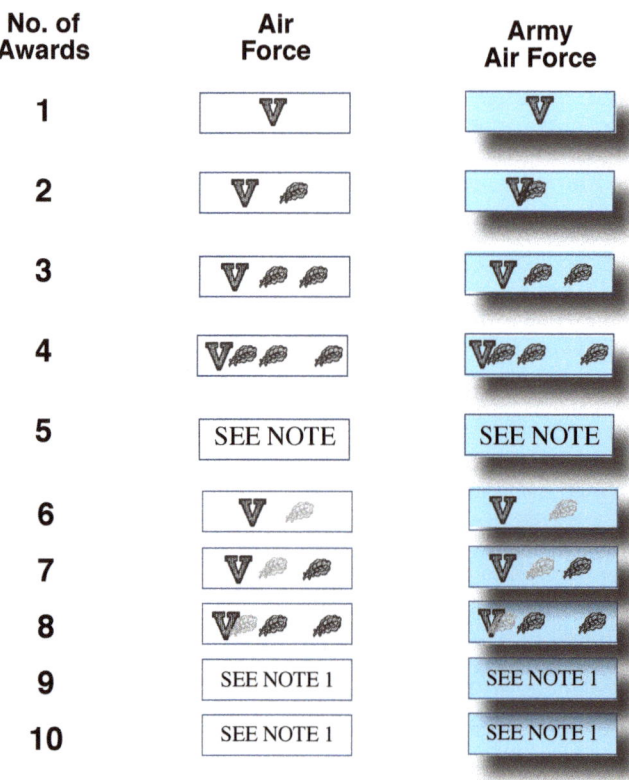

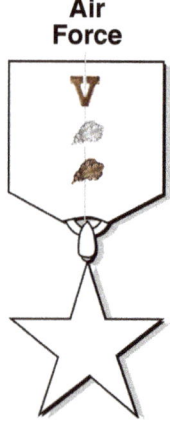

Same as ribbons to the left–but placed vertically

NOTE:

1. Army and Air Force regulations limit the number of devices which may be worn on a single ribbon to a maximum of four. If more than four devices are authorized, a second ribbon is worn containing the excess devices.

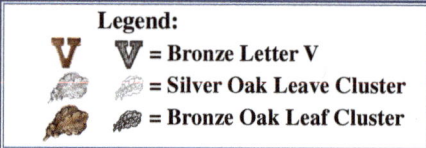

❖ Placement of Devices on the Armed Forces Reserve Medal

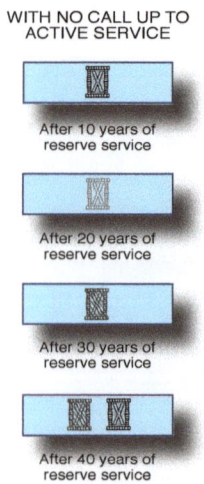

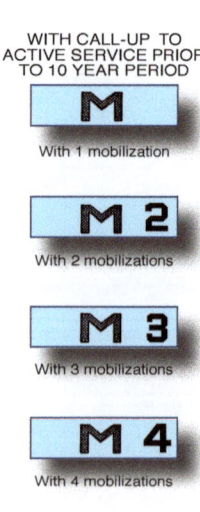

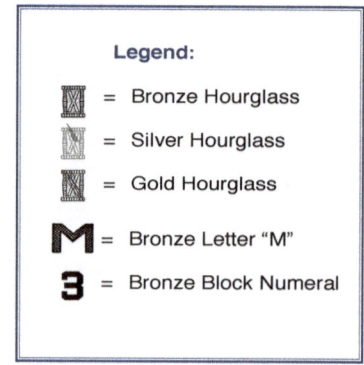

Note: The M device is always goes in the center of the ribbon.

❖ Placement of Silver Devices on the Ribbon

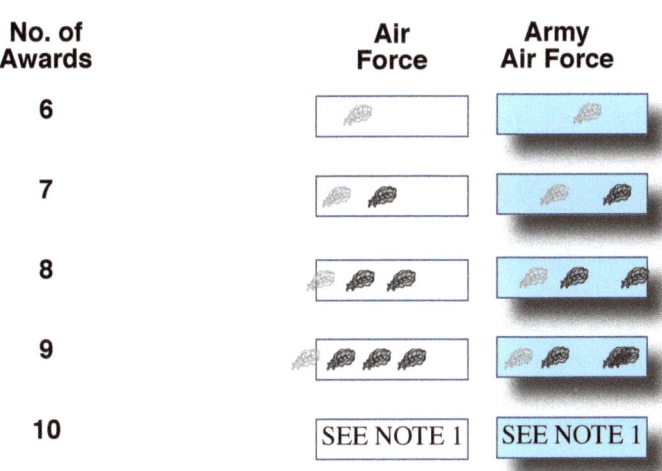

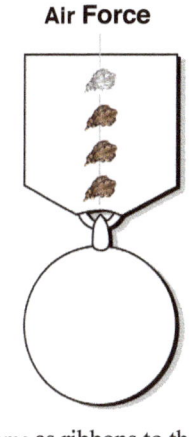

Same as ribbons to the left but placed vertically

NOTE:
1. Army and Air Force regulations limit the number of oak leaf clusters which may be worn on a single ribbon to a maximum of four (4). If more than four devices are authorized, a second ribbon is worn containing the excess devices.

Legend:
- ★ = 5/16" Bronze Star
- ☆ = 5/16" Silver Star
- 🍂 = Bronze Oak Leaf Cluster
- 🍂 = Silver Oak Leaf Cluster

❖ Placement of Silver Campaign Stars on the Ribbon

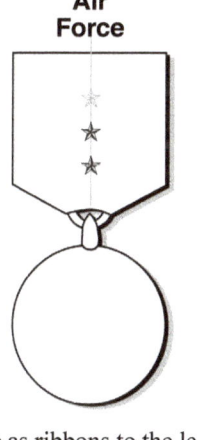

Same as ribbons to the left but placed vertically

NOTE:
1. Army and Air Force regulations limit the number of devices which may be worn on a single ribbon to a maximum of four. If more than four devices are authorized, a second ribbon is worn containing the excess devices.
2. Campaign stars are often referred to as "Battle Stars".

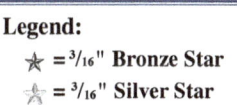

Legend:
- ★ = 3/16" Bronze Star
- ☆ = 3/16" Silver Star

Medals of America 65

❖ The United States Air Force Pyramid of Honor

The Pyramid of Honor

As mentioned earlier the Air Force award system has evolved into a highly structured program which is called the "Pyramid of Honor." The system is designed to reward services ranging from heroism on the battlefield to superior performance of noncombatant duties and even includes the completion of entry level airman training.

Since World War II the Air Force has generally embraced Napoleon's concept of liberally awarding medals and ribbons to enhance morale and esprit de corps. The large number of Air Medal awarded in World War II is an example of this policy. Air Force losses were second only to the infantry and the leadership wanted an immediate way to recognize the extraordinary

service of the air crews. Over the years an expanded and specifically-tailored awards program became generally very popular in the all-volunteer Air Force and has played a significant part in improving morale, job performance, recruitment and reenlistments among junior officers and enlisted personnel.

The decorations and awards which represent the rich United States Air Force military heritage are presented on the following pages. The details of these awards tell the story of the dedication to the ideals of freedom and sacrifices required to earn them.

The color plates display multiply versions of each medal and describe the Service or Services to which the award is authorized, the date instituted and the criteria for award along with appropriate attachments and in some cases examples of how they were earned. Generally every variation, official and unofficial, of the medal, miniature, ribbon and pin is shown. This is probably the only publication in the world that does that.

The medals and ribbons are presented in the Air Force order of precedence beginning with the Medal of Honor and ending with the commonly awarded foreign medals and ribbons. The foreign section also includes an expanded area on the awards which may have been received by Air Force personnel from the Republic of South Vietnam.

The Air Force issues and present all decorations and many of the service medals. With the exception of the Medal of Honor all of the medals and ribbons presented in this book can be purchased by veterans, their family, active-duty, Guard and Reserve. *Make no mistake, it is absolutely against the law to buy or sell a United States Medal of Honor.*

The Stolen Valor Act

The Stolen Valor Act of 2005, signed into law by President George W. Bush, was a statute that broadened the provisions of a previous law and addressed the unauthorized wear, manufacture or sale of certain military decorations and medals. The law made it a federal misdemeanor to falsely represent oneself as having received any U.S. military decoration or medal. If convicted, defendants might have be imprisoned for up to six months, (up to one year in the case of the Medal of Honor). In United States v. Alvarez the U.S. Supreme Court ruled on June 28, 2012, that the Stolen Valor Act was too restrictive and an unconstitutional abridgment of freedom of speech under the First Amendment, striking down the law in a 6 to 3 decision. In 2012, a new bill was introduced in the House of Representatives which passed by a vote of 410-3. The sponsors argued that the bill would survive judicial review since it resolved the constitutional issues involved and targets those who falsely claim to have earned certain major military decorations or any medal signifying combat service. A companion bill, the Stolen Valor Act of 2013 was ratified by the United States Senate on May 22, 2013 and signed into law by the President on June 3, 2013.

Army Medal of Honor

Navy Medal of Honor

Army Medal of Honor (1862-1896)

Air Force Medal of Honor

Army Medal of Honor (1896-1904)

Medal of Honor

In the United States the Government is based on a totally democratic society, therefore, it is fitting that the first medal to reward valor on the battlefield was for private soldiers and seamen (although extended in later years to officers).

The Congressional Medal of Honor (referred to universally as the Medal of Honor in all official documents) was born in conflict, steeped in controversy during its early years and finally emerged, along with Britain's Victoria Cross, as one of the world's premier awards for bravery.

The medal is actually a statistical oddity, proving the unlikely equation that "Three equals One". Although there are three separate medals representing America's highest reward for bravery (illustrated above), there is now only a single set of directives governing the award of this, the most coveted of all U.S. decorations.

Many Americans today are confused by the term: "Congressional Medal of Honor" when, in fact, the proper term is "Medal of Honor". Part of this confusion stems from a law that was passed on July 1918 authorizing the President to present the medal" ... in the name of Congress". The fact that all Medals of Honor recipients belong to the Congressional Medal of Honor Society, an official organization chartered by Congress, does not help the situation. However, suffice it to state that the medal is referred to universally as the "Medal of Honor" in all statues, awards manuals, uniform regulations and official documents.

Air Force Medals of Honor

Army Medal of Honor (1904-1944)

While Captain Eddie Rickenbacker did not start flying combat missions until 7 months before the war ended, he shot down a total of 26 German aircraft. That was the highest total of any American pilot in the war, making him officially the American "ace of aces."

He was awarded the Medal of Honor for his actions in the World War I. He was known to Americans simply as "Captain Eddie."

Rosette

Army Medal of Honor (1944-Present)

Ribbon

Army Medal of Honor

The Army Medal of Honor was first awarded in 1862 but, owing to extensive copying by veterans groups, was redesigned in 1904 and patented by the War Department to ensure the design exclusivity.

The present medal, a five pointed golden star, lays over a green enamelled laurel wreath. The center of the star depicts Minerva, Goddess of righteous war and wisdom, encircled by the words: "United States of America".

Medal of Honor (Army)

Awarded to members of the Army Air Force and United States Air Force until May 1954.

Medals of America 69

Air Force Medals of Honor

Rosette

Ribbon

Medal of Honor (Air Force)

For conspicuous gallantry and intrepidity at the risk of one's own life, above and beyond the call of duty, in action involving actual conflict with an opposing armed force.

Reverse

Congress authorized the Air Force Medal of Honor in 1960, 13 years after the establishment of the Air Force as an independent Service (prior to 1960, airmen received the Army medal). The medal design is fashioned after the Army version and is a five pointed star with a green enameled laurel wreath. The center depicts the head of the Statue of Liberty surrounded by 34 stars. The star hangs from a representation of the Air Force coat of arms and is suspended from a bar inscribed "VALOR".

Establishing Authority: The Air Force design of the Medal of Honor was established by Congress on July 6, 1960 and presented to all Air Force recipients of the MOH on or after November 1, 1965. Air Force decorations are generally considered as deriving from their earlier comparable Army awards; that is, they are not legally "new" decorations but rather the Air Force design versions of previously established Army decorations. The Air Force is authorized to issue its own version of the Army Medal of Honor by Section 8741 of Title 10 of the U.S. Code.

Criteria: Criteria for awarding the Air Force Medal of Honor is the same as for the Army and Navy, to wit: "conspicuous gallantry and intrepidity at the risk of one's own life above and beyond the call of duty."

Each recommendation for the Medal of Honor must incontestably prove that the self sacrifice or personal bravery involved conspicuous risk of life.

The Air Force Medal of Honor became effective on November 1, 1965 and was designed by Lewis J. King, Jr. of the Army's Institute of Heraldry. The first recipient of the Air Force Medal of Honor was Major Bernard E. Fisher on January 19, 1967 for his heroic actions in rescuing a fellow pilot who had crash landed on a landing strip in the A Shau Valley on March 10, 1966. Airman First Class John L. Levitow was the first USAF enlisted person to receive the Medal. He was awarded the MOH for saving his AC-47 gunship and crew in Vietnam. Five airmen received the Medal of Honor during the Vietnam War.

The medal is officially described as follows: within a wreath of laurel in green enamel, a gold-finished five-pointed star, one point down, tipped with trefoils and each point containing a crown of laurel and oak on a green enamel background. Centered upon the star is an annulet of thirty-four stars which surround the profile of the head from the Statue of Liberty. The star is suspended by a connecting bar and pinned hinge from a trophy consisting of a bar inscribed with the word, "VALOR", above an adaptation of a thunderbolt. The bar is suspended from a pale blue moire silk neck band behind an elongated square pad in the center, with the corners turned back and charged with thirteen white stars in the form of a triple chevron. The star is a replica of the design originally adopted by the Navy and the Army. The profile taken from the Statue of Liberty represents those ideals for which the United States is known throughout the world. The thunderbolt is taken from the Air Force coat of arms and distinguishes the medal as an Air Force decoration. The medal is two inches in overall height and two and one-sixteenth inches in overall width, making it larger than either the Army or Navy Medals of Honor. The reverse is plain, providing space for the name of the recipient.

Although referred to here and in most texts as the "Air Force Medal of Honor", the nation's highest award for valor for Air Force personnel is properly referred to as the "Medal of Honor - Air Force design."

Colonel George E. Day's Medal of Honor Citation

Rank and organization: Colonel DAY, GEORGE E. (then Major), U.S. Air Force, Forward Air Controller Pilot of an F-100 aircraft. Place and date: North Vietnam, 26 August 1967. Entered service at: Sioux City, Iowa. Born: 24 February 1925, Sioux City, Iowa.

Citation:

On 26 August 1967, Col. Day was forced to eject from his aircraft over North Vietnam when it was hit by ground fire. His right arm was broken in 3 places, and his left knee was badly sprained. He was immediately captured by hostile forces and taken to a prison camp where he was interrogated and severely tortured. After causing the guards to relax their vigilance, Col. Day escaped into the jungle and began the trek toward South Vietnam. Despite injuries inflicted by fragments of a bomb or rocket, he continued southward surviving only on a few berries and uncooked frogs. He successfully evaded enemy patrols and reached the Ben Hai River, where he encountered U.S. artillery barrages. With the aid of a bamboo log float, Col. Day swam across the river and entered the demilitarized zone. Due to delirium, he lost his sense of direction and wandered aimlessly for several days. After several unsuccessful attempts to signal U.S. aircraft, he was ambushed and recaptured by the Viet Cong, sustaining gunshot wounds to his left hand and thigh. He was returned to the prison from which he had escaped and later was moved to Hanoi after giving his captors false information to questions put before him. Physically, Col. Day was totally debilitated and unable to perform even the simplest task for himself. Despite his many injuries, he continued to offer maximum resistance. His personal bravery in the face of deadly enemy pressure was significant in saving the lives of fellow aviators who were still flying against the enemy. Col. Day's conspicuous gallantry and intrepidity at the risk of his life above and beyond the call of duty are in keeping with the highest traditions of the U.S. Air Force and reflect great credit upon himself and the U.S. Armed Forces.

George Everett "Bud" Day (24 February 1925–27 July 2013) was a United States Air Force Colonel and pilot who served during World War II, the Korean War, and the Vietnam War, including five years and seven months as a prisoner of war in North Vietnam. Day was a recipient of the Medal of Honor and the Air Force Cross. As of 2013, he is the only person to be awarded both medals.

Medals of America 71

❖ Old Distinguished Service Cross

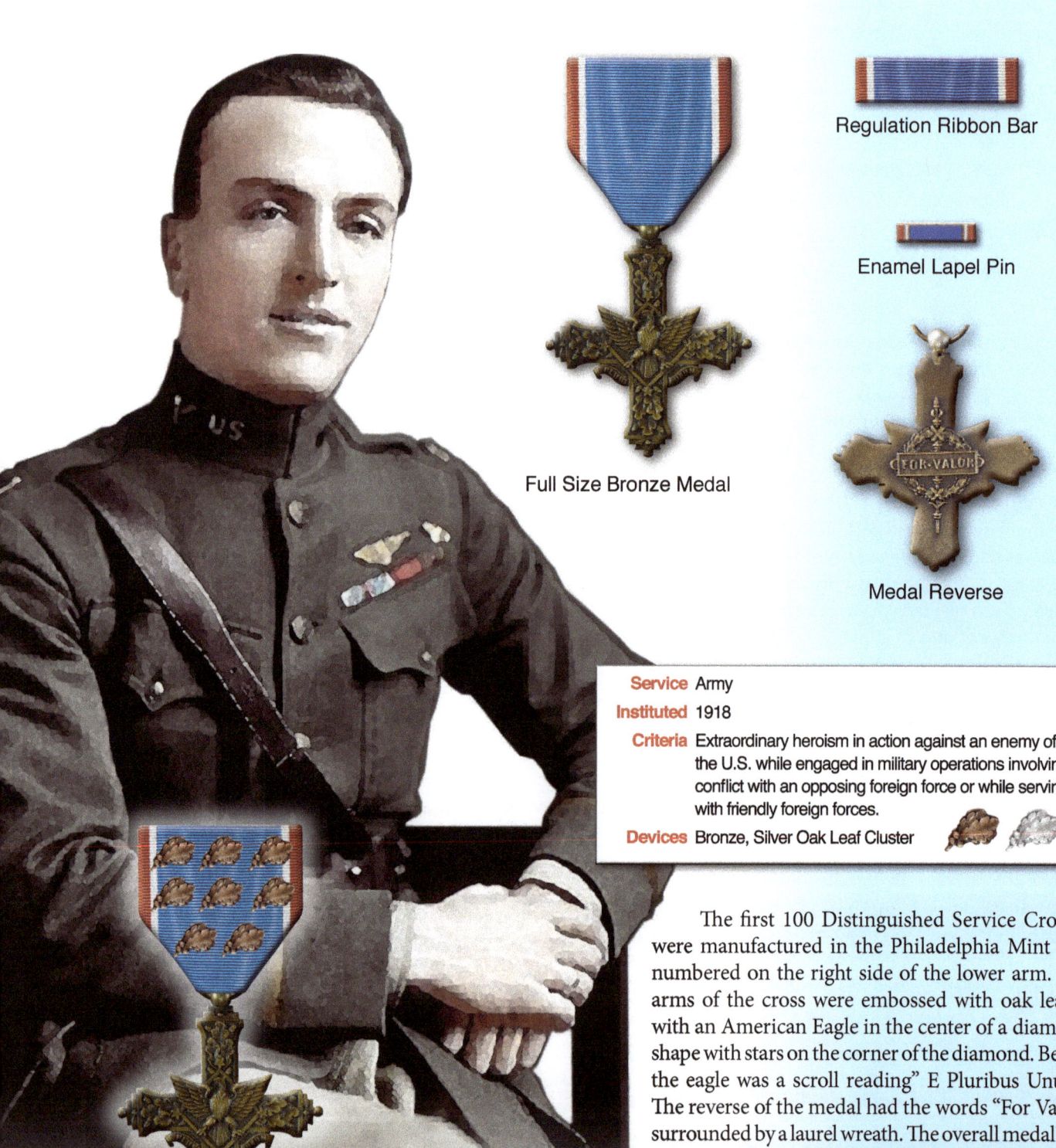

Full Size Bronze Medal

Regulation Ribbon Bar

Enamel Lapel Pin

Medal Reverse

Service	Army
Instituted	1918
Criteria	Extraordinary heroism in action against an enemy of the U.S. while engaged in military operations involving conflict with an opposing foreign force or while serving with friendly foreign forces.
Devices	Bronze, Silver Oak Leaf Cluster

Captain Eddie Rickenbacker was awarded nine Distinguished Service Crosses.

The first 100 Distinguished Service Crosses were manufactured in the Philadelphia Mint and numbered on the right side of the lower arm. The arms of the cross were embossed with oak leaves with an American Eagle in the center of a diamond shape with stars on the corner of the diamond. Below the eagle was a scroll reading" E Pluribus Unum". The reverse of the medal had the words "For Valor" surrounded by a laurel wreath. The overall medal was influence by the art deco design of the period and was soon replaced by a second design with decorative, fluted edges and a small ornamental scroll topped by a ball at the end of each arm. The diamond and stars design was replaced by a wreath behind an enlarged eagle. Several variations of the first type DSC were made in France and are generally thinner and slightly smaller in size. None of the French made DSCs were numbered.

Lieutenant FRANK LUKE, JR.

(Air Service), U.S. Army Pilot, 27th Aero Squadron, 1st Pursuit Group, Air Service, A.E.F.

Date of Action: September 12 - 15, 1918

Citation: (First Award)
The Distinguished Service Cross is presented to Frank Luke, Jr., Second Lieutenant (Air Service), U.S. Army, for extraordinary heroism in action near St. Mihiel, France, September 12 to 15, 1918. Lieutenant Luke, by skill, determination, and bravery, and in the face of heavy enemy fire, successfully destroyed eight enemy observation balloons in four days.

Other Award: Medal of Honor (WWI), Distinguished Service Cross w/OLC (WWI)

Lieutenant ELLIOTT WHITE SPRINGS

(Air Service), U.S. Army Pilot, 148th Aero Squadron, 4th Pursuit Group, Air Service, A.E.F.

Date of Action: August 22, 1918

Citation:
The Distinguished Service Cross was presented to Elliott White Springs, First Lieutenant (Air Service), U.S. Army, for extraordinary heroism in action near Bapaume, France, August 22, 1918. Attacking three enemy planes (type Fokker), who were diving on one of our planes. Lieutenant Springs, after a short and skillful fight, drove off two of the enemy and shot down the third. On the same day he attacked a formation of five enemy planes (type Fokker), and after shooting down one plane was forced to retire because of lack of ammunition.

Lieutenant FRANK KERR HAYS

(Air Service), U.S. Army Pilot, 13th Aero Squadron, 2d Pursuit Group, Air Service, A.E.F.

Date of Action: September 13, 1918

Citation:
The Distinguished Service Cross was presented to Frank Kerr Hays, Second Lieutenant (Air Service), U.S. Army, for extraordinary heroism in action in the region of Chambley, France, September 13, 1918. Lieutenant Hays was one of an offensive patrol of five planes, attacked by seven enemy scouts (Fokker type), that dived down on them from the clouds, catching the American patrol in a disadvantageous position. In the course of the combat which followed, both of Lieutenant Hays' machine guns jammed. By an extraordinary effort he cleared his guns and drove off the adversary. He then observed his flight commander in a dangerous situation with two enemy planes behind him. He attacked and destroyed one and forced the other to withdraw.

❖ Distinguished Service Cross

Bronze

Anodized or Gold-Plated

Regulation Ribbon Bar

Enamel Lapel Pin

Medal Reverse

Miniature Medals

Mini Ribbon (unofficial)

Hat Pin

Authorized by Congress on July 9, 1918. Awarded for extraordinary heroism against an armed enemy but of a level not justifying the award of the Medal of Honor. It may be awarded to both civilians and military personnel serving in any capacity with the Army who distinguish themselves by heroic actions in combat. The act or acts of heroism must be so notable and have involved risk of life so extraordinary as to set the individual apart from his comrades. The medal had been initially proposed for award to qualifying members of the American Expeditionary Forces in Europe during World War I but was authorized permanently by Congress in the Appropriations Act of 1918. The Cross was designed by 1st Lt. Andre Smith and Captain Aymar Embury with the final design sculpted by John R. Sinnock at the Philadelphia Mint.

While DSCs were originally numbered, the practice was discontinued during World War II. In 1934 the DSC was authorized to be presented to holders of the Certificate of Merit which had been discontinued in 1918 when the Distinguished Service Medal was established. The medal is a cross with an eagle with spread wings centered on the cross behind which is a circular wreath of laurel leaves. The cross has decorative fluted edges with a small ornamental scroll topped by a ball at the end of each arm. The laurel wreath is tied at its base by a scroll which upon which are written the words, "FOR VALOR." The eagle represents the United States and the laurel leaves surrounding the eagle representing victory and achievement. The reverse of the cross features the same decorations at the edges that appear on the front. The eagle's wings, back and tips also show. Centered on the reverse of the cross is a laurel wreath. In the center of the wreath is a decorative rectangular plaque for engraving the soldier's name. The ribbon has a one inch wide center of national blue edged in white and red. The national colors taken from the flag stand for sacrifice (red), purity (white) and high purpose (blue).

Service	Army
Instituted	1918
Criteria	Extraordinary heroism in action against an enemy of the U.S. or while serving with friendly foreign forces.
Devices	Bronze, Silver Oak Leaf Cluster
Notes	100 copies of earlier design cross were issued with a European-style (unedged) ribbon.

EISENHOWER VISITS DEBDEN. (l. to r.) General Eisenhower, C.G., SHAEF Capt. Don Gentile, Col. Don Blakeslee. Award of the Distinguished Service Cross, April 1944.

General William "Billy" Mitchell, regarded as the father of the United States Air Force, enlisted as an Army private early in the Spanish-American war. Later commissioned, he predicted in 1906 that the future of the Armed Forces was in the air. He became head of the Army Signal Corps Aviation Section in May 1916. He was the first American officer to fly over German lines in World War I. Promoted to Colonel in 1917 by September 1918 he planned and led an allied air force of over 1000 planes in the battle of St. Mihiel, the first coordinated air ground offense in the history of modern warfare. Promoted to brigadier general in 1918, he became Chief of the Air Service of the American Expeditionary Forces.

A strong advocate of air power he was court-martialed in 1925 for accusing Army and Navy leaders of almost treasonable conduct for investing limited American defense funds in battleships instead of aircraft. Found guilty of insubordination by an old line military tribunal he resigned. After his death in 1936 the President commissioned him a Major General. He is the only Air Force officer that a military aircraft was named after; the B-25 Mitchell.

World War I was the first conflict which American military personnel could accept foreign decorations. Shown in this remarkable photograph Gen. Mitchell's decorations are listed below:

Senior Pilot Wings
Expert Rifle Marksmanship Badge
French Pilot Wings

U.S. Army Decorations
Distinguished Service Cross (1918)
Distinguished Service Medal (1919)

U.S. Army Service Medals
Spanish War Service Medal (1918)
Philippine Campaign Medal, 1905
Army of Cuban Occupation Medal (1915)
Cuban Pacification Medal (1909)
Mexican Service Medal (1917)
First World War Victory Medal with 8 campaign clasps (1919)

International Orders, Decorations and Medals
Grand Officer of the Order of the Crown of Italy
Companion of the Order of St Michael and St George (United Kingdom)
Commander of the French Legion of Honor
Commander of the Order of Saints Maurice and Lazarus (Italy)
Cross of War (France) with one silver palm, 3 bronze palms and one silver star
Verdun Medal (France)
War Merit Cross (Italy)

❖ Air Force Cross

Full Size Medal Bronze — Medal Reverse

Regulation Ribbon Bar

Enamel Lapel Pin

Miniature Medals

Mini Ribbons (unofficial)

Enamel Hat Pin (unofficial)

Service	Air Force
Instituted	1960
Criteria	Extraordinary heroism in action against an enemy of the U.S. or while serving with friendly foreign forces.
Devices	Bronze, Silver Oak Leaf Cluster
Notes	Created with the same legislation which established the Distinguished Serrvice Cross.

Authorized on July 6, 1960 for extraordinary heroism while engaged in a military action against an enemy of the United States. Before July 6, 1960, deserving Air Force personnel received the Army Distinguished Service Cross (DSC). The Air Force Cross is awarded for heroic actions not justifying the Medal of Honor and is presented in the name of the President.

The first actual award of the Air Force Cross was made in 1968 posthumously to Major Rudolf Anderson, Jr. who was shot down and killed over Cuba during the Cuban missile crisis while flying a U-2 aircraft. The first living enlisted man to receive the award was Sgt. Duane D. Hackney who received it for rescuing a downed Air Force pilot in Vietnam. As of this writing, the latest awards of the Air Force Cross were the result of actions occurring during Operation Enduring Freedom in Afghanistan.

Major Rudolf Anderson, Jr.

The design of the Air Force Cross medal and ribbon are based on the design of the Army Distinguished Service Cross. The medal is a bronze cross containing a gold-plated American bald eagle with wings against a cloud formation encircled by a green laurel wreath. The awardees name may be engraved on the reverse. The ribbon has a very wide center stripe of Brittany blue with narrow stripes of white and red at the edges. The blue in the center of the ribbon is a lighter shade than that of the Army Distinguished Service Cross indicating the close connection of these awards. Additional awards are denoted by bronze and silver oak leaf clusters.

The Air Force Cross is the second highest Air Force award for valor and was designed by Eleanor Cox of the United States Air Force awards division and was sculpted by Thomas Hudson Jones of the Institute of Heraldry. The Air Force Cross has been awarded fewer than 200 times. Multiple awards are very rare with Col. John Dramesi, Capt. Leland Kennedy, and Lt. Col. Robinson Risner being the only two-time recipient's (all during the Vietnam War). Lt. Col. James Kasler, an F105 pilot, was awarded two Air Force Crosses in Vietnam and a third for his heroic service as a POW during the Vietnam war.

76 Decorations, Medals, and Ribbons of the United States Air Force

❖ Air Force Cross
HEROES

Captain Barry F. Crawford, Jr. was awarded the Air Force Cross for extraordinary heroism for action in Afghanistan as Special Tactics Officer near Laghman Province, Afghanistan, on 4 May 2010. Attached to Army Special Forces Operational Detachment Alpha and their Afghan partner force, Captain Crawford conducted a helicopter assault into Hendor Village. Upon landing, Captain Crawford received reports that multiple groups of armed enemy were maneuvering into prepared fighting positions in the high ground around the village. As the assault force initiated clearance operations, they received heavy machine gun and sniper fire from an enemy force of over 100 fighters. As the assault force was attacked, Captain Crawford took decisive action to save the lives of three wounded Afghan soldiers and evacuate two Afghan soldiers killed in action. Recognizing that the wounded Afghan soldiers would die without evacuation he ran into the open to guide the helicopter into the landing zone. Once the pilot had eyes on Captain Crawford who remained exposed, despite having one of his radio antennas shot off inches from his face, he guided in the aircraft. Captain Crawford then bounded across open terrain, engaged enemy positions with his assault rifle and called in AH-64 strafe attacks to defeat the ambush allowing the aid-and-litter teams to move toward the casualties. While the casualties were being moved the team's exposed position once again came under from two enemy trucks threatening the medial evacuation landing zone. As the medical evacuation helicopter took direct hits from small arms fire, it departed with only four casualties leaving one wounded Afghan soldier on the ground. Captain Crawford executed a plan to suppress the enemy, enabling the helicopter to return to the hot landing zone to retrieve the last casualty. While Captain Crawford's element exfiltrated the village, the assault force conducted a two kilometer movement over steep terrain with little to no cover. During this movement the ground force commander and Captain Crawford's element were ambushed and pinned down in the open from multiple enemy fighting positions, some as close as 150 meters away. Without regard for his own life, Captain Crawford moved alone across open terrain in the kill zone to locate and engage enemy positions with his assault riffle while directing AH-64 30-mm. strafe attacks. Continuing to move with minimal cover, Captain Crawford again engaged the enemy with his assault rifle while integrating AH-64s and F-15E's in a coordinated air-to-ground attack plan that included strafing runs along with 500 and 2,0000-pound bomb and Hellfire missile strikes. Throughout the course of the ten hour firefight, Captain Crawford braved effective enemy fire and consciously placed himself at grave risk on four occasions while controlling over 33 aircraft and more than 40 airstrikes on a well-trained and well-prepared enemy force. His selfless actions and expert airpower employment neutralized a numerically superior enemy force and enabled friendly elements to exfiltrate the area without massive casualties. Through his extraordinary heroism, superb airmanship, and aggressiveness in the face of the enemy, Captain Crawford has reflected great credit upon himself and the United States Air Force.

Air Force Chief of Staff Gen. Norton Schwartz presents the Air Force Cross to Staff Sgt. Robert Gutierrez, Special Tactics and Training Squadron combat controller, during a ceremony at Hurlburt Field, Fla., Oct. 27, 2011. Gutierrez was awarded the Air Force Cross, the second highest military decoration, for displaying extraordinary heroism in combat while deployed in support of Operation Enduring Freedom. (U.S. Air Force photo/Staff Sgt. Sharida Jackson)

Colonel William J. "Dixie" Sloan, First in history to be awarded the Air Force Cross.

During World War II "Dixie" Sloan became a DOUBLE ACE with a total of 12 victories. He was originally submitted and approved for award of the Distinguished Service Cross for his actions, but the award was never acted upon. In 1968 Sloan's son contacted General Tooey Spaatz who had originally approved the DSC, and the former Air Force Commander requested that the record be corrected. In February 1969 Colonel Sloan was awarded the Air Force Cross in lieu of the DSC he had never received, making his actions on July 5, 1943, the first in history to merit award of the Air Force Cross. He retired as an Air Force Colonel on September 30, 1963.

◆ DOD Distinguished Service Medal

Bronze

Anodized or Gold-Plated

Regulation Ribbon Bar

Enamel Lapel Pin

Medal Reverse

Miniature Medals

Mini Ribbons (unofficial)

Enamel Hat Pin (unofficial)

Authorized on July 9, 1970 and awarded to military officers for exceptionally meritorious service while assigned to a Department of Defense joint activity. The Secretary of Defense is the awarding authority for the medal, which is usually awarded to very senior officers. Examples of assignments that may allow qualification for this medal are: Chairman, Joint Chiefs of Staff; Chiefs and Vice Chiefs of the Military Services, including the Commandant and Assistant Commandant of the Marine Corps and Commanders and Vice Commanders of Unified and Specified Commands. It may also be awarded to other senior officers who serve in positions of great responsibility or to an officer whose direct and individual contributions to national security or defense are also recognized as being so exceptional in scope and value as to be equivalent to contributions normally associated with positions encompassing broader responsibilities. Subsequent awards are denoted by bronze and silver oak leaf clusters.

The medal depicts an American bald eagle with wings spread and the United States shield on its breast; the eagle is superimposed on a medium blue pentagon (which represents the five services) and is surrounded by a gold circle that has thirteen stars in the upper half and a laurel and olive wreath in the lower half. On the reverse of the medal is the inscription, "FROM THE SECRETARY OF DEFENSE TO...FOR DISTINGUISHED SERVICE." Space is provided between the TO and FOR for engraving of the recipient's name. The ribbon has a central stripe of red flanked by stripes of gold and blue. The red represents zeal and courageous action, the gold denotes excellence and the medium blue represents the Department of Defense.

Service	All Services (By Sec. of Defense)
Instituted	9 July 1970
Criteria	Exceptionally meritorious service to the United States while assigned to a Joint Activity in a position of unique and great responsibility.
Devices	Bronze & Silver Oak Leaf Cluster

The Defense Distinguished Service Medal was designed by Mildred Orloff and sculpted by Lewis J. King, Jr., both of the Institute of Heraldry.

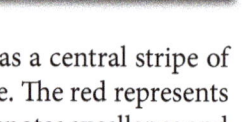
The Defense Distinguished Service Ribbon with an oak leaf for second award is a the top of this senior officers ribbon chest. Two other ribbons are also DOD awards indicating a long period of assignment on the Joint Staff. All of the decorations shown here are awards for meritorious service.

❖ Distinguished Service Medal *(Army)*

Regulation Ribbon Bar
Enamel Lapel Pin
Miniature Medals
Mini Ribbons (unofficial)
Medal Reverse
Enamel Hat Pin (unofficial)

Bronze — Anodized or Gold-Plated

Authorized by Congress on July 9, 1918 for exceptionally meritorious service to the United States while serving in a duty of great responsibility with the U.S. Army. It was originally intended for qualifying actions during wartime only but was later authorized during both wartime or peacetime. As this country's highest award for meritorious service or achievement, it has been awarded to both military and civilians, foreign and domestic. In 1918 the first American to receive this medal was General John J. Pershing, Commanding General of the American Expeditionary Forces during World War I. Individuals who had received the Certificate of Merit before its disestablishment in 1918 were authorized to receive the DSM. The Army DSM is seldom awarded to civilians and personnel below the rank of Brigadier General.

Service	Army (Army Air Service)
Instituted	1918
Criteria	Exceptionally meritorious service to the United States Government in a duty of great responsibility.
Devices	All Services: Bronze & Silver Oak Leaf Cluster
Notes	Originally issued with European (unedged) ribbon ("French Cut")

The medal is a circular design containing the U.S. Coat of Arms encircled by a blue ring with the inscription, "FOR DISTINGUISHED SERVICE MCMXVII". Subsequent awards are denoted by the attachment of a bronze oak leaf cluster to the medal and ribbon. In the center of the reverse of the medal, amidst several flags and weapons, is a blank scroll for engraving the awardees name.

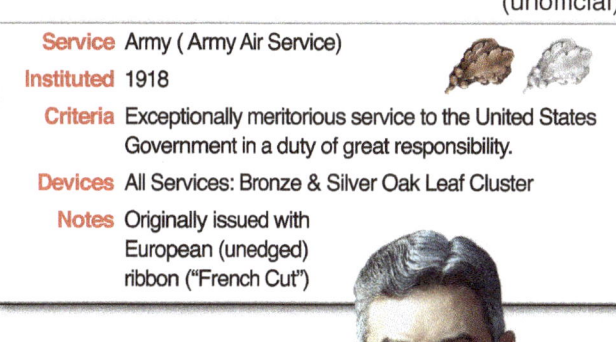

General Curtis Emerson LeMay was the fifth chief of staff of the U.S. Air Force, and is shown wearing the Army DSM with two clusters.

The ribbon has a central wide white stripe edged with blue and an outer red band representing the colors of the U.S. flag. The Army Distinguished Service Medal was designed by Captain Aymar E. Embury III and sculpted by Private Gaetano Cecere.

◆ Air Force Distinguished Service Medal

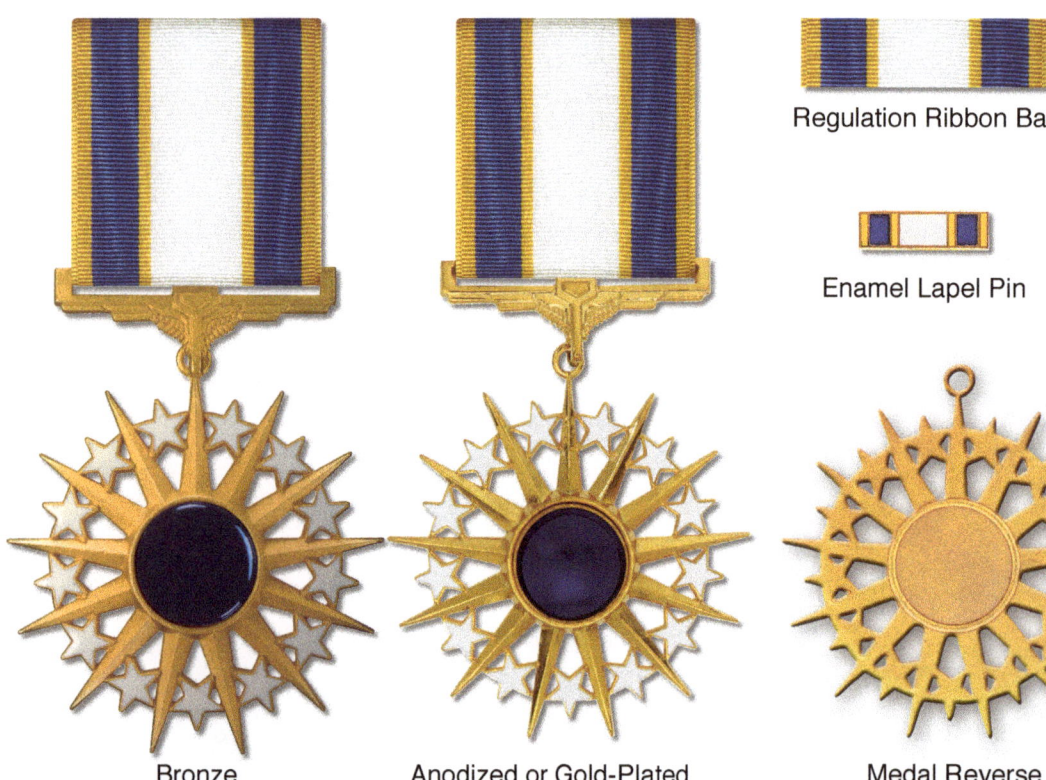

Bronze

Anodized or Gold-Plated

Medal Reverse

Regulation Ribbon Bar

Enamel Lapel Pin

Miniature Medals

Mini Ribbon (unofficial)

Enamel Hat Pin (unofficial)

The Air Force Distinguished Service Medal was authorized by Congress on July 6, 1960; it evolved from the Army Distinguished Service Medal authorized in 1918. The medal is awarded for exceptionally meritorious service to the U.S. in a duty of great responsibility; the term "great responsibility" denotes the success of a major operation or program attributed to the proper exercise of authority and judgement. This is the highest peacetime Air Force decoration awarded. It is presented to all recipients who are awarded this decoration on or after November 1, 1965; AAF and USAF personnel who were awarded this decoration prior to this date received the Army version. The Air Force Distinguished Service Medal is rarely awarded to officers below the rank of Brigadier General. The medal should be referred to as "Distinguished Service Medal – Air Force design." Major General Osmond J. Ritland, Air Force Systems Command, was the first recipient of the Air Force Distinguished Service Medal on November 30, 1965 for his efforts as Deputy Commander for Manned Space Flight. Subsequent awards are denoted by bronze and silver oak leaf clusters. The medal is a blue stone centered within 13 gold rays, each separated by 13 white stars. The recipient's name may be engraved on the reverse of the medal.

Service	Air Force
Instituted	1960
Criteria	Exceptionally meritorious service to the United States Government in a duty of great responsibility.
Devices	Bronze & Silver Oak Leaf Cluster
Notes	Original design was modified and used as the Airman's Medal.

Air Force Chief of Staff Gen. Norton Schwartz awards Lt. Gen. Richard Y. Newton III, Assistant Vice Chief of Staff and Director, Air Staff, Headquarters U.S. Air Force, the Distinguished Service Medal at his retirement ceremony on Joint Base Anacostia-Bolling, D.C., on April 27, 2012. (U.S. Air Force photo)

Lt. Gen. Frank Gorenc, outgoing Commander, Third Air Force, the war-fighting headquarters of U.S. Air Forces in Europe is presented the Air Force DSM at change-of-command ceremony. Lt. Gen. Gorenc was awarded the DSM after more than 30 months commanding 33,000 airmen and civilians and 10 wings throughout Europe. A naturalized U.S. citizen, Lt. Gen. Gorenc and his family came to the United States from Yugoslavia when he was four years old, with nothing except a few suitcases and $100.

USAF Image

United Kingdom's DFC

The Air Force Distinguished Service Medal was designed by Mr. Frank Alston of the U.S. Army Institute of Heraldry. The sunburst design is a striking example of the medalist's art and an extraordinary departure from the normal designs developed 40 years earlier in the Art Deco era for the Distinguished Service Medals of the other services. The front design has a sunburst of 13 gold rays separated by 13 white enameled stars, with a semiprecious blue stone in the center. The back of the medal is flat for engraving. The star is suspended from the ribbon by a wide slotted bar which consists of stylized wings symbolic of the Air Force. The slotted bar and wings came from the United Kingdom's 1918 DFC's slotted bar design. A touch of tradition on the most modern of medal designs.

Ribbon Description

The ribbon has a wide center stripe of white flanked on either side by a thin stripe of old gold, a wide stripe of ultramarine blue and a narrow stripe of old gold at the edges. The blue stone in the center represents the vault of the heavens; the 13 stars represent the original colonies and man's chain of achievements. The sunburst represents the glory that accompanies great achievements, and the rays depict man's quest for light and knowledge.

❖ Silver Star

Bronze   Anodized or Gold-Plated

Regulation Ribbon Bar
Enamel Lapel Pin
Miniature Medals
Medal Reverse
Mini Ribbons (unofficial)
Enamel Hat Pin (unofficial)

Notes: Derived from the 3/16" silver "Citation Star" previously worn on Army campaign medals.

Awarded for gallantry in action against an enemy of the United States or while engaged in military operations involving conflict against an opposing armed force in which the United States is not a belligerent party. The level of gallantry required, while of a high degree, is less than that required for the Medal of Honor, Army, Air Force or Navy Cross. The Silver Star is derived from the Army's "Citation Star", a 3/16" dia. silver star device which was worn on the ribbon bar and suspension ribbon of the "appropriate Army campaign medal" by any soldier cited in orders for gallantry in action. Although most applicable to the World War I Victory Medal, it was retroactive to all Army campaign medals dating back to the Civil War.

The Silver Star Medal was instituted in 1932 with the first award presented to General Douglas MacArthur, the Army's then-Chief-of-Staff. The Silver Star was designed by Rudolf Freund of the firm of Bailey, Banks and Biddle. On August 7, 1942, the award was extended to Navy personnel and, later that year, authorized for civilians serving with the armed forces who met the stated criteria specified in the initial regulation.

The medal is a five-pointed star finished in gilt-bronze. In the center of the star is a three-sixteenths inch silver five-pointed star within a wreath of laurel, representing the silver [citation] star prescribed by the original legislation. The rays of both stars align. The top of the medal has a rectangular-shaped loop for the suspension ribbon. The laurel wreath signifies achievement and the larger gilt-bronze star represents military service. The reverse contains the inscription, "FOR GALLANTRY IN ACTION" with a space to engrave the name of the recipient.

The ribbon, based on the colors of the National flag, has a center stripe of red flanked by a stripes of white which are flanked by blue bands with borders of white edged in blue. Additional awards are denoted by a bronze or silver oak leaf clusters or gold and silver stars depending on the recipient's Branch of Service.

Service	All Services (Originally Army only)
Instituted	1932
Criteria	Gallantry in action against an armed enemy of the United States or while serving with friendly foreign forces.
Devices	Army/Air Force: Bronze, Silver Oak Leaf Cluster; Navy/Marine Corps/Coast Guard: Gold, Silver Star.
Notes	Derived from the 3/16" silver "Citation Star" previously worn on Army campaign medals.

Lt. Col. Walter T. Holmes, wearing the Silver Star, DFC, Purple Heart, Air Medal and Great Britian's DFC probably in 1944 or 1945, after the Ploesti raid.

Silver Star Tie

Silver Star Certificate

U.S. Air Force Maj. Gen. Frank Padilla, Deputy Inspector General of the Air Force, pins a Silver Star on Staff Sgt. Zachary Kline, 306th Rescue Squadron pararescueman during a ceremony at Davis-Monthan Air Force Base, Ariz., July 14, 2013. Kline earned the medal while serving in Afghanistan April 23, 2011. (U.S. Air Force photo)

(U.S. Air Force photo)

Medals of America 83

❖ Defense Superior Service Medal

Bronze

Anodized

Medal Reverse

Regulation Ribbon Bar

Enamel Lapel Pin

Miniature Medals

Mini Ribbon (unofficial)

Enamel Hat Pin (unofficial)

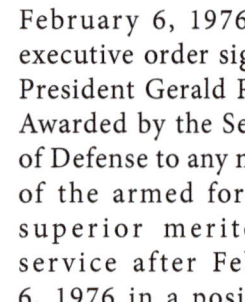

Authorized on February 6, 1976 by an executive order signed by President Gerald R. Ford. Awarded by the Secretary of Defense to any member of the armed forces for superior meritorious service after February 6, 1976 in a position of significant responsibility while assigned to a DOD joint activity, including the Office of the Secretary of Defense, the Joint Chiefs of Staff, and specified and unified commands. The medal was created to provide recognition to those assigned to joint duty on a level equivalent to that recognition provided by the Legion of Merit. Prior to establishment of the Defense Superior Service Medal, the Office of the Secretary of Defense had to provide recognition through equivalent awards that were approved through individual service channels. Although it was established as equivalent to the Legion of Merit, its precedence is before the Legion of Merit when both are worn. Oak leaf clusters denote additional awards.

Service	All Services (by Secretary of Defense)
Instituted	6 February 1976
Criteria	Superior meritorious service to the United States while assigned to a Joint Activity in a position of significant responsibility.
Devices	Bronze & Silver Oak Leaf Cluster

The medal depicts a silver American bald eagle with wings spread and the United States shield on its breast; the eagle is superimposed on a medium blue pentagon (which represents the five services) and is surrounded by a silver circle that has thirteen stars in the upper half and a laurel and olive wreath in the lower half. On the reverse of the medal is the inscription, "FROM THE SECRETARY OF DEFENSE TO...FOR SUPERIOR SERVICE." Space is provided between the TO and FOR for engraving of the recipient's name. The ribbon consists of a central stripe of red, flanked on either side by stripes of white, blue and gold.

> **Did You Know?** At the time of its creation it was decided that this medal would be obtained at the lowest possible cost and "with as little involvement as possible." For these reasons and because it would rank just below the Defense Distinguished Service Medal for similar service, it was decided to use the same design as the Defense Distinguished Service Medal, except that it would be finished in silver rather than gold and the inscription on the reverse would be modified.

❖ Legion of Merit

Bronze — Anodized or Gold-Plated

Regulation Ribbon Bar

Enamel Lapel Pin

Miniature Medals

Medal Reverse

Mini Ribbon (unofficial)

Enamel Hat Pin (unofficial)

Authorized by Congress on July 20, 1942 for award to members of the Armed Forces of the United States for exceptionally meritorious conduct in the performance of outstanding service. Superior performance of normal duties will not alone justify award of this decoration. It is not awarded for heroism in the Air Force but rather for service and achievement while performing duties in a key position of responsibility. It may be presented to foreign personnel but is not authorized for presentation to civilian personnel. There are four degrees of this decoration that are awarded to foreign personnel only (Chief Commander, Commander, Officer and Legionnaire). The first two degrees are comparable in rank to the Distinguished Service Medal and are usually awarded to heads of state and to commanders of armed forces, respectively. The last two degrees are comparable in rank to the award of the Legion of Merit to U.S. service members. The Medal was designed by Colonel Robert Townsend Heard and sculpted by Katharine W. Lane.

The name and design of the Legion of Merit was strongly influenced by the French Legion of Honor. The medal is a white enameled five-armed cross with ten points, each tipped with a gold ball and bordered in red enamel. In the center of the cross, thirteen stars on a blue field are surrounded by a circle of heraldic clouds. A green enameled laurel wreath circles behind the arms of the cross. Between the wreath and the center of the medal, in between the arms of the cross are two crossed arrows pointing outward. The blue circle with thirteen stars surrounded by clouds is taken from the Great Seal of the United States and is symbolic of a "new constellation," as the signers of the Declaration of Independence called our new republic. The laurel wreath represents achievement, while the arrows represent protection of the nation. The reverse of the cross is a gold colored copy of the front with blank space to be used for engraving The raised inscription, "ANNUIT COEPTIS MDCCLXXXII" with a bullet separating each word encircles the area to be engraved. The words, "UNITED STATES OF AMERICA" and "ANNUIT COEPTIS" (He [God] Has Favored Our Undertaking) come from the Great Seal of the United States and the date, "MDCCLXXXII" (1782) refers to the year General Washington established the Badge of Military Merit. The ribbon is a purple-red called American Beauty Red which is edged in white. The color is a variation of the original color of the Badge of Military Merit.

Service	All Services
Instituted	1942 (retroactive to 8 Sept 1939)
Criteria	Exceptionally meritorious conduct in the performance of outstanding services to the United States.
Devices	Army/Air Force: Bronze, Silver Oak Leaf Cluster; Navy/Marine Corps/Coast Guard: Bronze Letter "V" (for valor), Gold, Silver Star.
Notes	Issued in four degrees (Legionnaire, Officer, Commander & Chief Commander) to foreign nationals.

President Franklin D. Roosevelt, established the rules for the Legion of Merit and required the President's approval for the award. However, in 1943, at the request of General George C. Marshall, approval authority for U.S. personnel was delegated to the War Department.

Executive Order 10600, dated March 15, 1955, by President Dwight D. Eisenhower, revised approval authority. Current provisions are contained in Title 10, United States Code 1121.

❖ Legion of Merit for Foreign Military Personnel

Chief Commander Legion of Merit

Commander Legion of Merit

Officer Legion of Merit

Legionnaire Legion of Merit

The Legion of Merit is awarded to members of armed forces of foreign nations in four degrees according to the level of responsibility, rank and position of the receiver of the award.

The degrees of Chief Commander, Commander, Officer, and Legionnaire are awarded only to members of armed forces of foreign nations under the criteria outlined in Army Regulation 672-7 and is based on the relative rank or position of the recipient as follows:[5]

Chief Commander: *Head of state or government. However this degree was awarded by President Roosevelt to some Allied World War II theater commanders usually for joint amphibious landings or invasions. (The President had this power under Executive Order 9260 of October 29, 1942 paragraph 3b.[6])*

Commander: *Equivalent of a U.S. military chief of staff or higher position, but not to a head of state.*

Officer: *General or flag officer below the equivalent of a U.S. military chief of staff; colonel or equivalent rank for service in assignments equivalent to those normally held by a general or flag officer in U.S. military service; or military attachés.*

Legionnaire: *All recipients not included above. When the Legion of Merit is awarded to members of the uniformed services of the United States it is awarded without reference to degree.*

The degrees and the design of the decoration were clearly influenced by the French Legion of Honor (Légion d'honneur) The Chief Commander Degree of the Legion of Merit Medal overall width is 2 15/16 inches (75 mm). The words "UNITED STATES OF AMERICA" are engraved in the center of the reverse. A miniature of the decoration in gold on a horizontal gold bar is worn on the service ribbon.

The Commander Degree of the Legion of Merit Medal overall width is 2 1/4 inches (57 mm). A gold laurel wreath in the v-shaped angle at the top connects an oval suspension ring to the neck ribbon that is 1 15/16 inches (49 mm) in width. The reverse of the five-pointed star is enameled in white, and the border is crimson. In the center, a disk for engraving the name of the recipient surrounded by the words "ANNUIT COEPTIS MDCCLXXXII." An outer scroll contains the words "UNITED STATES OF AMERICA." A miniature of the decoration in silver on a horizontal silver bar is worn on the service ribbon.

The Officer Degree of the Legion of Merit Medal is similar to the degree of Commander except the overall width is 1 7/8 inches (48 mm) and the pendant has a suspension ring instead of the wreath for attaching the ribbon. A gold replica of the medal, 3/4 inch (19 mm) wide, is centered on the suspension ribbon.

The Legionnaire Degree of the Legion of Merit Medal and the Legion of Merit Medal issued to U.S. personnel are basically the same as the degree of Officer, except the suspension ribbon does not have the medal replica. The date "MDCCLXXXII" (1782), which is the date of America's first decoration, the Badge of Military Merit, now known as the Purple Heart. The ribbon design also follows the pattern of the Purple Heart ribbon.

> The degrees and the design of the decoration were clearly influenced by the French Legion of Honor (Légion d'honneur)

❖ Legion of Merit Examples awarded to Foreign Military Officers

General Kayani (Pakistan) receiving the Legion of Merit from the United States for his service.

Lieutenant General Ehud Barak (Israeli Army) was decorated with the Legion of Merit in 1993.

❖ Distinguished Flying Cross

Full Size Medals

Bronze — Anodized or Gold-Plated — Medal Reverse

Regulation Ribbon Bar

Enamel Lapel Pin

Miniature Medals

Mini Ribbon (unofficial)

Enamel Hat Pin (unofficial)

The Distinguished Flying Cross was authorized on July 2, 1926 and implemented by an executive order signed by President Calvin Coolidge on January 28, 1927. It is awarded to United States military personnel for heroism or extraordinary achievement that is clearly distinctive involving operations during aerial flight that are not routine. It is the first decoration authorized in identical design and ribbon to all branches of the U.S. Armed Forces. Captain Charles A. Lindbergh was the first recipient of the Distinguished Flying Cross for his solo flight across the Atlantic. The Wright Brothers were awarded the DFC by an Act of Congress for their first manned flight at Kitty Hawk, North Carolina in 1903. Amelia Earhart became the only female civilian to be awarded the DFC when it was presented to her by the United States Army Air Corps for her aerial exploits. Such awards to civilians were prohibited on March 1, 1927 by Executive Order 4601.

While the Distinguished Flying Cross was never intended to be an automatic award, the Army Air Force did use it in that capacity many times during World War II by awarding DFCs for specific number of sorties and flying hours in a combat theater.

The front of the medal is a four-bladed propeller contained within a bronze cross suspended from a straight bar attached to the medal drape. The reverse is blank and provides space for the recipient's name and date of the award. The ribbon is blue with a narrow stripe of red bordered by white in the center. The ribbon edges are outlined with bands of white inside blue. Additional awards are denoted by bronze and silver oak leaf clusters or gold and silver stars depending on the recipient's Service Branch.

Service	All Services
Instituted	1926 (retroactive to 6 April 1917)
Criteria	Heroism or extraordinary achievement while participating in aerial flight.
Devices	Army/Air Force: Bronze, Silver Oak Leaf Cluster; Bronze Letter "V" (Air Force), Navy/Marine Corps: Bronze Letter "V" (for valor), Gold, Silver Star; Coast Guard: Gold, Silver Star.

This display of a 20th Air Force World War II veteran shows his awards of the Distinguished Flying Cross, Purple Heart, four Air Medals, American Campaign Medal, the Asiatic Pacific Campaign Medal with four battle stars, the World War II Victory Medal, the Philippine Liberation Medal, and the Philippine Independence Medal. The final medal is a World War II Victory Commemorative.

Distinguished Flying Cross Tie.

This display of a Fifth Air Force Korean war pilot veteran shows his awards of the Distinguished Flying Cross, Air Medal, National Defense Medal, the Korean Service Medal with two battle stars, the UN Korean Service Medal, ROK Korean War Service medal, and four Commemorative Medals, the last being the Cold War Victory Commemorative Medal.

This display of a Vietnam pilot veteran shows his awards of the Distinguished Flying Cross, Meritorious Service Medal, five Air Medals, the Air Force Commenation Medal, Combat Readines Medal, National Defense Service Medal, the Vietnam Service Medal, the Armed Forces Reserve Medal with Mobilization devices, RVN Staff Service Medal, and the RVN Campaign Medal.

Medals of America 89

◆ Soldier's Medal (Heroism)

Bronze

Anodized or Gold-Plated

Regulation Ribbon Bar

Enamel Lapel Pin

Medal Reverse

Miniature Medals

Mini Ribbon (unofficial)

Enamel Hat Pin (unofficial)

Authorized by Congress on July 2, 1926 to any member of the Army, National Guard or Reserves for heroism not involving actual conflict with an armed enemy.

The bronze octagonal medal has, as its central feature, a North American bald eagle with raised wings representing the United States. The eagle grasps an ancient Roman fasces symbolizing the State's lawful authority and conveys the concept that the award is to a soldier from the Government. There are seven stars on the eagle's left side and six stars and a spray of leaves to its right. The octagonal shape distinguishes the Soldier's Medal from other decorations. The stars represent the thirteen original colonies that formed the United States. The laurel spray balances the groups of stars and represents achievement. The reverse has a U.S. shield with sprays of laurel and oak leaves representing achievement and strength in front of a scroll. The words, "SOLDIER'S MEDAL" and "FOR VALOR" are inscribed on the reverse.

The ribbon contains thirteen alternating stripes of white (seven) and red (six) in the center, bordered by blue and are taken from the United States flag. The thirteen red and white stripes are arranged in the same manner as the thirteen vertical stripes in the U.S. Coat of Arms shield and also represent the thirteen original colonies.

Service	Army
Instituted	1926
Criteria	Heroism not involving actual conflict with an armed enemy of the United States.
Devices	Bronze Oak Leaf Cluster

Gaetano Cecere designed and sculpted the Soldier's Medal (the art deco influence of the 1920's can certainly be seen in this medal more than in any other Army award.) The Soldier's Medal is one of four decorations for which an enlisted soldier may increase his retirement by ten percent. The increase is not automatic, however; recipients of the Soldier's Medal must petition the Army Decorations Board for the bonus. Additional awards are denoted by oak leaf clusters.

Did You Know? The Soldier's Medal is awarded for risking one's life to save another's. The medal is awarded in peacetime for actions of heroism held to be equal to or greater than the level which would have justified an award of the Distinguished Flying Cross if the act had taken place in combat and involved actual conflict with an enemy. Any American Service Member who is eligible for retirement pay will receive an increase of 10 percent in retirement pay, if the level of valor was equal to that which would earn the Distinguished Service Cross.

❖ Airman's Medal (Heroism)

Bronze

Anodized or Gold-Plated

Regulation Ribbon Bar

Enamel Lapel Pin

Medal Reverse

Miniature Medals

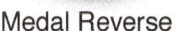

Mini Ribbon (unofficial)

Enamel Hat Pin (unofficial)

Authorized on August 10, 1956 and instituted on July 6, 1960, the authorizing directive was an amendment to the same order which created the Soldier's Medal (prior to that time, USAF personnel qualifying for such an award were awarded the Soldier's Medal). The medal's name is also fashioned as a carryover from the Soldier's Medal but does not make the casual observer aware of the medal's significance and the acts required to earn the decoration. The Airman's Medal is awarded for actions involving voluntary risk of life under conditions other than combat. A successful voluntary heroic act or the saving of a life is not essential to the award of this decoration. The first Airman's Medal was awarded to Captain John Burger on July 21, 1960 at McDill Air Force Base, Florida for saving a fellow airman's life by removing a live power line that laid across his body after having been severely shocked. Another example of the heroism required for the award was the bravery exhibited by Senior Airman Joe Sampson of Charleston Air Force Base, South Carolina when he saved an Army jumpmaster's life at the risk of his own aboard a C-141 aircraft carrying Army paratroopers. When the jumpmaster's reserve parachute inadvertently deployed and threatened to pull him out of the aircraft, Sr. Airman Sampson, without hesitation, grabbed the jumpmaster and his chute and pulled him back into the aircraft despite the tremendous forces of the airstream.

The American bald eagle is depicted on the face of the medal along with the Greek god Hermes, herald and messenger of other gods. Around the edge of the medal is the curved inscription, "AIRMAN'S" on the left and "MEDAL" on the right. The reverse contains space for engraving just below the inscription, "FOR VALOR." Additional awards of the Airman's Medal are denoted by oakleaf clusters.

Service	Air Force
Instituted	1960
Criteria	Heroism involving voluntary risk of life under conditions other than those of actual conflict with an armed enemy.
Devices	Bronze Oak Leaf Cluster
Notes	Derived from original design of the Air Force Distinguished Service Medal.

Staff Sgt. Chris Harlan was awarded the Airman's Medal. Sergeant Harlan and his friends saved the lives of four exchange students drowning at Turner Falls. (Air Force photo by Margo Wright)

Medals of America 91

❖ Bronze Star Medal

Bronze | Anodized or Gold-Plated

Notes: Awarded to World War II holders of Army Combat Infantryman Badge or Combat Medical Badge.

Regulation Ribbon Bar

Enamel Lapel Pin

Medal Reverse

Miniature Medals

Mini Ribbons (unofficial)

Enamel Hat Pin (unofficial)

Service	All Services
Instituted	1944 (retroactive to 7 Dec. 1941)
Criteria	The Bronze Star Medal is awarded to individuals who, while serving in the United States Armed Forces in a combat theater, distinguish themselves by heroism, outstanding achievement or by meritorious service not involving aerial flight.
Devices	Bronze Letter "V" (for Valor) Army/Air Force: Bronze, Silver Oak Leaf Cluster.

Authorized on February 4, 1944, retroactive to December 7, 1941. It is awarded to individuals who, while serving in the United States Armed Forces in a combat theater, distinguish themselves by heroism, outstanding achievement or by meritorious service not involving aerial flight.

The Bronze Star was originally conceived by the U.S. Navy as a junior decoration comparable to the Air Medal for heroic or meritorious actions by ground and surface personnel. The level of required service would not be sufficient to warrant the Silver Star if awarded for heroism or the Legion of Merit if awarded for meritorious achievement. In a strange twist of fate, the Bronze Star Medal did not reach fruition until championed by General George C. Marshall, the Army Chief of Staff during World War II. Marshall was seeking a decoration that would reward front line troops, particularly infantrymen, whose ranks suffered the heaviest casualties and were forced to endure the greatest danger and hardships during the conflict. Once established, the Bronze Star Medal virtually became the sole province of the Army in terms of the number of medals awarded.

Although Marshall wanted the Bronze Star Medal to be awarded with the same freedom as the Air Medal, it never came close to the vast numbers of Air Medals distributed during the war. The only exception was the award of the Bronze Star Medal to every soldier of the 101st Airborne Division who had fought in the Normandy invasion, Operation Market Garden in Holland, the Battle of the Bulge or were wounded.

After the war, when the ratio of Air Medals to airmen was compared to the numbers of Bronze Star Medals awarded to combat soldiers, it became clear that a huge disparity existed and many troops who deserved the award for their service had not received it. Therefore, in September 1947, the Bronze Star Medal was authorized for all personnel who had received either the Combat Infantryman's Badge (CIB) or the Combat Medical Badge (CMB) between December 7, 1941 to September 2, 1945. In addition, personnel who had participated in the defense of the Philippine Islands between December 7, 1941 and May 10, 1942 were awarded the Bronze Star Medal if their service was on the island of Luzon, the Bataan Peninsula or the harbor defenses on Corregidor Island and they had been awarded the Philippine Presidential Unit Citation.

The Bronze Star Medal is a five-pointed bronze star with a smaller star in the center (similar in design to the Silver Star Medal); the reverse contains the inscription, "HEROIC OR MERITORIOUS ACHIEVEMENT" in a circular pattern. The ribbon is red with a white-edged blue band in the center and white edge stripes. The Bronze Star Medal was designed by Rudolf Freund of Bailey, Banks and Biddle.

US Air Force (USAF) SENIOR AIRMAN (SRA) Alex Sutherland, holds a Bronze Star to be awarded to CHIEF MASTER Sergeant (CMSGT) Barford, second from right, by Major General (MGEN) James Skiff, second from left, the Deputy Adjutant General (DAGEN) for the Pennsylvania Air National Guard (ANG). Also being awarded a Bronze Star is Lieutenant Colonel (LCOL) Tony Carrelli at the Willow Grove Air Reserve Station (ARS), Willow Grove, Pennsylvania (PA). At right is the Command CHIEF MASTER (CCM) Sergeant CMSGT Louis Boykin, (USAF Photo)

Army Air Force medic's decorations and medals include the Bronze Star for Meritorious service authorized in 1947 to all recipients of the Combat Medics Badge. Note American Defense Service Medal for service before WW II and the World War II Occupation of Germany Medal for occupation service after the war. The last medal is the French Cross of War which was presented to many American military personnel by the Free French Republic.

Example of Bronze Star car plate authorized for veterans in many states.

Bronze Star Tie

❖ Purple Heart

Service	All Services (Originally Army Only)
Instituted	1932; The Purple Heart is retroactive to 5 April 1917; however, awards for qualifying prior to that date have been made.
Criteria	Awarded to any member of the Armed Forces of the United States or to any civilian national of the United States who, while serving under competent authority in any capacity with one of the U.S. Armed Forces, since 5 April 1917 has been wounded, killed, or who has died or may die of wounds received from an opposing enemy force while in armed combat or as a result of an act of international terrorism or being a Prisoner of War.
Devices	Army/Air Force: Bronze, Silver Oak Leaf Cluster

The Purple Heart is America's oldest military decoration. It was originally established on August 7, 1782 by General George Washington who designed the original award called the "Badge of Military Merit." The Badge of Military Merit was awarded for singularly meritorious action to a deserving hero of the Revolutionary War. There were only three known recipients of the award, all of whom were noncommissioned officers of the Continental Army. The Badge of Military Merit was intended by Washington to be a permanent decoration but was never used again after the three initial presentations until it was reestablished as the Purple Heart Medal on February 22, 1932 (the 200th anniversary of Washington's birth) by the Army War Department.

During the First World War, War Department General Order No. 134 of October 12, 1917 authorized a red ribbon with a narrow white center stripe to be worn on the right breast for wounds received in action. However, the order was rescinded 32 days later and the ribbon never became a reality. Instead the Army authorized wound chevrons which were worn on the lower right sleeve of the tunic.

On July 21, 1932, General Douglas MacArthur, who was a key figure in its revival, received the first Purple Heart after it was reestablished. President Franklin D. Roosevelt signed an executive order on December 3, 1942 that expanded the award to members of the Navy, Marine Corps and Coast Guard as well. Although the Purple Heart was awarded for meritorious service between 1932 and 1943, the primary purpose of the award has always been to recognize those who received wounds while in the service of the United States military.

Later Presidential Executive Orders extended eligibility for the Purple Heart to military and civilian personnel who received wounds from a terrorist attack or while performing peace keeping duties. Currently, it is awarded for wounds received while serving in any capacity with one of the U.S. Armed Forces after April 5, 1917; it may be awarded to civilians as well as military personnel. The wounds may have been received while in combat against an enemy, while a member of a peacekeeping force, while a Prisoner of War, as a result of a terrorist attack or as a result of a friendly fire incident in hostile territory. The 1996 Defense

WW II Display with Purple Heart

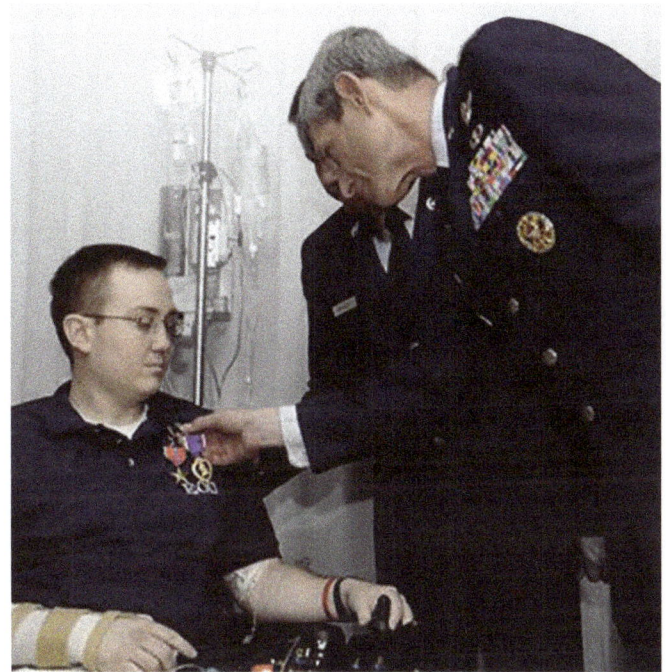

Air Force Chief of Staff Gen. Norton Schwartz thanks Staff Sgt. David Flowers for service to the nation June 22 at Walter Reed Army Hospital in Washington, D.C. Sergeant Flowers was awarded a Bronze Star, a Purple Heart and a Combat Action Medal during a ceremony at the hospital. (U.S. Air Force photo/Scott M. Ash)

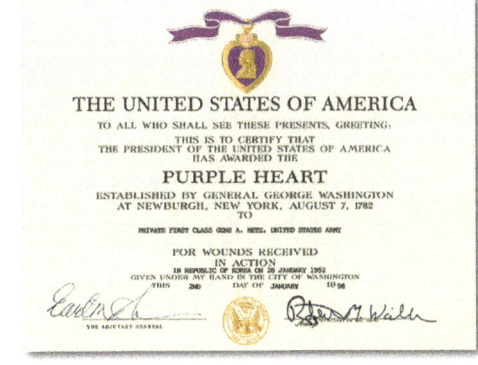

Authorization Act extended eligibility for the Purple Heart to prisoners of war before April 25, 1962; previous legislation had only authorized the medal to POWs after April 25, 1962. Wounds that qualify must have required treatment by a medical officer and must be a matter of official record.

The Purple Heart was originally last in precedence of all other personal decorations but was elevated in 1985 by an act of Congress to a position just behind the Bronze Star.

The medal is a heart-shaped, gold-rimmed medallion with a profile of George Washington on a purple enameled base. Above Washington's profile is the shield from his family's coat of arms. "FOR MILITARY MERIT" is inscribed on the reverse. The ribbon is a dark purple with narrow white edges. The original Badge of Military Merit was a satin purple heart edged in white. The design may have been used since the strongest wood available for gun carriages and weapons during the Revolution was called "Purpleheart", a very strong smooth grain wood from Latin America that was stronger than the famous English oak. Here was an American wood that was stronger, more resistant to rot and termites than any other known wood. Perhaps General Washington chose the American Purpleheart wood as a symbol of strength and resistance over the British hearts of English Oak (a popular English military song of the time).

Additional awards of the Purple Heart are denoted by bronze and silver oak leaf clusters or gold and silver stars, depending on the recipient's Service Branch.

World War II and Vietnam Veteran's awards.

Medals of America 95

World War II Purple Heart Presentation Case

The Japanese Armed Forces determination to fight to the death during the Pacific campaign led everyone, especially the Navy and Marines to anticipate heavy casualties. The government requested so many Purple Hearts be manufactured that it was not until almost 1947 that all the contracts were completed. Meanwhile the Air Force bombing campaign and the use of the first atomic bombs lead to the capitulation of Japan and ended the requirement for the huge order of Purple Heart medals.

The Purple Heart medal has always been highly respected by military personnel since it was earned by giving one's life or being wounded while in military service of our country. Shown above is a World War II Purple Heart and its WW II period presentation box. The presentation came with the medal, a ribbon and a lapel pin. During World War II contracts were issued for over a million and a half Purple Heart medals with the largest number being produced in anticipation of the invasion of Japan.

Approximately a half million Purple Hearts went into the military inventories after World War II. Even with many of these medals presented during the Korean and Vietnam eras there were over 100,000 World War II Purple Heart medals still in the military supply chain during the Liberation of Kuwait. Refurbished, many of these Purple Hearts continued to be awarded to veterans. The World War II Purple Hearts are generally identified by the high quality of workmanship and a single white stitch under the left and right edge of the ribbon bar of the medal drape. It is not improbable for an Iraq or an Afghanistan veteran to receive the Purple Heart medal that was originally manufactured for his grandfather's generation.

Purple Heart Tie

Purple Heart Stamp

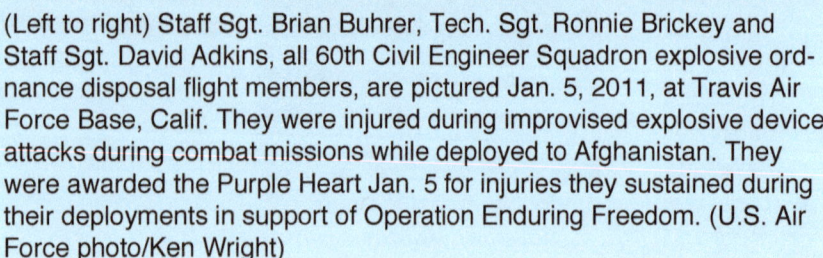

(Left to right) Staff Sgt. Brian Buhrer, Tech. Sgt. Ronnie Brickey and Staff Sgt. David Adkins, all 60th Civil Engineer Squadron explosive ordnance disposal flight members, are pictured Jan. 5, 2011, at Travis Air Force Base, Calif. They were injured during improvised explosive device attacks during combat missions while deployed to Afghanistan. They were awarded the Purple Heart Jan. 5 for injuries they sustained during their deployments in support of Operation Enduring Freedom. (U.S. Air Force photo/Ken Wright)

Purple Heart License Plate

❖ Defense Meritorious Service Medal

Bronze — Anodized or Gold-Plated — Medal Reverse

Regulation Ribbon Bar — Enamel Lapel Pin — Miniature Medals — Mini Ribbon (unofficial) — Enamel Hat Pin (unofficial)

Authorized on November 3, 1977. The Defense Meritorious Service Medal is awarded to any active member of the U.S. Armed Forces who distinguishes him/herself by noncombat meritorious achievement or service while serving in a Joint Activity after November 3, 1977. Examples of Joint assignments that may allow qualification for this medal are: Office of the Secretary of Defense, Office of the Joint Chiefs of Staff, Unified or Specified Commands, Joint billets in NATO or NORAD, Defense Agencies, National Defense University, National War College, Industrial College of the Armed Forces, Armed Forces Staff College and the Joint Strategic Target Planning Staff.

Service	All Services (by Secretary of Defense)
Instituted	3 November 1977
Criteria	Noncombat meritorious achievement or service while assigned to a Joint Activity.
Devices	Bronze & Silver Oak Leaf Cluster

The bronze medal has an eagle with spread wings in the center superimposed on a pentagon in the center of a laurel wreath. The reverse is inscribed with the words, "DEFENSE MERITORIOUS SERVICE" and "UNITED STATES OF AMERICA". The ribbon has a wide white center stripe with three light blue stripes in the middle. The white stripe is flanked by ruby red and white. The ruby red and white are copied from the ribbon of the Meritorious Service Medal with the blue stripes representing the Department of Defense. Subsequent awards are denoted by bronze and silver oak leaf clusters. The Defense Meritorious Service Medal was designed by Lewis J. King, Jr. of the Institute of Heraldry.

Maj. Gen. Darren W. McDew presents Maj. Eric J. Mottice, the Defense Meritorious Service Medal upon his retirement. (USAF photo)

❖ Meritorious Service Medal

Bronze   Anodized or Gold-Plated

Regulation Ribbon Bar

Enamel Lapel Pin

Medal Reverse

Miniature Medals

Mini Ribbon (unofficial)

Enamel Hat Pin (unofficial)

Authorized on January 16, 1969 and awarded to members of the Armed Forces for noncombat meritorious achievement or meritorious service after that date. The Meritorious Service Medal evolved from an initial recommendation in 1918 by General John J. Pershing, the Commander of the American Expeditionary Forces during World War I. He suggested that an award for meritorious service be created to provide special recognition to deserving individuals by the U.S. government. Although the request by General Pershing was disapproved, it was revisited several more times during World War II and afterwards. During the Vietnam War the proposal to create the medal received significant attention and was eventually approved when President Lyndon B. Johnson signed the executive order on January 16, 1969. The Meritorious Service Medal cannot be awarded for service in a combat theater. It has often been the decoration of choice for both end of tour and retirement recognition for field grade officers and senior enlisted personnel.

The MSM is a bronze medal with six rays rising from the top of a five-pointed star with beveled edges with two smaller stars outlined within. On the lower part of the medal in front of the star there is an eagle with its wings spread. It is standing on two curving laurel branches tied between the eagle's talons. The eagle, symbol of the nation, holds laurel branches representing achievement. The star represents military service with the rays symbolizing individual efforts to achieve excellence. The reverse of the medal has the inscription, "UNITED STATES OF AMERICA" at the top and "MERITORIOUS SERVICE" at the bottom; the space inside the circle formed by the text is to be used for engraving the recipient's name. The ribbon is ruby red with two white stripes and is a variation of the Legion of Merit ribbon. Jay Morris and Lewis J. King of the Institute of Heraldry designed and sculpted the Meritorious Service Medal. Additional awards are indicated by bronze and silver oak leaf clusters or gold and silver stars depending on the recipient's Service Branch.

Service	All Services
Instituted	16 January 1969
Criteria	Outstanding noncombat meritorious achievement or service to the United States.
Devices	Army/Air Force: Bronze, Silver Oak Leaf Cluster; Navy/Marine Corps: Gold, Silver Star; Coast Guard: Silver Letter "O", Gold, Silver Star

Did You Know? The Meritorious Service Medal was designed to provide appropriate recognition for non-combat achievement or service comparable to the Bronze Star for combat achievement or service. Today, most MSM recipients are field grade officers, pay grade (O-4 to O-6), senior warrant officers (W-3 to W-5), senior noncommissioned officers (E-7 to E-9) and individuals who have displayed a level of service that warrants an award of such magnitude. Normally, the acts or services rendered must be comparable to that required for the Legion of Merit but in a duty of lesser, though considerable, responsibility.

Company Grade Officer of the Year: Capt. Michael D. Fanton, U.S. Air Force Honor Guard. (courtesy photo) USAF Photos

❖ Air Medal

Authorized on May 11, 1942, the Air Medal is awarded for single acts of achievement after September 8, 1939 to any member of the U.S. Armed Forces who distinguishes him/herself by heroism, outstanding achievement or by meritorious service while participating in aerial flight. During World War II, the Air Medal was to be awarded for a lesser degree of heroism or achievement than required for the Distinguished Flying Cross. However, many Army Air Force units began to award the Air Medal on a quota basis, e.g., 20 missions equaled one Air Medal or an Air Medal for every enemy aircraft shot down. Some commands carried this to extremes by awarding a DFC for every five Air Medals. By the end of the war, over a million Air Medals were awarded (many of which were, of course, oak leaf clusters). While this might appear extreme, the generous award of the Air Medal provided combat aircrews a visible sign that their devotion and determination were appreciated by the country. The Air Medal helped keep morale up in a force that suffered the highest casualty rate of the war after the Infantry.

Although the Naval Services were authorized to award the Air Medal during World War II, the numbers never approached those received by the Army Air Force amidst the European bombing campaigns. Subsequent to World War II, however, with the increased role of the Navy in joint operations, the use of the Air Medal was subtly redefined. The Air Medal was still awarded for single acts of outstanding achievement which involve superior airmanship but of a lesser degree than would justify an award of a Distinguished Flying Cross. However, during the Korean, Vietnam and Gulf conflicts, awards for meritorious service were made for sustained distinction in the performance of duties involving regular and frequent participation in aerial

Service	All Services
Instituted	1942 (Retroactive to 8 September 1939)
Criteria	Heroic actions or meritorious service while participating in aerial flight, but not of a degree that would justify an award of the Distinguished Flying Cross.
Devices	Army: Air Force: Bronze, Silver Oak Leaf Cluster
Notes	During World War II, the Army Air Corps and U.S. Army Air Force employed bronze and silver oak leaf clusters as additional award devices on all decorations including the Air Medal. The same devices were used by the Army until the establishment of the bronze numeral as its unique additional award device for the Air Medal during the Vietnam War.

flight operations. These operations include "strikes" (sorties which deliver ordnance against the enemy; those which land or evacuate personnel in an assault; or, those which involve search and rescue operations which encounter enemy opposition), "flights" (sorties which involve the same kinds of operations as strikes but which do not encounter enemy opposition) or "direct combat support" (sorties which include such activities as reconnaissance, combat air patrol, electronic countermeasures support, psychological warfare, coastal surveillance, etc.). In addition, the Air Medal was awarded for noncombat aerial achievement, such as, to air weather crews who gather major storm data by flying into hurricanes. The Air Force ceased all noncombat awards of the Air Medal with the institution of the Aerial Achievement Medal in 1988 but without a comparable peacetime medal, the other Services still award the Air Medal under circumstances not involving actual combat.

Vietnam multiple Air Medal awards.

Senior Command Pilot Officer's Career Display.

The Air Medal was designed and sculpted by Walker Hancock and is a bronze sixteen point compass rose suspended by a fleur-de-lis. In the center there is an diving eagle carrying a lighting bolt in each talon. The compass rose represents the global capacity of American air power. The lightning bolts show the United States' ability to wage war from the air and the Fleur-de-lis, the French symbol of nobility, represents the high ideals of American airmen. The reverse of the compass rose is plain with an area for engraving the recipient's name. The ribbon is ultramarine blue with two golden orange stripes representing the original colors of the Army Air Force.

WW II Air Medal display

Lt. Col. Kurt Matthews salutes Master Sgt. Jeffrey McManus after awarding him two Air Medals and an Air Force Commendation Medal (with valor). (U.S. Air Force photo)

❖ Aerial Achievement Medal

Bronze — Anodized or Gold-Plated

Regulation Ribbon Bar
Enamel Lapel Pin
Medal Reverse
Miniature Medals
Mini Ribbon (unofficial)
Enamel Hat Pin (unofficial)

The Aerial Achievement Medal was established on February 3, 1988 and has been in effect since January 1, 1990. It is awarded to U.S. Air Force personnel for sustained meritorious achievement while participating in aerial flight. It is not awarded for single event flights. In contrast to the normal procedure for award of all other military decorations, the individual performance which may qualify for the Aerial Achievement Medal can vary based on the requirements and criteria established by each Major Air Force Command. This is due to the many variations posed by each Command's location, mission, environment, available aircraft types, local political conditions and the general world situation.

The American bald eagle is depicted on the front of the Aerial Achievement Medal just below 13 stars symbolic of the original colonies and in front of two intercepting arcs symbolic of flight paths. The eagle is clutching six lightning bolts which represent the U.S. Air Force. The reverse contains the words "FOR MILITARY MERIT" surrounding a space for engraving the awardees name. Additional awards of the Aerial Achievement Medal are denoted by bronze and silver oak leaf clusters.

Service	Air Force
Instituted	1988
Criteria	Sustained meritorious achievement while participating in aerial flight.
Devices	Bronze, Silver Oak Leaf Cluster
Notes	Considered on a par with the Air Medal but more likely to be awarded for peacetime actions.

Brig. Gen. Dean Despinoy, 434th Air Refueling Wing commander, left, presents an Aerial Achievement Medal to Col. Chris Nixon, 434th Aerospace Medicine Squadron commander. (U.S. Air Force photo/Tech. Sgt. Patrick Kuminecz)

❖ Joint Service Commendation Medal

Bronze

Anodized or Gold-Plated

Regulation Ribbon Bar

Enamel Lapel Pin

Medal Reverse

Miniature Medals

Mini Ribbons (unofficial)

Enamel Hat Pin (unofficial)

Authorized on June 25, 1963, this was the first medal specifically authorized for members of a Joint Service organization. Awarded to members of the Armed Forces for meritorious achievement or service while serving in a Joint Activity after January 1, 1963. The "V" device is authorized if the award is made for direct participation in combat operations.

The medal consists of four conjoined green enameled hexagons edged in gold which represent the unity of the Armed Forces. The top hexagon has thirteen gold five-pointed stars (representing the thirteen original states) and the lower hexagon has a gold stylized heraldic device (for land, air and sea). An eagle with spread wings and a shield on its breast is in the center of the hexagons. The eagle is grasping three arrows in its talons. The hexagons are encircled by a laurel wreath bound with gold bands (representing achievement). On the reverse there is a plaque for engraving the recipient's name. Above the plaque are the raised words, "FOR MILITARY" and below, "MERIT" with a laurel spray below. The words and laurel spray are derived from the Army and Navy Commendation Medals. The ribbon is a center stripe of green flanked by white, green, white and light blue stripes. The green and white are from the Army and Navy Commendation ribbons and the light blue represents the Department of Defense.

Service	All Services (by Secretary of Defense)
Instituted	June 25, 1963
Criteria	Meritorious service or achievement while assigned to a Joint Activity.
Devices	Bronze Letter "V" (for valor), Bronze, Silver Oak Leaf Cluster

The Joint Service Commendation Medal was designed by the Institute of Heraldry's Stafford F. Potter. Oak leaf clusters denote additional awards.

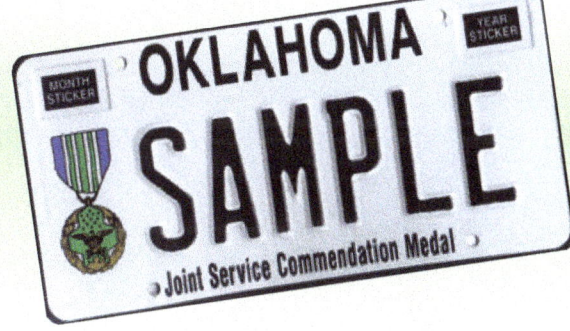

Medals of America 103

❖ Army Commendation Medal

Bronze

Anodized or Gold-Plated

Regulation Ribbon Bar

Enamel Lapel Pin

Medal Reverse

Miniature Medals

Mini Ribbon (unofficial)

Enamel Hat Pin (unofficial)

Authorized on December 18, 1945 as a commendation ribbon and awarded to members of the Army and Army Air Force for heroism, meritorious achievement or meritorious service after December 6, 1941. It was meant for award where the Bronze Star Medal was not appropriate, i.e., outside of operational areas.

The Army Commendation Medal, commonly called the ARCOM, is unique as it is the first and only Army award that started as a ribbon-only award and then became a medal. After World War II, it became the only award created for the express purpose of peacetime and wartime meritorious service as well as the only award designed expressly for presentation to junior officers and enlisted personnel.

In short, the ARCOM became the peacetime version of the Bronze Star Medal to recognize outstanding performance and boost morale. Subsequent to World War II, retroactive awards of the Commendation Ribbon were authorized for any individual who had received a Letter of Commendation from a Major General or higher before January 1, 1946.

In 1947, the rules were changed allowing the ARCOM to be awarded in connection with military operations for which the level of service did not meet the requirements for the Bronze Star or Air Medal. In 1949 the change from a ribbon-only award to a pendant was approved. Anyone who received the ribbon could apply for the new medal. The Army redesignated the Commendation Ribbon With Metal Pendant as the Army Commendation Medal in 1960. In 1962, it was authorized for award to a member of the Armed Forces of a friendly nation for the same level of achievement or service which was mutually beneficial to that nation and the United States. The next big change occurred on February 29, 1964 with the approval of the "V" device to denote combat heroism of a degree less than that required for the Bronze Star Medal.

Service	Army
Instituted	1945 (retroactive to 1941)
Criteria	Heroism, meritorious achievement or meritorious service.
Devices	Bronze letter "V" (for valor), Bronze, Silver Oak Leaf Cluster
Notes	Originally a ribbon-only award then designated "Army Commendation Ribbon with Metal Pendant". Redesignated: "Army Commendation Medal" in 1960.

Additionally, the ARCOM continued to be awarded for acts of courage not qualifying for the Soldier's Medal. Award is not authorized General Officers.

The medal, a bronze hexagon, depicts the American bald eagle with spread wings on the face. The eagle has the U.S. shield on its breast and is grasping three crossed arrows in its talons. On the reverse of the medal are inscriptions "FOR MILITARY" and "MERIT" with a plaque for engraving the recipient's name between the two inscriptions. A spray of laurel, representing achievement is at the bottom. The ribbon is a field of myrtle green with five white stripes in the center and white edges. The Army Commendation Medal was designed and sculpted by Thomas Hudson Jones of the Institute of Heraldry.

(USAF Photo)

❖ Air Force Commendation Medal

Bronze

Anodized or Gold-Plated

Medal Reverse

Authorized on March 28, 1958; awarded to personnel below the rank of Brigadier General for outstanding achievement, meritorious service or acts of courage that do not meet the requirements for award of the Airman's Medal or the Bronze Star Medal. Previous to its establishment, the Army Commendation Medal was awarded to Air Force personnel who met the criteria for the award. The medal has often been used for end of tour recognition, especially to junior officers and noncommissioned officers. In 1996, the Secretary of the Air Force authorized the award of a bronze letter "V" with this medal, retroactive to January 11, 1996, if the award's recipient distinguishes him/herself while under attack or during a hazardous situation

Service	Navy, Marine Corps
Instituted	1958
Criteria	Outstanding achievement or meritorious service rendered on behalf of the United States Air Force.
Devices	Bronze, Silver Oak Leaf Cluster, Bronze Letter "V"

resulting from hostilities. The "V" may be awarded for actions taken during single acts of terrorism and isolated combat incidents. The first instances of the "V" device being awarded with this medal occurred during the terrorist bombing in Saudi Arabia in 1996. The front of the medal contains an American eagle with outstretched wings in front of a cloud formation and perched above the Air Force Coat of Arms. The reverse contains the words, "FOR MILITARY MERIT" above a blank area which may be used to engrave the recipient's name. The ribbon stripe pattern was designed using the official Air Force colors. The center stripe and other blue stripes are ultramarine blue. They are flanked by stripes of golden yellow. (Displays continued on next page.)

A1C Franklin J. Vinson awarded the Air Force Commendation Medal 4 April 1961 (USAF Photo)

This Air Force NCO Korea and Vietnam veteran's display shows 2 awards of the AF Commendation Medal, Multiple awards of the AF Good Conduct Medal and a Army Good Conduct Medal from the Korean War.

Did You Know?
The Air Force Commendation Medal is not awarded to general officers.

This Air Force NCO veteran of the Southeast Asia Campaign display shows 3 awards of the AF Commendation Medal, as well as the AF Achievement Medal, Combat Readiness Medal, Multiple awards of the AF Good Conduct and National Defense Medal. The campaign Medal for Southwest Asia Service has one battle star and is joined by the Humanitarian Service Medal plus the Saudi Arabia and Kuwait Liberation Medals.

106 Decorations, Medals, and Ribbons of the United States Air Force

❖ Joint Service Achievement Medal

Bronze | Anodized or Gold-Plated

Regulation Ribbon Bar
Enamel Lapel Pin
Miniature Medals
Medal Reverse
Mini Ribbon (unofficial)
Enamel Hat Pin (unofficial)

The Joint Service Achievement Medal was established in 1983 specifically to complete the Department of Defense awards hierarchy and thereby provide a system of decorations for meritorious achievement comparable to those of the separate services. In so doing, the integrity of the more senior Joint Service medals was protected and the opportunity to earn recognition while assigned to a Joint Activity was provided.

It is awarded for meritorious service or achievement while serving in a Joint Activity after August 3, 1983 to military personnel below the rank of colonel. Oak leaf clusters denote additional awards.

The medal features an American eagle with the United States coat of arms on its breast holding three arrows in the center of the bronze medal which consists of a star of twelve points chosen to make it distinctive. The eagle was taken from the Seal designed for the National Military Establishment in 1947 by the President and the arrows were adapted from the seal of the Department of Defense. This is the same design seen on the Army and Navy Commendation Medals.

The reverse of the medal contains the inscriptions, "JOINT SERVICE" and "ACHIEVEMENT AWARD" in a circle. There is space in the center for inscribing the recipient's name. The ribbon consists of a center stripe of red flanked on either side by stripes of light blue, white, green, white and blue.

The Joint Service Achievement Medal was designed by Jay Morris and sculpted by Donald Borja, both of the Institute of Heraldry.

Service	All Services
Instituted	1983
Criteria	Meritorious service or achievement while serving with a Joint Activity.
Devices	Bronze, Silver Oak Leaf Cluster

Did You Know? ... The JSAM may not be awarded for any act or period of service for which a Military Department medal was awarded, and it should not be awarded for retirement. Bronze oak-leaf clusters are used to denote the 2nd through 5th award. No more than four bronze oak-leaf clusters can be worn. Bronze oak-leaf clusters may be worn with one or more silver oak-leaf clusters to denote 7 or more awards.

◆ Air Force Achievement Medal

Bronze | Anodized or Gold-Plated

Regulation Ribbon Bar

Enamel Lapel Pin

Medal Reverse

Miniature Medals

Mini Ribbon (unofficially)

Hat Pin (unofficially)

The Air Force Achievement Medal was established by the Secretary of the Air Force on October 12, 1980 and may be awarded to U.S. military personnel below the rank of colonel for meritorious service or outstanding achievement. This medal was designed by Captain Robert C. Bonn, Jr., USAF. The primary use of the medal has been to recognize specific individual achievements or accomplishments rather than continuing periods of service such as might be associated with a change in permanent assignment, although it has been used for end of tour recognition for some junior ranking personnel. A bronze letter "V" was authorized retroactive to January 11, 1996 for those receiving the award for actions during combat conditions, hostile acts or single acts of terrorism. The first instances of the "V" device being awarded with the medal were to airmen who received the medal for actions during the 1996 terrorist bombing of an Air Force dormitory in Saudi Arabia. The front of the medal has eleven cloud like shapes on the outer border; within the medal are a set of wings with four thunderbolts signifying striking power through aerospace, adapted from the Air Force's Seal. The reverse of the medal has a circular inscription, "AIR FORCE MERITORIOUS ACHIEVEMENT" around its outer edge.

Service	Air Force
Instituted	1980
Criteria	Outstanding achievement or meritorious service not warranting award of the Air Force Commendation Medal.
Devices	Bronze, Silver Oak Leaf Cluster, Bronze Letter "V"

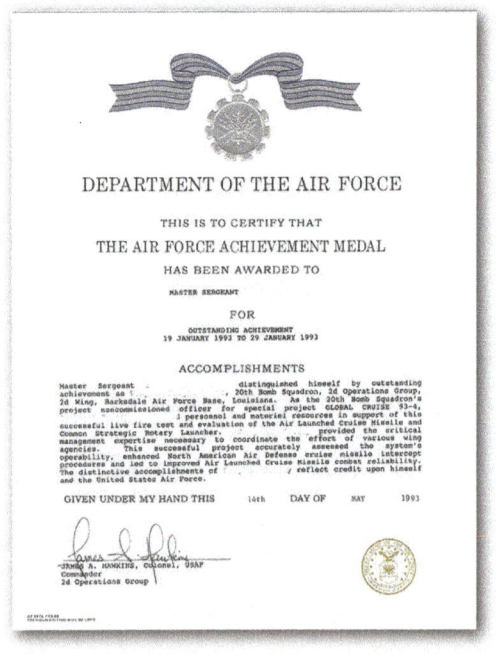

108 Decorations, Medals, and Ribbons of the United States Air Force

❖ Air Force Combat Action Medal

Silver colored

Silver plated

Regulation Ribbon Bar

Enamel Lapel Pin

Medal Reverse

Miniature Medals

Mini Ribbon (unofficial)

Enamel Hat Pin (unofficial)

On January 2007, the SECAF approved establishment of the Air Force Combat Action Medal (AFCAM) to recognize any military member of the Air Force (airman through colonel) who actively participated in combat (ground or air). The principal eligibility criterion is that the individual must have been under direct and hostile fire while operating in enemy domain (outside the wire) or physically engaging hostile forces with direct and lethal fire. "Outside the Wire" is a military term that describes when service members in a warzone travel outside the perimeter fence of a camp, base, or forward operating base.

Combat conditions defined: for the purposes of this award, combat conditions are met when: 1) individuals deliberately go outside the wire to conduct official duties—either ground or air; and 2) they come under enemy attack by lethal weapons while performing those duties; and 3) are at risk of grave danger. Or 1) individuals defending the base (on the wire); and 2) come under fire and engage the enemy with direct and lethal fire; and 3) are at risk of grave danger, also meet the intent of combat conditions for this award. Additionally, personnel in ground operations who actively engage the enemy with direct and lethal fire may qualify even if no direct fire is taken—as long as there was risk of grave danger and other criteria are met. Central to the integrity of this combat recognition is the adherence to those combat conditions prerequisites.

Service	Air Force
Instituted	2007 (retroactive to 11 Sept. 2001)
Criteria	Awarded to Airmen who have direct participated in active combat, either in the air or on the ground, as part of their official duties.
Devices	Gold and Silver Stars

Designed by Susan Gamble, the symbolism of the medal is as follows: The eagle represents strength and vigilance and embodies the American spirit of freedom. The star and eagle, as well as the ribbon colors are adapted from the art insignia on the aircraft of Billy Mitchell and give this medal the heritage and honor of that history. Gen. Mitchell was an airpower advocate who planned and led the first coordinated air ground offensive in history during World War I (see pg 75). The eagle is facing toward the olive branch for peace and emphasizes looking forward to peace while the arrows represent lethal capability. The laurel wreath is symbolic of respect and high achievement.

General Billy Mitchell's World War I personal aircraft insignia was used as a basis of the design for the new Air Force Combat Action Medal. (See page 75 for more about General Mitchell).

Medals of America 109

❖ Army Presidential Unit Citation

 The Army Presidential Unit Citation (PUC) was established on February 26, 1942 as the "Distinguished Unit Badge" or the "Distinguished Unit Citation" and redesignated as the Presidential Unit Citation in 1966. It is awarded to Army units that display the same degree of heroism in combat as would warrant the Distinguished Service Cross for an individual. Like all Army unit awards, the PUC is worn above the pocket on the right breast of the uniform. The gold-colored frame around the ribbon is worn with the open end of the "V" of the laurel leaf pattern pointing upward. The badge may only be worn permanently by those individuals who were assigned to the unit for the period for which it was cited. Current members of the unit who were not assigned to the unit for the award period are entitled to wear the ribbon but only for the duration of their assignment with the cited unit. Such personnel must remove it from their uniform upon reassignment. Additional awards of the Army Presidential Unit Citation are denoted by bronze oak leaf clusters.

Service	Army
Instituted	1942, Redesignated in 1966
Criteria	Awarded to Army units for extraordinary heroism in action against an armed enemy.
Devices	Bronze, Silver Oak Leaf Cluster
Notes	Original designation: Distinguished Unit Citation. Redesignated to present name in 1966.

"Distinguished Unit Citation" of the The 507th Fighter Group, U.S. Army Air Forces

The 507th Fighter group (SE) is cited for outstanding performance of duty in action against the Japanese on 13th of August 1945. On that date forty-eight aircraft of the group flew a very-long-range fighter sweep from their base on Le Shima (Ryukyu Retto) to Keijo, Korea. The flight involved was rendered unusually dangerous by the lack of weather information and by the incomplete intelligence of the anti-aircraft defenses available to the enemy held territory. Upon arriving in this remote target area the group was intercepted by a force of approximately fifty enemy aircraft of various types. Combat was sought by the 507th in spite of it being airborne approximately four hours in single seated P47s. For half an Hour the engagement continued while 507th Group carried on a aggressive attacks with great skill. While sustaining the loss of but one plane whose pilot was later rescued, the 507th Fighter Group destroyed twenty enemy airplanes in the air and probably destroyed another. On the ground one was destroyed and two damaged. The enemy was literally driven from the skies over Keijo, Korea. Thus did the group distinguish itself in aerial battle deep in enemy territory while flying an exhausting round-trip of 1580 miles requiring a full eight hours of flight in single place fighter planes. This extraordinary feat of combat efficiency was accomplished in spite of the extreme length of flight and the accompanying drain upon the energies of the pilots. As the 507th Fighter group engaged and overwhelmingly defeated the enemy in aerial combat, the enemy that day found his adversary to be a daring and determined foe who in this opening blow in virgin territory produced devastating results with extraordinary heroism although faced with uncommon difficulties, hazards, and uncertainties. The strength of the enemy's interception indicated his concern with the audacity of the attack. The entire action demonstrates the importance of the contribution of the 507th Fighter group through the outstanding success of this mission during the final hours of hostilities, materially increasing at this critical period the pressure upon the enemy to cease his resistance and surrender. The exemplary courage and skilled airmanship demonstrated by the 507th Fighter Group on this very important mission reflected great credit upon the group and were keeping with the highest traditions of the Army Air Forces.

❖ Air Force Presidential Unit Citation

The Air Force Presidential Unit Citation owes its heritage to the original Army award which was created in February 26, 1942 and modified by Executive Order on December 2, 1943. The order created the Distinguished Unit Citation which was re designated as the Presidential Unit Citation on January 10, 1957. It is conferred upon units of the Army and Air Force of the United States for extraordinary heroism in action against an armed enemy on or after December 7, 1941. The unit must display such gallantry, determination and esprit de corps as to set it apart from and above other units participating in the same campaign. The degree of heroism required is the same that which would warrant award of the Distinguished Service Cross or Air Force Cross to an individual. Unlike the Army, the Air Force PUC may only be worn by individuals who are assigned or permanently attached to and also present for duty with a unit in the action for which the Presidential Unit Citation is awarded. Subsequent awards of the Presidential Unit Citation are denoted by bronze oak-leaf clusters.

Service	Air Force
Instituted	1957
Criteria	Awarded to Air Force units for extraordinary heroism in action against an armed enemy.
Devices	Bronze, Silver Oak Leaf Cluster
Notes	Original designation: Distinguished Unit Citation. Re designated to present name in 1957.

Air Force Presidential Unit Citation, of the 483rd Tactical Airlift Wing, 535th Tactical Airlift Squadron

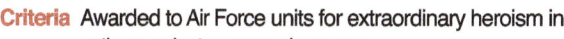

483rd Tactical Airlift Wing, 535th Tactical Airlift Squadron (C-7A Caribou) received the Air Force Presidential Unit Citation, Special Order GB-613 dated 3 September 1971, for extraordinary gallantry from 1 April 1970 to 30 June 1970 for participation in aerial resupply of the besieged Special Forces Camp at Deak Seang. Nearly all C-7A Caribous' sustained battle damage during this time. Six C-7A Caribous and fifteen airmen were lost during this time due to extreme enemy fire. This amounts to almost one-half of C-7A Caribous losses since the U.S. Air Force took over the C-7A Caribou mission from the U.S. Army in 1967. The primary mission for C-7A Caribou was to support Special Forces and Special Operations Group missions and bases located throughout South Vietnam, Cambodia, and Laos.

❖ Joint Meritorious Unit Award

 The Joint Meritorious Unit Award was authorized by the Secretary of Defense on June 10, 1981 (retroactive to January 23, 1979) and was originally called the Department of Defense Meritorious Unit Award. It is awarded in the name of the Secretary of Defense for meritorious service, superior to that which would normally be expected during combat, a declared national emergency or under extraordinary circumstances that involve national interest. The service performed by the unit would be similar to that performed by an individual awarded the Defense Superior Service Medal. The ribbon is similar to the Defense Superior Service Medal ribbon with a gold metal frame with

Service	All Services
Instituted	1981 (Retroactive to 1979)
Criteria	Awarded to Joint Service units for superior meritorious achievement or service.
Devices	Bronze, Silver Oak Leaf Cluster

laurel leaves. Like the Defense Superior Service Medal, the ribbon consists of a central stripe of red flanked on either side by stripes of white, blue and yellow, but with blue edges. Additional awards are denoted by oak leaf clusters.

❖ Air Force Gallant Unit Award

The Gallant Unit Citation (GUC) was established in 2004 by the Secretary of the Air Force and is awarded to active duty, Reserve and Guard units for extraordinary heroism in action against an armed enemy of the United States while engaged in military operations involving conflict with an opposing foreign force on or after September 11, 2001. The unit must have performed with marked distinction under difficult and hazardous conditions in accomplishing its mission so as to set it apart from and above other units participating in the same conflict. The degree of heroism is the same as

Service	Air Force
Instituted	2004
Dates	11 Sept. 2001 to Present
Criteria	Awarded to U.S. Air Force units for extraordinary heroism against an armed enemy of the United States.
Devices	Bronze, Silver Oak Leaf Cluster

that which would warrant award of the Silver Star to an individual. Bronze and silver oak leaf clusters are worn to denote additional awards.

❖ Army Meritorious Unit Commendation

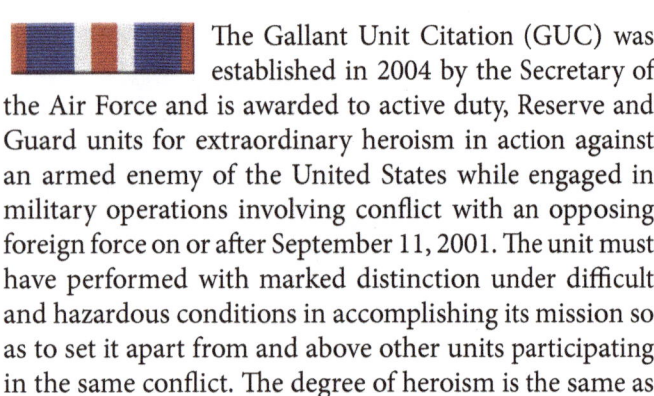

 The Army Meritorious Unit Commendation is awarded to units for exceptionally meritorious conduct in performance of outstanding services for at least six continuous months of military operations against an armed enemy occurring on or after January 1, 1944. Service in a combat zone is not required but must be directly related to the combat effort. Units based in the continental U.S. or outside the combat area of operation are excluded. The unit must display such outstanding devotion and superior performance of exceptionally difficult tasks as to set it apart and above other units with similar missions. The award is usually given to units larger than battalions.

 The degree of achievement required is the same as for award of the Legion of Merit to an individual. It was originally authorized as a wreath emblem that was worn on the

Service	Army and Army Air Force
Instituted	1944
Criteria	Awarded to U.S. Army units for exceptionally meritorious conduct in the performance of outstanding service.
Devices	Bronze, Silver Oak Leaf Cluster
Notes	Originally a golden wreath worn on the lower sleeve. Authorized in its present form in 1961.

lower right sleeve of the Army uniform but was redeveloped in its present form in 1961. As with other unit citations, it has a gold frame surrounding the ribbon; the open end of the "V" shaped design on the frame points upward. In the Army it goes with other unit citations on the right side of the uniform. Additional awards are denoted by bronze and silver oak leaf clusters.

112 Decorations, Medals, and Ribbons of the United States Air Force

❖ Air Force Meritorious Unit Award

The Meritorious Unit Award was established in 2004 by the Secretary of the Air Force to reward active duty, Reserve and Guard units for exceptionally meritorious conduct in the performance of outstanding services for at least 90 continuous days during a period of military operations against an armed enemy on or after September 11, 2001. The unit must display such outstanding devotion and superior performance of exceptionally difficult tasks so as to set it above and apart from other units with similar missions. The degree of achievement required is the same as that which would warrant award of the Legion of Merit to an individual. Bronze and silver oak leaf clusters are worn to denote additional awards.

Service	Air Force
Instituted	2004
Criteria	Awarded to U.S. Air Force units for exceptionally meritorious conduct in the performance of outstanding services against an armed enemy of the United States.
Devices	Bronze, Silver Oak Leaf Cluster 

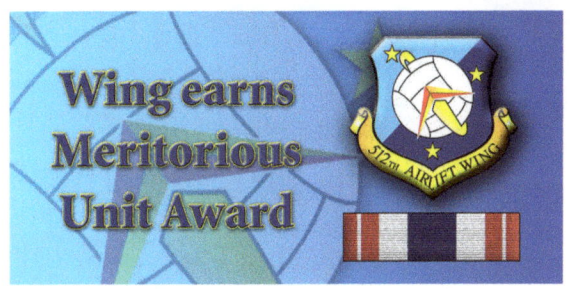

❖ Air Force Outstanding Unit Award

The Outstanding Unit Award was established on January 6, 1954 and is awarded by the Secretary of the Air Force to units for exceptionally meritorious service or outstanding achievement that clearly sets the unit above and apart from similar units. A unit must clearly perform at a high level for a sustained period of time to receive such recognition as afforded by this award. The exceptionally meritorious service must have been performed for a period of not more than two years and not less than one year. A bronze letter "V" for the ribbon was awarded for combat or direct combat support actions but was discontinued in 2014 and is no longer awarded. Bronze and silver oak leaf clusters are worn to denote additional awards.

Service	Air Force
Instituted	1954
Criteria	Awarded to U.S. Air Force units for exceptionally meritorious achievement or meritorious service.
Devices	Bronze Letter "V" no longer awarded, Bronze, Silver Oak Leaf Cluster

❖ Air Force Organizational Excellence Award

The Air Force Organizational Excellence Award was established on August 26, 1969 to recognize unique, unnumbered organizations/units that have performed exceptionally meritorious service for a nominated time period of not less than two years. It is awarded to recognize the achievements and accomplishments of Air Force organizations or activities that do not meet the eligibility requirements of the Air Force Outstanding Unit Awards such as Headquarters organizations and Air Force Academy units. The letter "V" was authorized until 2014 for combat or direct combat support actions. Additional awards are signified by bronze and silver oak leaf clusters.

Service	Air Force
Instituted	1969
Criteria	Same as Outstanding Unit Award but awarded to unique unnumbered organizations performing staff functions.
Devices	Bronze Letter "V" no longer awarded, Bronze, Silver Oak Leaf Cluster

Medals of America 113

❖ Prisoner of War Medal

Bronze Anodized or Gold-Plated

Regulation Ribbon Bar
Enamel Lapel Pin
Medal Reverse
Miniature Medals
Mini Ribbon (unofficial)
Enamel Hat Pin (unofficial)

The Prisoner of War Medal is awarded to any person who was taken prisoner of war and held captive after April 5, 1917. It was authorized by Public Law Number 99-145 in 1985 and may be awarded to any pterson who was taken prisoner or held captive while engaged in an action against an enemy of the United States, while engaged in military operations involving conflict with an opposing armed force or while serving with friendly forces engaged in armed conflict against an opposing armed force in which the United States is not a belligerent party. The recipient's conduct while a prisoner must have been honorable.

The Prisoner of War Medal is worn after all unit awards (after personal decorations in the case of the Army) and before the various Armed Service Good Conduct Medals (before the Combat Readiness Medal in the case of the Air Force).

The Prisoner of War Medal was designed by the Institute of Heraldry. The medal is a circular bronze disc with an American eagle centered and completely surrounded by a ring of barbed wire and bayonet points. The reverse of the medal has a raised inscription, "AWARDED TO" with a space for the recipient's name and, "FOR HONORABLE SERVICE WHILE A PRISONER OF WAR" set in three lines. Below this is the shield of the United States and the words, "UNITED STATES OF AMERICA." The ribbon is black with thin border stripes of white, blue, white and red. Additional awards are denoted by three-sixteenth inch bronze stars.

124,079 U.S. Army personnel were captured by the enemy In World War II. 41,057 were airmen of the Army Air Forces most of whom were shot down in aerial combat over enemy territory. 35,621 Americans were POWs of Germany and its Allies while Japan captured 5,436 American airmen. The most of the 235 airmen captured in the Korean War were held in solitary confinement for most of their captivity.

Service	All Services
Instituted	1985
Criteria	Awarded to any member of the U.S. Armed Forces taken prisoner during any armed conflict dating from World War I.
Devices	Bronze, Silver Star

Prisoners suffered from bitter cold and inadequate food, clothing, and medical care. Airmen, especially pilots, were considered potential sources of intelligence and subjected to frequent torture. Most of the 660 total Air Force POWs who survived the Vietnam war were held in North Vietnam. However some were held in South Vietnam (124), Cambodia (23), Laos (13) and China (2). Their experience as POWs was in some ways even more harsh.

Documents of Flight Officer Thomas Floyd who captured after his B17 was shot down in Feb 1945. War Department notification to his wife, POW postcard, German POW file and the hand written report all USAAF POWs were required to prepare when liberated, detailing how they were captured.

❖ Combat Readiness Medal

Bronze

Anodized or Gold-Plated

Regulation Ribbon Bar

Enamel Lapel Pin

Medal Reverse

Miniature Medals

Mini Ribbon (unofficial)

Enamel Hat Pin (unofficial)

The Combat Readiness Medal was authorized on March 9, 1964. Awarded for periods of qualifying service in a combat or mission ready status for direct weapon system employment. Direct weapon system employment is defined as: (1) An aircrew whose wartime mission places them into enemy territory or in the threat envelope of ground enemy defenses, (2) A missile operation which could employ weapons to destroy enemy targets and (3) Individuals who directly control in-flight manned aircraft whose wartime mission is to seek and destroy enemy targets. An individual must be a member of a unit subject to combat readiness reporting under Joint Chiefs of Staff requirements, must have completed all prerequisite training and be certified as combat or mission ready in performing the unit's mission and must be subject to a continuous individual positional evaluation program. In previous regulations, eligibility was extended to Air Force members on special duty with another U.S. military service provided they were certified as combat ready in that service and the combat ready status closely correlated to that of the Air Force. Originally an individual

Service	Air Force
Instituted	1964
Criteria	Awarded for specific periods of qualifying service in a combat or mission-ready status.
Devices	Bronze, Silver Oak Leaf cluster

was required to be combat ready for three years to earn this award. Currently, individuals must have 24 months of sustained combat ready status to receive the award. Eligibility for the award is certified by the individual's unit commander and is filed in the unit's personnel records group. An oak leaf cluster attachment is awarded for each additional 24 months of combat ready status provided there is no break greater than 120 days. The front of the medal has a border of concentric rays encircling a ring of stylized cloud forms with two intersecting triangles on a compass rose that has small triangles at his points. The reverse of the medal contains the inscription, "FOR COMBAT READINESS-AIR FORCE."

The Combat Crew Badge was established by the Air Force September 1, 1964. It was worn by USAF personnel serving where they were accruing creditable service towards the Combat Readiness Medal as outlined in Air Force regulation 900-48. It was a qualification badge and not a medal; and therefore not a permanent award. The Air Force eliminated the Combat Crew Badge in August 1993 to eliminate duplication, achieve standardization, and promote an uncluttered appearance on the uniform. The badge was worn on the wearer's right side above the name tag when it was authorized.

❖ Army Good Conduct Medal

Bronze

Anodized or Gold-Plated

Regulation Ribbon Bar

Enamel Lapel Pin

Medal Reverse

Miniature Medals

Mini Ribbon (unofficial)

Enamel Hat Pin (unofficial)

Authorized on June 28, 1941 for exemplary conduct, efficiency and fidelity and awarded to Army enlisted personnel who, on or after August 27, 1940, had honorably completed three years of active Federal military service. The medal could also be awarded for one year of service after December 7, 1941 while the U.S. was at war. The award was not automatic and required certification by a commanding officer (usually a battalion commander or higher).

The Army Good Conduct Medal was designed by Joseph Kiselewski with an eagle perched on a roman sword atop a closed book. Around the outside are the words, "EFFICIENCY, HONOR, FIDELITY." The reverse of the medal has a five pointed star just above center with a blank scroll for engraving the soldier's name. Above the star are the words, "FOR GOOD" and below the scroll is the word, "CONDUCT." A wreath of half laurel leaves, denoting accomplishment and half oak leaves, denoting bravery surrounds the reverse design.

The ribbon was designed by Arthur E. DuBois, the legendary Director of the Army Institute of Heraldry, and is scarlet with three narrow white stripes on each side. The ribbon is divided by the white stripes so as to form thirteen stripes representing the thirteen original colonies of the United States. During the Revolutionary War, the color scarlet symbolized the mother country and the white stripe symbolized the virgin land separated by force from the mother country.

Unlike other additional award devices, e.g., oak leaf clusters, bronze, silver, or gold clasps with knots (or loops) are used to indicate the **total** number of awards of the Army Good Conduct Medal. For instance, two awards of the medal are indicated by two bronze knots, three by three, etc. Six total awards are indicated by one silver knot, seven by two silver knots, etc. Eleven total awards are indicated by one gold knot, twelve by two gold knots, etc. While all regulations since World War II only authorize a clasp to be worn after the second award or higher; it was not unusual to see veterans with a clasp having

Service	Army
Instituted	1941
Criteria	Exemplary conduct, efficiency and fidelity during three years of active enlisted service with the U.S. Army (1 year during wartime).
Devices	Bronze, Silver, Gold Knotted clasp

a single bronze knot on their Army Good Conduct Medal or ribbon; this may have indicated either a single or second award and seems to have been an earlier unofficial practice.

Although the Good Conduct Medal was officially instituted by executive order in 1941, it really goes back to the American Revolution. When General George Washington established the Badge of Military Merit in 1782 he also created an award called the Honorary Badge of Distinction. This was the first good conduct award since it was to be conferred on veteran noncommissioned officers and soldiers of the Army who served more than three years with bravery, fidelity and good conduct. However, just as the Badge of Military Merit disappeared after the Revolution so did the Honorary Badge of Distinction.

When President Roosevelt signed executive order 9323 on March 31, 1943 he officially changed the policy that the Army Good Conduct Medal could be awarded after one year. It additional awards of the Good Conduct Medal cannot be given for each additional year of service in World War II but required completion of a subsequent additional three-year period.

During the Korean War, President Eisenhower approved a first award only which could be presented for service after June 27, 1950 with less than three years but more than one year service.

The Air Force ceased using the Army Good Conduct Medal June, 1 1963. Qualifying airmen were then awarded the Air Force Good Conduct Medal which differed from the Army Good Conduct Medal only in design of the ribbon. The medal remained the same. Personnel who earned the Army Good Conduct medal before earning the Air Force Good Conduct Medal can wear both with the Air Force Good Conduct Medal coming first.

There is often some discussion if the Army Good Conduct Medal is a decoration or service medal. Historically going back to World War II, the Good Conduct Medal was considered a decoration and was one of a few medals to be manufactured throughout the war when service medal production was restricted due to the need to divert metal to the arms industry. Today however, it is considered a service award.

There was no certificate to denote the award of the Army Good Conduct Medal until 1981; army regulations covering the issue of the paper certificate prohibited the issue of the certificate of those awarded the Good Conduct Medal prior to January 1, 1981.

Currently the Army authorizes engraving at the government's expense by the U.S. Army Support Activity in Philadelphia PA. The Good Conduct Medal is the last United States Army award established prior to World War II. It was also the last medal that the War Department attempted to issue with a serial number (a practice dropped in WW II). It is the only United States Army medal awarded which specifically excludes officers from eligibility and is only authorized for enlisted personnel.

World War II AAF Officer with previous enlisted service.

Korean War USAF NCO with Army Good Conduct Medal.

World War II and Cold War veteran with multiply Army and the Air Force Good Conduct Medals. The presence of American Defense Service Medal tells you he enlisted before World War II and served until at least 1965 to have earned the USAF Good Conduct.

❖ Air Force Good Conduct Medal

Bronze — Anodized or Gold Plated

Regulation Ribbon Bar / Enamel Label Pin / Medal Reverse / Miniature Medals / Mini Ribbon (unofficial) / Enamel Hat Pin (unofficial)

Service	Air Force
Instituted	1963
Criteria	Exemplary conduct, efficiency and fidelity during three years of active enlisted service with the U.S. Air Force.
Devices	Bronze, Silver Oak Leaf cluster

The Air Force Good Conduct Medal is the last version of the five Services Good Conduct Medals. Authorized by Congress in 1960, it became official 1 June 1963. Air Force personnel were issued the Army Good Conduct Medal between 1947 and 1963 and for those serving both before and after 1963, the Army and Air Force Good Conduct Medals can be worn simultaneously on an Air Force uniform.

The Air Force medallion is the same as the Army 1941 version, but the suspension and service ribbons for the medals are different. The Air Force ribbon is light sky blue with two sets of thin red, white and blue stripes representing the national colors. The medallion bears the inscription, "EFFICIENCY, HONOR, FIDELITY," surrounding the American eagle which stands on a closed book and sword. On the reverse is a five-pointed star above a blank scroll for engraving the airman's name; the words, "FOR GOOD" are above the star and below the scroll is the word, "CONDUCT." Additional awards of the Air Force Good Conduct Medal are denoted by bronze or silver oak leaf clusters.

The Air Force Good Conduct medal is awarded to enlisted personnel for three-years of active military service or a one-year period of service during war. Airmen awarded the medal must have had character and efficiency ratings of excellent or higher throughout the qualifying period and no convictions of court martial or non-judicial punishment during this period. In 2005, the 97th Air Force Uniform Board recommended discontinuing the Good Conduct Medal with the rationale that good conduct of Airmen is the expected standard. The decision was finalized February 2006 and the medal was no longer issued. Airmen who had previously earned the Good Conduct Medal were still authorized to wear it. Air Force officials reconsidered the policy and in February 2009 the medal was reinstated and made retroactive to 8 February 2006, with all eligible recipients being awarded the medal automatically.

(USAF Photo)

❖ Air Reserve Forces Meritorious Service Medal

Originally established by the Secretary of the Air Force as a ribbon bar on April 1, 1964 and later amended to be a medal on May 1, 1973.

The medal may be awarded on specific recommendation of the unit commander to enlisted members of the Air Reserve Forces for exemplary behavior, efficiency and fidelity for a period of four continuous years service prior to July 1, 1972 and for three years on/after July 1, 1972. Creditable service ends when the Reservist is called to active duty or is appointed a commissioned officer. The medal may be awarded to individuals who accrue at least one year, but less than three years, toward award of the medal and terminate their enlisted Reserve status as a commissioned or warrant officer, regardless of the beginning eligibility date. The medal is awarded to individuals who accrue at least one year, but less than three years, toward award of the medal and terminate their enlisted Reserve status as a commissioned or warrant officer, regardless of the beginning eligibility date. A period of more than 24 hours between Reserve enlistments counts as a break in service. Credit must begin anew after the break. An active duty period is not a break in service. Service in the U.S. Army, Navy, Marine Corps or Coast Guard Reserve components is not creditable for award of the medal nor is service as a commissioned officer.

Service	Air Force
Instituted	1964
Criteria	Exemplary behavior, efficiency and fidelity during three years of active enlisted service with the Air Force Reserve.
Devices	Bronze, Silver Oak Leaf cluster

The circular bronze medal was designed by the Army's Institute of Heraldry. The front of the medal has the American eagle perched atop a small circle containing a five-pointed star. A banner sits above the eagle and contains the words, "MERITORIOUS SERVICE." On the outer edge of the medal are the words, "AIR RESERVE FORCES." On the reverse is a cloud design with thunderbolts and wings with the word, "TO" inscribed below it with space to engrave the recipient's name. Along the circular outer edge, the words, "EXEMPLARY BEHAVIOR" are in raised letters on the upper half of the ring and "EFFICIENCY-FIDELITY" appear on the lower half.

The ribbon has a wide, light blue center with stripes of, reading outward from the center on each side, dark blue, yellow, dark blue, white and light blue selvedges. Additional awards are denoted by bronze and silver oak leaf clusters.

Air Force Outstanding Airmen of the Year 2010 (USAF Photo)

❖ Outstanding Airman of the Year Ribbon

Authorized February 21, 1968 it is awarded to 12 airmen chosen from nominees throughout the Air Force, field operation agencies, the Air Force Reserve and Air National Guard in the 12 Outstanding Airmen of the Year Program. The award of the ribbon is retroactive to include those selected for this program as of June 1970. The 12 finalist wear a bronze service star and multiple winners wear oak leaf clusters to denote additional awards. The Outstanding Airman of the Year Ribbon is the highest personal ribbon award of the United States Air Force.

Each year, 12 airmen are selected by the office of the Chief Master Sergeant of the Air Force as the best enlisted personnel in the Air Force. They stand out among their peers for their superior leadership, job performance, community involvement, and personal achievements. The Chief Master Sergeant of the Air Force, a general officer and selected Major Command chiefs form the selection board. The Air Force Chief of Staff reviews the selections. The Twelve Outstanding Airmen are awarded the Outstanding Airmen ribbon with the bronze service star device and wear the Outstanding Airmen badge for one year. They also serve on the Air Force Enlisted Council for one year.

Service Air Force
Instituted 1968
Criteria Awarded to airmen for selection to the "12 Outstanding Airmen of the Year" Competition Program.
Devices Bronze, Silver Oak Leaf Cluster, Bronze Star

❖ Air Force Recognition Ribbon

The Air Force Recognition Ribbon is a military award which was authorized on October 12, 1980 and effective January 1, 1981. Awarded to individual recipients of Air Force level special trophies and awards, as listed in appropriate Air Force regulations, except the 12 Outstanding Airmen of the Year nominees. It is not awarded to individuals of a unit which receives a special award. The ribbon is intended to recognize those who have received "non-portable" awards for accomplishment and excellence while serving on active duty in the United States Air Force.

To receive the Air Force Recognition Ribbon, a service member must receive a designated trophy, plaque, or other award (such as the Sijan Leadership Award) through an achievement as specified by Air Force regulations. The ribbon is thus intended to recognize awards which cannot otherwise be displayed on a military uniform; as such, this award is typically presented in combination with an Air Force level annual award. The ribbon is not awarded retroactively. The ribbon design is patterned after the Air Force Cross ribbon with a red stripe in the center. Bronze and silver oak leaf clusters are used to denote additional awards.

Service Air Force
Instituted 1980
Criteria Awarded to individual recipients of Air Force-level special trophies and awards.
Devices Bronze, Silver Oak Leaf Cluster

In 1981 the Lance P. Sijan USAF Leadership Award was established to recognize individuals who demonstrated the highest qualities of leadership in their jobs and in their lives. It is one of the U.S. Air Force's most prestigious awards. Captain Sijan, an Air Force fighter pilot, died while a POW in Vietnam. Prior to his capture, the USAF Academy graduate and posthumous Medal of Honor recipient evaded the North Vietnamese for six weeks after being shot down in November 1967. Recipients of the Sijan Award are entitled to wear the Air Force Recognition Ribbon

❖ The Early Medals

Mexican Service Medal (Army)

Service: Army
Instituted: 1917
Dates: 1914-1919
Criteria: Awarded to Army personnel who participated in engagements or expeditions in Mexico during 10 specific time periods from April 1914 to June, 1919.
Devices: Silver Citation Star

Bronze   Medal Reverse

Mexican Border Service Medal (Army)

Service: Army
Instituted: 1918
Dates: 1916-1917
Criteria: Awarded to Army and National Guard troops who served on the Mexican border between January 1916 and April 1917.

Bronze   Medal Reverse

The Mexican Service Medal was awarded to Army Air Service personnel who actually served in Mexico. On the front of the medal is the Yucca plant symbolizing the area of the campaign while the thorny, sharp pointed leaves stood for the raids by Mexican bandits. The background mountains show the type of terrain the Army was fighting in. "Mexican Service" and dates tell the campaign and the period. The green and yellow colors stand for the Aztecs of ancient Mexico's standard of a gold sun surrounded by the green plumes carried in the battle of Otumba in 1520.

The Mexican Service Medal was a one time decoration and no service stars were authorized for multiple engagements. Army members cited for gallantry in combat, were authorized the Citation Star as a device to the Mexican Service Medal.

The Mexican Border Service Medal recognizes soldiers who served on the U.S.-Mexico border between the dates of January 1, 1916 and April 6, 1917, when the US-Mexico border was perceived to be threatened by a German-funded invasion (according to the interception of the Zimmermann Telegram). The Roman sword stands for military strength and while sheathed symbolizes service in the United States rather than combat. Rifles, sabers, and cannons represent the Infantry, Cavalry, and Artillery while the circular wreath is for achievement. The ribbon colors come from the Mexican Service Medal.

To recieve the Mexican Border Service Medal, a soldier must have served with the United States Army, along the Mexican border, or must have been assigned as a Regular or National Guard member to the Mexican Border Patrol. Those who had received the Mexican Service Medal were not eligible for the Mexican Border Service Medal. The Mexican Border Service Medal held dual status as both a Federal and a United States National Guard medal.

Regulation Ribbon Bar

World War I Victory Medal

Service: All Services
Instituted: 1919
Dates: 1917-1918
Criteria: Awarded to all military personnel who served in the Continental United States or overseas between April, 1917 and April, 1920.
Devices:

WW I Style Ribbon with Silver Star

Bronze   Medal Reverse

Battle Clasp   Service Clasp

The 14 Allied Nations decided on a single ribbon, but pendant design was left up to each Nation. Mr. James E. Fraser was the designer of the U.S. Victory Medal. The bronze medal front shows a Winged Victory holding a shield and sword. The back of the medal reads "The Great War For Civilization" curved along the top of the medal. On the bottom of the back of the medal are six stars, three on either side of the center column of seven Roman staffs wrapped in a cord. The top of the staff has a round ball on top and is winged on the side. The staff overlays a shield saying "U" on the left side of the staff and "S" on the right side. Left of the staff are listed World War I Allied countries: France, Italy, Serbia, Japan, Montenegro, Russia, and Greece. On the right side of the staff are: Great Britain, Belgium, Brazil, Portugal, Rumania (now spelled Romania), and China.

A 3/16 inch Silver Citation Star was authorized to be worn on the ribbon of the Victory Medal by any member of the U.S. Army who had been cited for gallantry in action between 1917 and 1920. In 1932, the Silver Citation Star was redesigned as the Silver Star and, upon application, any holder of the Silver Citation Star could have it converted to a Silver Star decoration. Only one bronze star was authorized for wear on the ribbon requardless of the number of campaign bars earned.

Army of Occupation of Germany Medal (Army)

Regulation Ribbon Bar

Service: Army
Instituted: 1942
Dates: 1918-1923
Criteria: Awarded to Army personnel who served in the occupation of Germany or Austria-Hungary between November, 1918 and July, 1923. Navy personnel on shore duty were also eligible.

First Ribbon Bar

The medal was designed by Mr. T. A. Rovelstad, of the Army Heraldic Division, in June 1942, and was approved 8 July 1942. The first ribbon had a wavy blue stripe to represent the Rhine river but was changed for ease of manufacture.

The front of the medal shows General Pershing and includes the dates of the U.S. Occupation of Germany. The reverse depicts the eagle standing on the Castle of Ehrenbreitstein, overlooking the Rhine in Coblenz, Germany. The three stars on the reverse symbolize the Third Army, which was the occupation force of Germany.

Bronze   Medal Reverse

Medals of America

❖ American Defense Service Medal

Bronze | Anodized or Gold-Plated | Regulation Ribbon Bar | Enamel Lapel Pin | Medal Reverse | Miniature Medals | Mini Ribbon (unofficial) | Hat Pin (unofficial)

Authorized on June 28, 1941 for military service during the limited emergency proclaimed by President Roosevelt on Sept. 8, 1939 or during the unlimited emergency proclaimed on May 27, 1941 until December 7, 1941 if under orders to active duty for 12 months or longer. A Foreign Service Clasp was issued by the Army for military service outside the continental limits of the United States, including service in Alaska. It is a Bronze bar 1/8 inch in width and 1-1/2 inches in length with the

Service	All Services
Instituted	1941
Dates	1939-41
Criteria	12 months of active duty service during the above period.
Devices	All Services: Bronze Star (denotes bars);
Bars	Army: Foreign Service for service outside the continental United States (CONUS).

words FOREIGN SERVICE, with a star at each end of the inscription A bronze star is worn on the service ribbon to denote receipt of any of the bars.

On the front of the medal a female Grecian figure, Columbia, representing America or Liberty, holding a shield and sword while standing on an oak branch, symbolic of strength. The oak leaves represent the strength of the Army, Navy, Marine Corps and Coast Guard. The inscription, "American Defense," is around the outside upper edge. The reverse of the medal carries the inscription, "For Service During the Limited Emergency Proclaimed By the President on September 8, 1939 or During the Unlimited Emergency Proclaimed By the President on May 27, 1941."

The single-seat P-40 Warhawk was first flown in 1938 and was the most available fighter when World War II started. Over 17,000 P-40s were built during the war before being repaced by the P38 Lightning, P 47 Thunderbolt, and P 51 Mustang.

The golden yellow color of the ribbon symbolizes the golden opportunity of United States youth to serve the nation, represented by the blue, white and red stripes on both sides of the ribbon. The medal was designed by Mr. Lee Lawrie, a civilian sculptor from Easton, Maryland and approved by the Commission of Fine Arts on May 5, 1942.

❖ Women's Army Corps Service Medal

Bronze

Regulation Ribbon Bar

Medal Reverse

Service	Army
Instituted	1943
Dates	1942-45
Criteria	Service with both the Women's Army Auxiliary Corps and Women's Army Corps during the above period.
Devices	None
Notes	Only U.S. award authorized for women only

Authorized on July 29, 1943 for service in both the Women's Army Auxiliary Corps (WAAC) between July 10, 1942 and August 31, 1943 and the Women's Army Corps (WAC) between September 1, 1943 and September 2, 1945. After 1945, members of the WAC received the same medals as other members of the Army. No attachments are authorized for the medal.

The front of the medal contains the head of Pallas Athena, goddess of victory and wisdom, superimposed on a sword crossed with oak leaves and a palm branch. The sword represents military might; the oak leaves represent strength and the palm branch represents peace. The reverse contains thirteen stars, an eagle and a scroll along with the words, "FOR SERVICE IN THE WOMEN'S ARMY AUXILIARY CORPS," and the dates "1942-1943." The dates on the medal, 1942-1943, remained the same even after the WAAC became the WAC. The ribbon is moss green with old gold edges, the branch colors of the Women's Army Corps. Green indicates merit and gold refers to achievement.

Fewer than 100,000 women in World War II qualified for the Women's Army Corps Service Medal; over 40,000 WAC members were assigned to the U.S. Army Air Force by 1945. By January 1945, only 50 percent of AAF WACs worked in the assignments traditionally seen as appropriate for women, such as stenography, typing, and filing. Instead, Air WACs served increasingly as weather observers, cryptographers, radio operators, aerial photograph analyzers, control tower operators, parachute riggers, maintenance specialists, and sheet metal workers. More than 7,000 Air WACs served overseas in every theater of operations, and three WACs received the Air Medal. This is the only U.S. service medal specifically created and authorized for women in the military.

Air WACs in WWII with new 15th AF shoulder sleeve insignia. (AAF photo)

WACs pose by the tail guns of a 401st BG B-17 at an 8th Air Force base in England in January 1944. (AAF photo)

❖ American Campaign Medal

For service during World War II within the American Theater of Operations. The American Campaign Medal was established by Executive Order on November 6, 1942 and amended on March 15, 1946, which established a closing date. The medal is awarded to any member of the Armed Forces who served in the American Theater of Operations during the period from December 7, 1941 to March 2, 1946 or was awarded a combat decoration while in combat against the enemy. The service must have been an aggregate of one year within the continental United States, thirty consecutive days outside the continental United States, or sixty nonconsecutive days outside the continental United States, but within the American Theater of Operations. Maps of the three theaters of operations during World War II were drawn on November 6, 1942 to include the American Theater, European- African - Middle Eastern Theater and Asiatic-Pacific Theater.

The American Campaign Medal was designed by the Army's Institute of Heraldry. The medal is a circular bronze disc showing a Navy cruiser, a B-24 bomber and a sinking enemy submarine above three waves. Shown in the background are buildings representing the United States. Above is the raised inscription, "AMERICAN CAMPAIGN." The reverse of the medal shows an American eagle standing on a rock. On the left of the eagle are the raised inscribed dates, "1941-1945" and on the right, "UNITED STATES OF AMERICA." The ribbon is azure blue with three narrow stripes of red, white and blue (United States) in the center and four stripes of white, red (Japan), black and white (Germany) near the edges. Three-sixteenth inch bronze stars indicated participation in specialized antisubmarine, escort or special operations. The American Campaign Medal is worn after the Women's Army Corps Service Medal by Army & Air Force personnel.

Service	All Services
Instituted	1942
Criteria	Service outside the U.S. in the American theater for 30 days, or within the continental United States (CONUS) for one year.
Devices	All Services: Bronze star ★

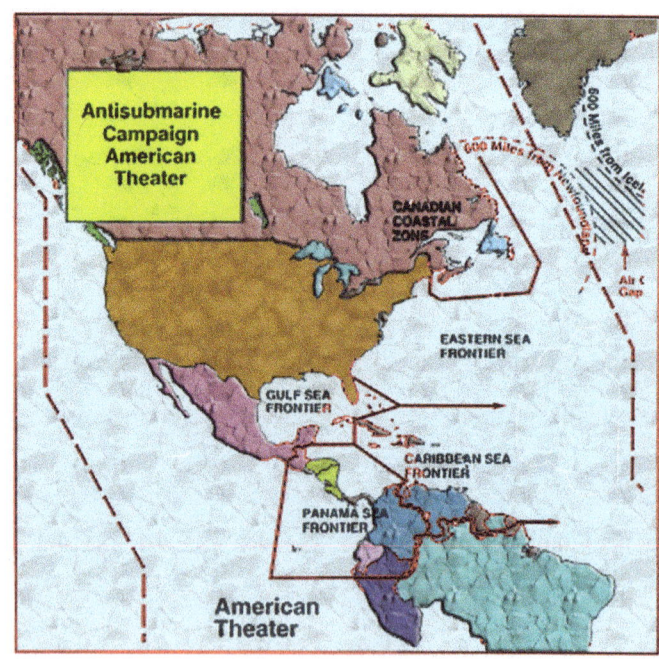

126 Decorations, Medals, and Ribbons of the United States Air Force

Does the Victory Medal appear slightly larger than the other medals? Well it is. The bronze World War II Victory medal is 1 3/8 inches in width while the regular campaign medals are are 1 1/4 inches wide.

Most all USAAF aircrews earned the American Campaign Medal by virtue of their time spent training in the United States before going overseas as shown by the two display cases below. An enlisted airman or member of the Women's Army Corps serving in the AAF stationed in the United States would normally have received the three medals shown above especially since the Good Conduct Medal was issued for just one year of service during the war. Since these medals were not really available at the end of the war most veterans only received ribbons.

❖ Asiatic-Pacific Campaign Medal

Authorized on November 6, 1942 and amended on March 15, 1946. Awarded to members of the U.S. Armed Forces for at least 30 consecutive (60 nonconsecutive) days service (less if in combat) within the Asiatic-Pacific Theater between December 7, 1941 and March 2, 1946.

The front of the medal shows a palm tree amidst troops with an aircraft overhead and an aircraft carrier, battleship and submarine in the background. The reverse has the American eagle, symbolizing power, on a rock, symbolizing stability, with the inscription, "UNITED STATES OF AMERICA" on the eagle's back. The orange yellow of the ribbon represents Asia while the white and red stripes toward each edge represent Japan. The center blue, white and red thin stripes are taken from the American Defense Service Medal, referring to America's continued defense preparedness after Pearl Harbor.

Service	All Services
Instituted	1942
Dates	7 December 1941 to 2 March 1946
Criteria	Service in the Asiatic-Pacific theater for 30 days or receipt of any combat decoration.
Devices	All Services: Bronze, Silver Star; Army/Air Force: Bronze arrowhead

A bronze star denoted participation in a campaign. A silver star attachment is used to represent five bronze stars. An arrowhead attachment is authorized by the Army and Air Force for participation in a combat parachute jump, combat glider landing or amphibious assault landing (only one arrowhead may be worn on the medal/ribbon despite the number of qualification events). The ribbon is worn with the center blue stripe on the wearer's right.

Designated Army & AAF campaigns for the Asiatic-Pacific Campaign Medal are:

Burma, 1941-1942
Philippine Islands, 1941-1942
Central Pacific, 1941-1943
East Indies, 1942
Aleutian Islands, 1942-1943
Guadalcanal, 1942-1943
Papua, 1942-1943

Air Offensive, Japan, 1942-1945
China Defensive, 1942-1945
India-Burma, 1942-1945
Bismark Archipelago, 1943-1944
New Guinea, 1943-1944
Northern Solomons, 1943-1944
Eastern Mandates (Air), 1943-1944
Eastern Mandates (Ground), 1944
Leyte, 1944-1945

Luzon, 1944-1945
Western Pacific, 1944-1945
Central Burma, 1945
China Offensive, 1945
Ryukyus, 1945
Southern Philippines, 1945
Air Combat, 1941-1945
Antisubmarine, 1941-1945
Ground Combat, 1941-1945

Lt. Col. Jimmy Doolittle accepts a medal from the skipper of the USS Hornet, Capt. Marc A. Mitscher. The medal, once given to a U.S. Navy officer by the Japanese, was wired to a 500-pound bomb for return to Japan "with interest." (U.S. Air Force photo)

European-African-Middle Eastern Campaign Medal

Authorized on November 6, 1942, as amended on March 15, 1946. Awarded to members of the U.S. Armed Forces for at least 30 days of consecutive (60 days nonconsecutive) service within the European Theater of Operations between December 7, 1941 and November 8, 1945 (lesser periods qualify if individual was in actual combat against the enemy during this period).

The front of the bronze medal shows a Landing Ship, Tank (LST) unloading troops while under fire with an airplane overhead. The reverse has the American eagle, symbol of power, standing on a rock, symbol of stability, with the inscription, "UNITED STATES OF AMERICA" and dates, "1941-1945."

Three-sixteenth inch diameter bronze and silver stars denoted participation in the specific campaigns described below. A bronze arrowhead indicated participation in a combat parachute jump, combat glider landing or amphibious assault landing. The ribbon's central blue, white and red stripes represent the United States. The wide green stripes represent the green fields of Europe, the brown edges represent the African desert sands, the thin green, white, and red stripes represent Italy and the thin black and white stripes represent Germany.

Service	All Services
Instituted	1942
Dates	7 December 1941 to 2 March 1946
Criteria	Service in the European-African-Middle Eastern theater for 30 days or receipt of any combat decoration.
Devices	All Services: Bronze, Silver Star; Army/Air Force: Bronze Arrowhead

Designated Army (& AAF) campaigns for the European-African-Middle Eastern Campaign Medal are as follows:

- ★ Algeria-French Morocco, 1942
- ★ Egypt-Libya, 1942-1943
- ★ Tunisia, 1942-1943
- ★ Air Offensive, Europe, 1942-1944
- ★ Sicily, 1943
- ★ Naples-Foggia, 1943-1944
- ★ Anzio, 1944
- ★ Rome-Arno, 1944
- ★ Normandy, 1944
- ★ Northern France, 1944
- ★ Southern France, 1944
- ★ North Apennines, 1944-1945
- ★ Rhineland, 1944-1945
- ★ Ardennes-Alsace, 1944-1945
- ★ Central Europe, 1945
- ★ Po Valley, 1945
- ★ Air Combat, 1941-1945
- ★ Antisubmarine, 1941-1945
- ★ Ground Combat, 1941-1945

(USAF Photo)

Medals of America 131

World War II Victory Medal

Bronze

Anodized or Gold-Plated

Regulation Ribbon Bar

Enamel Lapel Pin

Medal Reverse

Miniature Medals

Mini Ribbon (unofficial)

Hat Pin (unofficial)

Authorized by an Act of Congress on July 6, 1945 and awarded to all members of the Armed Forces who served at least one day of honorable, active federal service between December 7, 1941 and December 31, 1946, inclusive. The World War II Victory Medal was intially issued as a service ribbon called the "Victory Ribbon." Not until after the war in 1946 was a full medal designed and struck with a new title: World War II Victory Medal.

The front of the medal depicts the Liberty figure resting her right foot on a war god's helmet with the hilt of a broken sword in her right hand and the broken blade in her left hand. The reverse contains the words, "FREEDOM FROM FEAR AND WANT, FREEDOM OF SPEECH AND RELIGION, and UNITED STATES OF AMERICA 1941-1945." The red center stripe of the ribbon is symbolic of Mars, the God of War, representing both courage and fortitude. The twin rainbow stripes, suggested by the World War I Victory Medal, allude to the peace following a storm. A narrow white stripe separates the center red stripe from each rainbow pattern on both sides of the ribbon. The World War II Victory Medal provides deserving recognition to all of America's veterans who served during World War II.

Service	All Services
Instituted	1945
Dates	7 December 1941 to 31 December 1946
Criteria	Awarded for service in the U.S. Armed Forces during the above period.
Devices	None

No attachments are authorized although some veterans received the ribbon with an affixed bronze star which, according to rumors at the time, was to distinguish those who served in combat from those who did not. No official documentation has ever been found to support this supposition. Although eligible for its award, many World War II veterans never actually received the medal since many were discharged prior to the medal's institution.

❖ Army of Occupation Medal

Bronze

Anodized or Gold-Plated

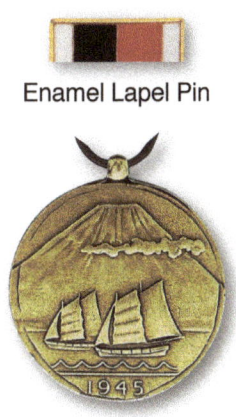
Medal Reverse

Regulation Ribbon Bar

Enamel Lapel Pin

Miniature Medals

Mini Ribbon (unofficial)

Hat Pin (unofficial)

Authorized on June 7, 1946 and awarded to both Army and Army Air Force personnel for at least 30 consecutive days of service in formerly held enemy territories, including Germany (1945-1955), Berlin (1945-1990), Austria (1945-1955), Italy (1945-1947), Japan (1945-1952) and Korea (1945-1949).

The front of the medal depicts the Remagen Bridge on the Rhine River with the inscription, "ARMY OF OCCUPATION" at the top. The reverse depicts Mount Fujiyama in Japan with two Japanese junks in front of the mountain. Although not specifically authorized by regulations, many veterans received Occupation Medals with reversed medallions, apparently to indicate the theater of occupation service, i.e., if occupation service was in Japan, the reverse side showing Mount Fujiyama became the front of the medal. The white and black colors of the ribbon represent Germany and the white and red colors represent Japan.

A gold-colored C-54 airplane device is authorized to denote participation in the Berlin Airlift. Medal clasps inscribed: Germany and Japan are authorized for the suspension ribbon of the medal for occupation service in those respective territories. An individual who performed occupational service in both areas is authorized to wear both clasps with the upper clasp representing the area where occupation was first performed. However, regardless of the clasp configuration, no attachment is authorized for the ribbon bar.

Service	Army/Air Force
Instituted	1946
Dates	1945-55 (Berlin: 1945-90)
Criteria	30 consecutive days of service in occupied territories of former enemies during above period.
Devices	Gold Airplane
Bars	"Germany", "Japan"

Italy, May 9, 1945 - Sept. 15, 1947
Germany (except West Berlin), May 9, 1945 - May 5, 1955
Austria, May 9, 1945 - Jul. 27, 1945 - Oct. 2, 1990
Germany (West Berlin), May 9, 1945 - Oct. 2, 1990
Korea, Sept. 3, 1945 - Jun. 29, 1949
Japan, Sept. 3, 1945 - Apr. 27, 1952

❖ Medal for Humane Action

Bronze | Anodized or Gold-Plated

Regulation Ribbon Bar

Enamel Lapel Pin

Medal Reverse

Miniature Medals

Mini Ribbon (unofficial)

Hat Pin (unofficial)

Authorized for members of the U.S. Armed Forces on July 20, 1949 for at least 120 days of service while participating in or providing direct support for the Berlin Airlift during the period June 26, 1948 and September 30, 1949. The prescribed boundaries for qualifying service include the area between the north latitudes of the 54th and the 48th parallels and between the 14th east longitude and the 5th west longitude meridians. Posthumous award may be made to any person who lost his/her life while, or as a direct result of, participating in the Berlin Airlift, without regard to the length of such service.

The front of the medal depicts the C-54 aircraft, which was the primary aircraft used during the airlift, above the coat of arms of Berlin which lies in the center of a wreath of wheat. The reverse has the American eagle with shield and arrows and bears the inscriptions, "FOR HUMANE ACTION and TO SUPPLY NECESSITIES OF LIFE TO THE PEOPLE OF BERLIN GERMANY."

Service	All Services
Instituted	1949
Dates	1948-49
Criteria	120 consecutive days of service participating in, or in support of the Berlin Airlift.
Devices	None

On the ribbon, the black and white colors of Prussia refer to Berlin, capital of Prussia and Germany. Blue alludes to the sky and red represents the fortitude and zeal of the personnel who participated in the airlift.

No attachments are authorized. However, instances have been noted where the gold C-54 airplane device was incorrectly placed on this award rather than its proper usage, the Occupation Medal.

(USAF Photo)

134 Decorations, Medals, and Ribbons of the United States Air Force

❖ National Defense Service Medal

Bronze | Anodized or Gold-Plated | Regulation Ribbon Bar | Enamel Lapel Pin | Medal Reverse

Miniature Medals | Mini Ribbon (unofficial) | Hat Pin (unofficial)

Initially authorized by executive order on April 22, 1953. It is awarded to members of the U.S. Armed Forces for any honorable active federal service during the Korean War (June 27, 1950 - July 27, 1954), Vietnam War (January 1, 1961- August 14, 1974), Desert Shield/Desert Storm (August 2, 1990 - November 30, 1995) and/or Operations Iraqi Freedom and Enduring Freedom (Afghanistan) (September 11, 2001 to a date TBD). President Bush issued an Executive Order 12776 on October 8, 1991 authorizing award of the medal to all members of the Reserve forces whether or not on active duty during the designated period of the Gulf War.

The latest award of the medal was promulgated in a memo, dated April 2, 2002, from the Office of the Deputy Secretary of Defense, Mr. Paul Wolfowitz who authorized the award to all U.S. Service Members on duty on or after September 11, 2001 to a date TBD. Today, there are probably more people authorized this medal than any other award in U.S. history. Circumstances not qualifying as active duty for the purpose of this medal include: (1) Members of the Guard and Reserve on short tours of active duty to fulfill training obligations; (2) Service members on active duty to serve on boards, courts, commissions, and like organizations; (3) Service members on active duty for the sole purpose of undergoing a physical examination; and (4) Service members on active duty for purposes other than extended active duty. Reserve personnel who have received the Armed Forces Expeditionary Medal or the Vietnam Service Medal are eligible for this medal. The National Defense Service Medal is also authorized to those individuals serving as cadets or midshipmen at the Air Force, Army or Naval Academies. The front of the medal shows the American bald eagle with inverted wings standing on a sword and palm branch and contains the words, "NATIONAL DEFENSE"; the reverse has the United States shield amidst an oak leaf and laurel spray. Symbolically, the eagle is the national emblem of the United States, the sword represents the Armed Forces and the palm is symbolic of victory. The reverse contains the shield from the great seal of the United States flanked by a wreath of laurel and oak representing achievement and strength. The ribbon has a broad center stripe of yellow representing high ideals. The red, white and blue stripes represent the national flag. Red for hardiness and valor, white for purity of purpose and blue for perseverance and justice. No more than one medal is awarded to a single individual and today a three-sixteenth inch diameter bronze star denotes an additional award of the medal in lieu of the bronze oak leaf used earlier.

Service	All Services
Instituted	1953
Dates	1950-54, 1961-74, 1990-95, 2001-TBD
Criteria	120 consecutive days of service participating in, or any honorable active duty service during any of the above periods.
Devices	Bronze Star, Bronze Oak Leaf Cluster
Notes	Reinstituted in 1966, 1991 and 2001 for Vietnam, Southwest Asia (Gulf War) and Iraq/Afghanistan actions respectively.

❖ Korean Service Medal

Bronze   Anodized or Gold-Plated   Regulation Ribbon Bar   Enamel Lapel Pin   Medal Reverse   Miniature Medals   Mini Ribbon (unofficial)   Hat Pin (unofficial)

Authorized by executive order on November 8, 1950 and awarded for service between June 27, 1950 and July 27, 1954 in the Korean theater of operations. Members of the U.S. Armed Forces must have participated in combat or served with a combat or service unit in the Korean Theater for 30 consecutive or 60 nonconsecutive days during the designated period. Personnel who served with a unit or headquarters stationed outside the theater but in direct support of Korean military operations are also entitled to this medal. The combat zone designated for qualification for the medal encompassed both North and South Korea, Korean waters and the airspace over these areas.

The first campaign began when North Korea invaded South Korea and the last campaign ended when the Korean Armistice cease-fire became effective. The period of Korean service was extended by one year from the cease fire by the Secretary of Defense; individuals could qualify for the medal during this period if stationed in Korea but would not receive any campaign credit. An award of this medal qualifies personnel for award of the United Nations (Korean) Service Medal and the Republic of Korea War Service Medal (approved 1999)

Service	All Services
Instituted	1950
Dates	1950-54
Criteria	Participation in military operations within the Korean area during the above period.
Devices	All Services: Bronze, Silver Star, Army, Air Force: Bronze Arrowhead

A Korean gateway is depicted on the front of the medal along with the inscription, "KOREAN SERVICE" and on the reverse are the "Taeguk" symbol from the Korean flag that represents unity and the inscription. "UNITED STATES OF AMERICA." A spray of oak and laurel line the bottom edge. The suspension ribbon and ribbon bar are both blue and white representing the United Nations. Bronze and silver stars are affixed to the suspension drape and ribbon bar to indicate participation in any of the 10 designated campaigns in the Korean War (see below). Army and Air Force personnel who participated in an amphibious assault landing are entitled to wear the arrowhead attachment.

Campaigns designated by the Army and Air Force for the Korea Service Medal are:

- ★ UN Defensive, 27 June - 15 Sept, 1950
- ★ UN Offensive, 16 Sept - 2 Nov, 1950
- ★ CCF Intervention, 3 Nov, 1950 - 24 Jan, 1951
- ★ 1st UN Counteroffensive, 25 Jan - 21 Apr, 1951
- ★ CCF Spring Offensive, 22 Apr - 8 July, 1951
- ★ UN Summer-Fall Offensive, 9 July - 27 Nov, 1951
- ★ Second Korean Winter, 28 Nov, 1951 - 30 Apr, 1952
- ★ Korea, Summer-Fall, 1 May - 30 Nov, 1953
- ★ Third Korean Winter, 1 Dec, 1952 - 30 Apr, 1953
- ★ Korea, Summer, 1 May - 27 July, 1953

Examples of veterans displays with and without Commemorative Medals.

❖ Antarctica Service Medal

Bronze

Anodized or Gold-Plated

Medal Reverse

Regulation Ribbon Bar

Mini Ribbon (unofficial)

Miniature Medals

Service	All Services
Instituted	July 7, 1960
Dates	1946 to Present
Criteria	30 calendar days of service on the Antarctric Continent.
Devices	All Services: Bronze, Gold, Silver disks
Bars	Wintered Over" in Bronze, Gold, Silver

Authorized on July 7, 1960 and awarded to any member of the Armed Forces who, from January 2, 1946, as a member of a U.S. Antarctic expedition, participates in, or performs services in direct support of scientific or exploratory operations on the Antarctic Continent. Qualifying service includes personnel who participate in flights or naval operations supporting operations in Antarctica. The medal may also be awarded to any U.S. citizen who participates in Antarctic expeditions under the same conditions as Service personnel.

The front of the medal depicts a figure appropriately clothed in cold weather gear with his hood thrown back, arms extended and legs spread, symbolizing stability, determination, courage and devotion. The reverse depicts a map of the Antarctic continent in polar projection across which are three centered lines containing the inscription, "COURAGE SACRIFICE DEVOTION."

A clasp containing the raised inscription, "WINTERED OVER" is worn on the medal and a disc of the same metal, containing the outline of the Antarctic Continent is worn on the ribbon bar if the individual remains on the continent during the winter months. For the first stay, the disc and bar are made of bronze, for the second stay, they are gold-colored and for the third and all subsequent winter tours, the devices are silver. The Coast Guard alone specifies the small three-sixteenths inch diameter bronze star as an additional award device.

Medals of America 137

❖ Armed Forces Expeditionary Medal

Bronze   Anodized or Gold-Plated

Regulation Ribbon Bar

Enamel Lapel Pin

Medal Reverse

Miniature Medals

Mini Ribbon (unofficial)

Hat Pin (unofficial)

President John F. Kennedy characterized the post World War II period as: "a twilight that is neither peace nor war." During the period commonly referred to as the Cold War, the Armed Services agreed to one medal to recognize major actions not otherwise covered by a specific campaign medal.

The Armed Forces Expeditionary Medal was authorized on December 4, 1961 to any member of the United States Armed Forces for U.S. military operations, U.S. operations in direct support of the United Nations and U.S. operations of assistance to friendly foreign nations after July 1, 1958. Operations that qualify for this medal are authorized in specific orders. Participating personnel must have served at least 30 consecutive (60 nonconsecutive) days in the qualifying operation or less if the operation was less than 30 days in length. The medal may also be authorized for individuals who do not meet the basic criteria but who do merit special recognition for their service in the designated operation.

Service	All Services
Instituted	1961
Dates	July 1, 1968 to Present
Criteria	Participation in military operations not covered by specific war medal.
Devices	All Services: Bronze, Silver Star
Notes	Authorized for service in Vietnam until establishment of Vietnam Service Medal.

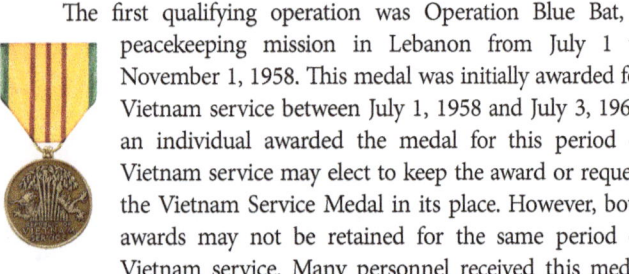

The first qualifying operation was Operation Blue Bat, a peacekeeping mission in Lebanon from July 1 to November 1, 1958. This medal was initially awarded for Vietnam service between July 1, 1958 and July 3, 1965; an individual awarded the medal for this period of Vietnam service may elect to keep the award or request the Vietnam Service Medal in its place. However, both awards may not be retained for the same period of Vietnam service. Many personnel received this medal for continuing service in Cambodia after the Vietnam cease-fire. The medal was also authorized for those serving in the Persian Gulf area who previously would have qualified for the Southwest Asia Service Medal and the National Defense Service Medal whose qualification periods for that area terminated on November 30, 1995. Individuals who qualify for both the Southwest Asia Service Medal and the Armed Forces Expeditionary Medal must elect to receive the Expeditionary medal.

The front of the medal depicts an American eagle with wings raised, perched on a sword. Behind this is a compass rose with rays coming from the angles of the compass points. The words "ARMED FORCES EXPEDITIONARY SERVICE" encircle the design. The reverse of the medal depicts the Presidential shield with branches of laurel below and the inscription, "UNITED STATES OF AMERICA." The American national colors are located at the center position or honor point of the ribbon. The light blue sections on either side suggest water and overseas service, while various colors representing areas of the world where American troops may be called upon to serve run outward to the edge.

F-15E Strike Eagles, from the 335th Expeditionary Fighter Squadron, drop 2,000 pound Joint Direct Attack Munitions on a cave in eastern Afghanistan, 26 Nov. 2009.

(USAF Photo)

The qualifying campaigns:

- Lebanon, Jul. 1, 1958 - Nov. 1, 1958
- Taiwan Straits, Aug. 23, 1958 - Jan. 1, 1959
- Quemoy & Matsu Islands, Aug. 23, 1958 - Jun. 1, 1963
- Vietnam, Jul. 1, 1958 - Jul. 3, 1965
- Congo, Jul. 14, 1960 - Sep. 1, 1962
- Laos, Apr. 19, 1961 - Oct. 7, 1962
- Berlin, Aug. 14, 1961 - Jun. 1, 1963
- Cuba, Oct. 24, 1962 - Jun. 1, 1963
- Congo, Nov. 23-27, 1964
- Dominican Republic, Apr. 23. 1965 - Sep. 21, 1966
- Korea, Oct. 1, 1966 - Jun. 30, 1974
- Cambodia, Mar. 29, 1973 - Aug. 15, 1973
- Thailand, Mar. 29, 1973 - Aug. 15, 1973 (Only those in direct support of Cambodia)
- Operation Eagle Pull - Cambodia, Apr. 11-13, 1975 (Includes evacuation)
- Operation Frequent Wind - Vietnam, Apr. 29-30, 1975
- Mayaquez Operation, May 15, 1975
- El Salvador, Jan. 1 , 1981 - Feb. 1, 1992
- Lebanon, Jun. 1, 1983 - Dec. 1, 1987
- Operation Urgent Fury-Grenada, Oct. 23, 1983 - Nov. 21, 1983
- Eldorado Canyon - Libya, Apr. 12-17, 1986
- Operation Earnest Will - Persian Gulf, Jul. 24, 1987 - Aug. 1, 1990 (Only those participating in, or in direct support)
- Operation Just Cause - Panama, Dec. 20, 1989 - Jan. 31, 1990 (USS Vreeland & other SVS-designated aircrew mbrs. outside the Conus in direct support)
- United Shield - Somalia, Dec. 5, 1992 - Mar. 31, 1995
- Operation Restore Hope - Somalia, Dec. 5, 1992 - Mar. 31, 1995
- Operation Uphold Democracy - Haiti, Sept. 1994 - Mar. 31, 1995
- Operation Joint Endeavor - Bosnia, Croatia, the Adriatic Sea & Airspace, Nov. 20, 1995 - Dec. 19, 1996
- Operation Vigilant Sentinel - Iraq, Saudi Arabia, Kuwait, & Persian Gulf Dec. 1, 1995 - Sep. 1, 1997
- Operation Southern Watch - Iraq, Saudi Arabia, Kuwait, Persian Gulf, Bahrain, Qatar, UAE, Oman, Gulf of Oman W of 62° E Long., Yemen, Egypt, & Jordan
- Operation Maritime Intercept - Iraq, Saudi Arabia, Kuwait, Red Sea, Persian Gulf, Gulf of Oman W of 62° E Long., Bahrain, Qatar, UAE, Oman, Yemen, Egypt & Jordan Dec. 1, 1995 - Open
- Operation Joint Guard - Bosnia, Herzegovina, Croatia, Adriatic Sea & Airspace, Dec. 20, 1996 - Jun. 20, 2008
- Operation Northern Watch - Iraq, Saudi Arabia, Kuwait, Persian Gulf of W of 56° E Long., and Incirlik AB, Turkey (Only pers. TDY to ONW), Jan. 1, 1997 - 18 March 2003
- Operation Joint Forge - Bosnia-Herzegovina, Croatia, Adriatic Sea & Airspace, Jun. 21, 1998 - Open
- Operation Desert Thunder - Iraq, Saudi Arabia, Kuwait, Bahrain, Qatar, UAE, Omar, Yemen, Egypt, Jordan, Persian Gulf, Gulf of Oman, Red Sea support, Nov. 11, 1998 - Dec. 22, 1998
- Operation Desert Fox - Iraq, Saudi Arabia, Kuwait, Bahrain, Qatar, UAE, Oman, Yemen, Egypt, Jordan, Persian Gulf, Gulf of Oman, USN Red Sea support, 16 Dec. -22 Dec. 1998
- Operation Desert Spring, Haiti, Southwest Asia, 31 Dec.1998-18 Mar. 2003
- Operation Secure Tomorrow, 29 Feb. 2004- 15 Jun. 2004

The Defense Department announced the transition of the Kosovo Campaign Medal to the Armed Forces Expeditionary Medal, effective Jan. 1, 2014.
As smaller contingencies of U.S. forces continue to support Operation Joint Guardian and NATO headquarters in Sarajevo, the AFEM will be awarded to recognize that support of operations in the Balkans.
The AFEM area of eligibility mirrors that of the KCM with the addition of Bosnia-Herzegovina, Croatia and Hungary. The eligible area also encompasses Serbian land and airspace including Vojvodina, Montenegro, Albania, Macedonia.
The Department of Defense Manual 1348.33, Volume 2, "Manual of Military Decorations and Awards" contains specific eligibility criteria.

❖ Vietnam Service Medal

Authorized by executive order on July 8, 1965 for U.S. military personnel serving in the Vietnam Theater of Operations after July 3, 1965 through March 28, 1973. Personnel must have served in Vietnam on temporary duty for at least 30 consecutive/60 non-consecutive days or have served in combat with a unit directly supporting a military operation in Southeast Asia. Military personnel serving in Laos, Cambodia or Thailand in direct support of operations in Vietnam are also eligible for this award. The Armed Forces Expeditionary Medal was awarded for earlier service in Vietnam from July 1, 1958 to July 3, 1965, inclusive; personnel receiving that award may be awarded the Vietnam Service Medal but are not authorized both awards for Vietnam service. The front of the medal depicts an oriental dragon behind a grove of bamboo trees; below the base of the trees is the inscription, "REPUBLIC OF VIETNAM SERVICE." The reverse of the medal depicts a crossbow with a torch through the center and contains the inscription, "UNITED STATES OF AMERICA" along the bottom edge. The colors of the suspension drape and ribbon suggest the flag of the Republic of Vietnam (the red stripes represent the three ancient Vietnamese empires of Tonkin, Annam, and Cochin China) and the green represents the Vietnamese jungle. Bronze and silver stars are authorized to signify participation in any of the 17 designated campaigns during the inclusive period.

Service	All Services
Instituted	1965
Dates	1965-73
Criteria	Service in Vietnam, Laos, Cambodia or Thailand during the above period.
Devices	USAF, Bronze, Silver star

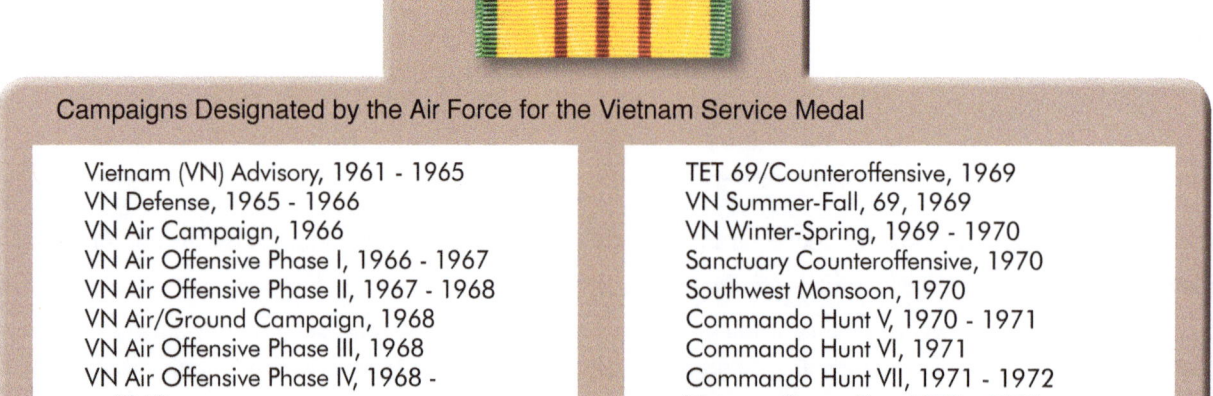

Campaigns Designated by the Air Force for the Vietnam Service Medal

- Vietnam (VN) Advisory, 1961 - 1965
- VN Defense, 1965 - 1966
- VN Air Campaign, 1966
- VN Air Offensive Phase I, 1966 - 1967
- VN Air Offensive Phase II, 1967 - 1968
- VN Air/Ground Campaign, 1968
- VN Air Offensive Phase III, 1968
- VN Air Offensive Phase IV, 1968 - 1969
- TET 69/Counteroffensive, 1969
- VN Summer-Fall, 69, 1969
- VN Winter-Spring, 1969 - 1970
- Sanctuary Counteroffensive, 1970
- Southwest Monsoon, 1970
- Commando Hunt V, 1970 - 1971
- Commando Hunt VI, 1971
- Commando Hunt VII, 1971 - 1972
- Vietnam Cease-Fire, 1972 - 1973

❖ Vietnam Veterans Service Displays

USAF Awards Displays for Vietnam Service.
Every display tells a different story of a veteran's military service.

❖ Southwest Asia Service Medal

Bronze

Anodized or Gold-Plated

Regulation Ribbon Bar

Lapel pin

Medal Reverse

Miniature Medals

Mini Ribbon (unofficial)

Hat Pin (unofficial)

Awarded to members of the United States Armed Forces who participated in, or directly supported, military operations in Southwest Asia or in surrounding areas between August 2, 1990 and November 30, 1995 (Operations Desert Shield, Desert Storm and follow-up). The medal was established by an executive order signed by President George Bush on March 15, 1991.

The front of the medal depicts the tools of modern desert warfare, i.e., aircraft, helicopter, tank, armored personnel carrier, tent and troops, battleship, in both desert and sea settings along with the inscription, "SOUTHWEST ASIA SERVICE" in the center. The reverse of the medal contains a sword entwined with a palm leaf representing military preparedness and the maintenance of peace and the inscription "UNITED STATES OF AMERICA" around the periphery. The ribbon is predominately tan, symbolizing the sands of the desert and contains thin stripes of the U.S. national colors towards each edge. The green and black center stripes and the black edges, along with the red and white, suggest the flag colors of most Arab nations in the region of Southwest Asia.

Service	All Services
Instituted	1992
Dates	1991-1995
Criteria	Active participation in, or support of, Operations Desert Shield, Desert Storm and/or subsequent follow-on operations in southwest Asia.
Devices	All Services: Bronze Star; ★
Notes	Recipients of this medal are usually entitled to the Saudi Arabian Medal for the Liberation of Kuwait and the Emirate of Kuwait Medal for the Liberation of Kuwait.

Approved campaigns for the Southwest Asia Service Medal, each being represented by a bronze star:

Operation Desert Shield, August 2, 1990 - January 16, 1991

Operation Desert Storm, January 17, 1991 - April 11, 1991

Southwest Asia Cease-fire Campaign, April 12, 1991- November 30, 1995

Operation Provide Comfort, June 1, 1992 - November 30, 1995

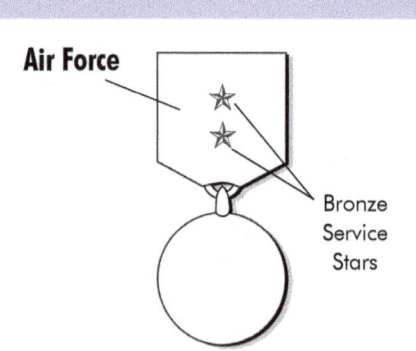

142 Decorations, Medals, and Ribbons of the United States Air Force

❖ Kosovo Campaign Medal

Bronze — Anodized or Gold-Plated

Regulation Ribbon Bar — Lapel Pins — Medal Reverse — Miniature Medals — Mini Ribbon (unofficial) — Hat Pin (unofficial)

For participation in, or in direct support of Kosovo operations. The Kosovo Campaign Medal is worn after the Southwest Asia Service Medal and before the Afghanistan Campaign Medal. The Kosovo Campaign Medal was established by executive order on May 15, 2000. The medal is awarded to all members of the Armed Forces who participated in or provided direct support to Kosovo operations within established areas of eligibility (AOE) from March 24, 1999 to December 31, 2013. The service member must have been a member of a unit participating in, or engaged in support of one or more of the following operations for 30 consecutive days or 60 nonconsecutive days.

Service	All Services
Instituted	2000
Dates	1999 - 2013
Criteria	Active participation in, or direct support of, Kosovo operations.
Devices	Bronze Star ★

Allied Force: 24 March - 10 June 1999
Task Force Hawk: 5 April - 24 June 1999
Joint Guardian: 11 June 1999- TBD
Task Force Saber: 31 March - 8 July 1999
Allied Harbour: 4 April - 1 Sept 1999
Task Force Falcon: 11 June - TBD
Sustain Hope/Shining Hope: 4 April - 10 July 1999
Task Force Hunter: 1 April - 1 Nov 1999
Noble Anvil: 24 March - 20 July 1999

the top. To date, there are two bronze service stars authorized for the Kosovo Campaign Medal as follows:

(1) Kosovo Air Campaign - 24 March 1999 to 10 June 1999
(2) Kosovo Defense Campaign - 11 June 1999 to a date TBD

The Kosovo Campaign Medal was designed by the Institute of Heraldry. The medal is a circular bronze disk depicting rocky terrain, a fertile valley and sunrise behind a mountain pass in Kosovo. Above the scene, on two lines, are the words, "KOSOVO CAMPAIGN." At the lower edge is a stylized wreath of grain reflecting the agricultural nature of the area. The reverse shows an outline of the province of Kosovo with the curved inscription, "IN DEFENSE OF HUMANITY" across

144 Decorations, Medals, and Ribbons of the United States Air Force

Example of a Senior USAF Officer's Service covering Southwest Asia, Afghanistan, NATO and War on Terrorism

Interesting to note the Colonel in this example has received an Army decoration and a Joint Service Meritorious Unit Award. The four oak leaf clusters on his Air Force Longevity Service Award ribbon indicated over 20 years honorable service. What else can you tell?

Medals of America 145

❖ Afghanistan Campaign Medal

Bronze | Anodized or Gold-Plated

Regulation Ribbon Bar | Enamel Lapel Pin | Medal Reverse | Miniature Medals | Mini Ribbon (unofficial) | Enamel Hat Pin (unofficial)

The Afghanistan Campaign Medal was signed into law by President George W. Bush, May 28, 2004 and implemented by Executive Order 13363, Nov. 29, 2004. It is awarded to Service members who have served in direct support of Operation Enduring Freedom on or after Oct. 24, 2001 until 31 December 2014. Effective 1 January 2015, Operation Freedom's Sentinel (OFS) is an approved operation for award of the ACM. The area of eligibility encompasses all land areas of the country of Afghanistan and all air spaces above the land.

Service members must have been assigned, attached or mobilized to units operating in these areas of eligibility for 30 consecutive days or for 60 non-consecutive days or meet one of the following criteria:

a. Be engaged in combat during an armed engagement, regardless of the time in the area of eligibility; or
b. While participating in an operation or on official duties, is wounded or injured and requires medical evacuation from the area of eligibility; or
c. While participating as a regularly assigned air crewmember flying sorties into, out of, within or over the area of eligibility in direct support of the military operations; each day of operations counts as one day of eligibility.

Service members qualified for the Global War on Terrorism Expeditionary Medal by reasons of service between Oct. 24, 2001, and April 30, 2005, in an area for which the Afghanistan Campaign Medal was subsequently authorized and between March 19, 2003, and Feb. 28, 2005, in an area for which the Iraq Campaign Medal was subsequently authorized remain qualified for the medal.

Service	All Services
Instituted	2004
Dates	2001 to 31 Dec. 2014, 1 Jan. 2015 until a date TBD
Criteria	Active service in direct support of Operation ENDURING FREEDOM, and FREEDOM'S SENTINEL.
Devices	Bronze Star, Silver Star

Upon application, any such service member may be awarded the Afghanistan Campaign Medal in lieu of the Global War on Terrorism Expeditionary Medal for such service. No service member shall be entitled to both medals for the same act, achievement or period of service.

The medal may be awarded posthumously.

Only one award of the Afghanistan Campaign Medal may be authorized for any individual. A bronze service star is worn on the suspension and campaign ribbon for one or more days of participation in each designated campaign phase. The Afghanistan Campaign Medal shall be positioned below the Kosovo Campaign Medal and above the Iraq Campaign Medal.

On the front of the medal, above a range of mountains is a map of Afghanistan in the center with the inscription, "AFGHANISTAN CAMPAIGN" around the top. On the reverse side on top is a radiating demi-sun superimposed by an eagle's head. Inscribed on the bottom half of the reverse side are three lines, "FOR SERVICE IN AFGHANISTAN" all enclosed by a laurel wreath symbolizing victory.

Deployed U.S. Air Force members of the 123rd Airlift Wing, Kentucky Air National Guard, pose with their Lockheed C-130H Hercules aircraft (s/n 91–1232, 91–1233) on a flightline in Afghanistan, 22 April 2009.

(USAF Photo)

The designated Afghanistan Campaign Medal campaigns for "Enduring Freedom" are:

Liberation of Afghanistan: 11 September 2001 - 30 November 2001

Consolidation I: 1 December 2001 - 30 September 2006

Consolidation II: 1 October 2006 - 30 November 2009

Consolidation III: 1 December, 2009–30 June 2011

Transition I: 1 July 2011–31 December 2014.

The designated Afghanistan Campaign Medal campaigns for "Freedom's Sentinel" are:

The transition from Operation Enduring Freedom to Freedom's Sentinel also marks a new campaign phase, "Transition II," for the Afghanistan Campaign Medal.

Transition II: 1 January, 2015 to a date to be determined.

U.S. Air Force A-10 Thunderbolt II aircraft taxi toward a parking area upon arriving at Bagram Airfield in Parwan province, Afghanistan, March 31, 2013.

(USAF Photo)

❖ Iraq Campaign Medal

Bronze — Anodized or Gold-Plated

Regulation Ribbon Bar — Enamel Lapel Pin — Medal Reverse — Miniature Medals — Mini Ribbon (unofficial) — Enamel Hat Pin (unofficial)

On Nov. 29, 2004, Public Law 108-234 and Executive Order 13363 approved the Iraq Campaign Medal (ICM) to recognize service members who are serving or have served in Iraq and the contiguous water area out to 12 nautical miles, and all air spaces above the land and above the contiguous water area out to 12 nautical miles of Iraq.

Eligibility for the ICM requires Air Force personnel to have served in direct support of *Operation Iraqi Freedom* (OIF). The period of eligibility is on or after March 19, 2003 to 31 December 2011.

Service members qualified for the Global War on Terrorism Expeditionary Medal (GWOT-E) by reasons of service between March 19, 2003 and Feb. 28, 2005, in an area for which the ICM was subsequently authorized, shall remain qualified for that medal. Upon application, any such service members may be awarded the ICM in lieu of the GWOT-E for such service. No service members shall be entitled to both medals for the same deployment, action, achievement or period of service.

Service members must have been assigned, attached or mobilized to units operating in the area of eligibility for 30 consecutive days or for 60 non-consecutive days or meet one of the following criteria:

1) Be engaged in combat during an armed engagement, regardless of the time in the area of eligibility; 2) While participating in an operation or on official duties, is wounded or injured and requires medical evacuation from the area of eligibility; 3) While participating as a regularly assigned aircrew member flying sorties into, out of, within or over the area of eligibility in direct support of the military operations; each day of operations counts as one day of eligibility. The Iraq Campaign Medal may be awarded posthumously.

Service	All Services
Instituted	2004
Dates	2003 to 31 December 2011
Criteria	Active service in direct support of Operation IRAQI FREEDOM.
Devices	Bronze Star, Silver Star

Only one award of the ICM may be authorized for any individual. In April 2008, the Dept. of Defense authorized service stars to recognize service members for participating in the different campaigns. The Iraq Campaign Medal is positioned below the Afghanistan Campaign Medal and above the Global War on Terrorism Expeditionary Medal.

The medal's obverse features a relief map of Iraq displaying two irregular lines representing the Tigris and Euphrates Rivers surmounting a palm wreath. Above is the inscription, "IRAQ CAMPAIGN". The Statue of Freedom is shown on the reverse surmounting a sunburst, encircle by two scimitars, points down, crossed at the tips of the blades, all above the inscription, "FOR SERVICE IN IRAQ".

A bronze star is worn on the suspension and campaign ribbon for one or more days of participation in each designated campaign phases. A silver campaign service star device is used for participation in five campaigns.

Note:

Under most circumstances, no personnel or unit should receive the Iraqi Campaign Medal, the Global War on Terrorism Expeditionary Medal (GWOT-E), the Global War on Terrorism Service Medal (GWOT-S), the Afghanistan Campaign Medal (ACM) or the Armed Forces Expeditionary Medal (AFEM) for the same deployment, action or period of service.

The designated Iraqi Freedom campaigns are:

Liberation of Iraq: 19 March 2003 - 1 May 2003
Transition of Iraq: 2 May 2003 - 28 June 2004
Iraqi Governance: 29 June 2004 - 15 December 2005
National Resolution: 16 December 2005 - 9 January 2007
Iraqi Surge: 10 January 2007–31 December 2008
Iraqi Sovereignty: 1 January 2009–31 August 2010
New Dawn: 1 September 2010–31 December 2011

◆ Global War on Terrorism Expeditionary Medal

Bronze · Anodized or Gold-Plated

Regulation Ribbon Bar
Enamel Lapel Pin

Medal Reverse

The medal has been redesigned and is slightly smaller in diameter and word medal has been removed from the reverse. Original first medals are still official.

Miniature Medals

Mini Ribbon (unofficial)
Enamel Hat Pin (unofficial)

Awarded for deployed service abroad in support of Global War on Terrorism operations on, or after September 11, 2001. The Global War on Terrorism Expeditionary Medal is worn after the Iraq Campaign Medal and before the Global War on Terrorism Service Medal.

The Global War on Terrorism Expeditionary Medal was authorized by executive order. The medal is awarded to any member of the Armed Forces who is deployed in an approved operation, such as ENDURING FREEDOM. The Chairman of the Joint Chiefs of Staff has designated the specific area of deployed eligibly per qualifying operation. To be eligible personnel must have participated in the operation by authority of written order. Qualification includes at least 30 consecutive days or 60 nonconsecutive days, or be engaged in actual combat (hostile weapons fire is exchanged), or duty that is equally as hazardous as combat duty, or wounded or injured requiring evacuation from the operation, or while participating as a regularly assigned air crewmember flying sorties into, out of, within or over the are of eligibility in direct support of the military operations.

Personnel may receive both the Global War on Terrorism Expeditionary Medal and the Global War on Terrorism Service Medal if they meet the requirements of both awards; however,

Instituted	2003
Dates	2001 to present
Criteria	Active participation in, or support of, Operations ENDURING FREEDOM, IRAQI FREEDOM, NOMAD SHADOW or follow-on operations while deployed abroad for service in the Global War on Terrorism.
Devices	Bronze Star

service eligibility for one cannot be used to justify service eligibility for the other.

The Global War on Terrorism Expeditionary Medal was designed by the Institute of Heraldry. The medal is a circular bronze disc which displays a shield adapted from the Great Seal of the United States surmounting two sword hilts enclosed within a wreath of laurel; overall an eagle, wings displayed, grasping a serpent in its claws. The reverse of the medal displays the eagle, a serpent and swords from the front of the medal within the encircling inscription, "WAR ON TERRORISM EXPEDITIONARY." The ribbon is scarlet, white and blue representing the United States; light blue refers to worldwide cooperation against terrorism; gold denotes excellence. *Effective 2005, the GWOTEM is no longer authorized to be awarded for service in Afghanistan and/or Iraq.*

To date, the Areas of Eligibility associated with the operations ENDURING FREEDOM, IRAQI FREEDOM and NOMAD SHADOW are:

Afghanistan	Jordan	Syria	Gulf of Aden	
Bahrain	Kazakhstan	Tajikistan	Gulf of Aqaba	
Bulgaria	Kenya	Turkey (east of 35	Gulf of Oman	
Crete	Kuwait	degrees east lat.)	Gulf of Suez	
Cyprus	Kyrgyzstan	Turkmenistan	That portion of the	
Diego Garcia	Lebanon	United Arab Emirates	Mediterranean Sea	
Djibouti	Oman	Uzbekistan	east of 28 degrees	
Egypt	Pakistan	Yemen	east longitude	
Eritrea	Philippines	That portion of the Arabian	Persian Gulf	
Ethiopia	Qatar	Sea north of 10 degrees	Red Sea	
Iran	Romania	north latitude and west of		
Iraq	Saudi Arabia	68 degrees longitude	Strait of Hormuz	
Israel	Somalia	Bab el Mandeb	Suez Canal	

The six approved operations and effective dates for the award of the Global War on Terrorism Expeditionary Medal are:

- Enduring Freedom, Sept. 11, 2001 – to be determined.
- Iraqi Freedom, March 19, 2003-Aug. 31, 2010.
- Nomad Shadow, Nov. 5, 2007 – to be determined.
- New Dawn, Sept.1, 2010-Dec. 31, 2011.
- Inherent Resolve, June 15, 2014 – to be determined.
- Freedom's Sentinel, Jan. 1, 2015 – to be determined.

❖ Global War on Terrorism Service Medal

Bronze

Anodized or Gold-Plated

Regulation Ribbon Bar

Enamel Lapel Pin

Medal Reverse

Miniature Medals
Orignial Design

Mini Ribbon
(unofficial)

Enamel Hat Pin
(unofficial)

Awarded to members of the United States Armed Forces who participated in, or served in support of operations relating to the Global War on Terrorism between September 11, 2001 and a date to be determined at a later date. The medal was established by an executive order signed by President George W. Bush on October 28, 2003. Initial award of the Global War on Terrorism Service Medal was limited to Airport Security Operations from September 27, 2001 until May 31, 2002 and to Service members who supported Operations ENDURING FREEDOM, NOBLE EAGLE and IRAQI FREEDOM.

Qualifying Air Force members must be assigned, attached or mobilized to a unit participating in or service in direct support of designated for 30 consecutive days or 60 nonconsecutive days. It is to be noted that eligibility for the Global War on Terrorism Service Medal is defined as support for the War on Terrorism in a non-deployed status, whether stationed at home or overseas. By contrast, service in an operationally deployed status abroad within a designated area of eligibility merits primary eligibility for the Global War on Terrorism Expeditionary Medal. Personnel may receive both the Global War on Terrorism Service and Expeditionary Medals if they meet the requirements of both awards. However, the qualifying period for one cannot be used to justify eligibility for the other. Establishing the award of the GWOTSM for general support of the war on terror makes the medal similar to the award of the National Defense Service Medal. The major difference between the National Defense Service Medal and GWOTSM is that the NDSM is authorized when an individual joins the Armed Forces and the GWOTSM is only authorized after 30 days of active service or 60 days non consecutive service for reserve forces.

Although qualifying circumstances would be extremely rare, Battle Stars may be applicable for personnel who were engaged in actual combat against the enemy under circumstances involving grave danger of death or serious bodily injury from enemy action.

Instituted	2004
Dates	2001 to Present
Criteria	Active participation in, or service in support of Global War on Terrorism operations on or after 11 September, 2001.
Devices	Bronze Star

The Global War on Terrorism Service Medal was designed by the Institute of Heraldry. The medal is a circular bronze disc which displays an eagle, wings displayed, with a stylized shield of thirteen vertical bars on its breast and holding in dexter claw an olive branch and in sinister claw three arrows, all in front of a terrestrial globe with the inscription above, "WAR ON TERRORISM SERVICE." The reverse of the medal displays a laurel wreath on a plain field. The ribbon is scarlet, white and blue representing the United States; gold denoting excellence.

The Original Medal

The new version of the medal has been redesigned and is slightly smaller in diameter and word "medal" has been removed from the front. The original issued medals are still official and are issued until the current stock is exhausted.

❖ Korea Defense Service Medal

Bronze

Anodized or Gold-Plated

Regulation Ribbon Bar

Enamel Lapel Pin

Medal Reverse

Miniature Medals

Mini Ribbon (unofficial)

Enamel Hat Pin (unofficial)

The Korea Defense Service Medal is authorized for Armed Forces members who served in support of the defense of the Republic of Korea after the signing of the Korean Armistice Agreement. To qualify a service member must serve at least 30 consecutive days in the Korean theater. The medal is also awarded for 60 non-consecutive days of service to include reservists on annual training in Korea.

Exceptions are made for the time requirement if a service member participated in a combat armed engagement, was wounded or injured in the line of duty requiring medical evacuation, or participated as a regularly assigned aircrew member in flying sorties which totaled more than 30 days of duty in Korean airspace. In such cases, the KDSM is authorized regardless of time served in theater.

The medal is retroactive to the end of the Korean War and is granted for any service performed after July 28, 1954. An official exception to policy entitles military personnel to both the Armed Forces Expeditionary Medal, and the KDSM for being in operations in Korea between October 1, 1966 - June 30, 1974. Only one award of the Korea Defense Service Medal is authorized, regardless of the time served in the Korean theater. The Korea Defense Service Medal is worn after the Global War on Terrorism Service Medal and before the Armed Forces Service Medal.

Service	All Services
Instituted	2003
Dates	1954 to date TBD
Criteria	For service in the Republic of Korea, or the waters adjacent thereto, for a qualifying period of time between 28 July, 1954 and a date to be determined.
Devices	None

Designed by John Sproston of the Institute of Heraldry, the medal is a bronze disc with a Korean circle dragon within a scroll inscribed, "KOREA DEFENSE SERVICE" with two sprigs of laurel at the base. The four-clawed dragon is a traditional Korean symbol representing intelligence and strength of purpose. The sprig of laurel denotes honorable endeavor and victory, the bamboo refers to the land of Korea. The reverse displays two swords placed over a map of Korea to signify defense of freedom and the readiness to engage in combat. The enclosing circlet represents the five-petal symbols common in Korean armory.

The dark green ribbon represents the land of Korea, blue indicates overseas service and commitment to achieving peace. Gold denotes excellence, white symbolizes idealism and integrity. Light blue with a thin white stripe in the center and narrow white stripes at the edges.

The Original Medal

The Institute of Heraldry changed the specifications for the Korea Defense Service Medal. At first glance you might not notice the change, but the new medals being manufactured have a slightly different look and the word medal has been removed from the front of the medallion. The original medal is still authorized for wear and may still be issued as long as they are in the supply system.

❖ Armed Forces Service Medal

Bronze New Design | Anodized or Gold-Plated Old Design

Regulation Ribbon Bar
Enamel lapel Pin
Medal Reverse
Miniature Medals
Mini Ribbon (unofficial)
Enamel Hat Pin (unofficial)

Authorized on January 11, 1996 for U.S. military personnel who, on or after June 1, 1992, participate in a U.S. military operation deemed to be a significant activity in which no foreign armed opposition or imminent hostile action is encountered and for which no previous U.S. service medal is authorized. The medal can be awarded to service members in direct support of the United Nations or North Atlantic Treaty Organization and for assistance operations to friendly nations. The initial awards of this medal were for operations that have occurred in the Balkans since 1992. Qualifications include at least one day of participation in the designated area. Direct support of the operation and aircraft flights within the area also qualify for award of this medal as long as at least one day is served within the designated area. Recent operations that qualify for the medal are *Provide Promise, Joint Endeavor, Able Sentry, Deny Flight, Maritime Monitor* and *Sharp Guard*.

The front of the medal contains the torch of liberty within its center and contains the inscription "ARMED FORCES SERVICE" around its periphery. The reverse of the medal depicts the American eagle with the U.S. shield in its chest and spread wings clutching three arrows in its talons encircled by a laurel wreath and the inscription, "IN PURSUIT OF DEMOCRACY." Bronze and silver service stars are worn to denote additional awards.

Service	All Services
Instituted	1995
Dates	1995 to Present
Criteria	Participation in military operations not covered by a specific war medal or the Armed Forces Expeditionary Medal.
Devices	All Services: Bronze, Silver Star

The Original Medal

The Institute of Heraldry redesigned the Armed Forces Service Medal to conform to changes made to three other medals. Unless you compare the original medal first authorized in 1995 with the new ones being struck you might not notice the change. The new medals being manufactured have a slightly different look and the word "Medal" has been removed from the front of the medallion. The change to the AFSM is one of 4 medals: GWOT Exp, GWOT Service and the Korea Defense Service Medal that the Institution of Heraldry has made minor modifications to and removed the word "Medal" from. The original medal is still authorized for wear and may still be issued as long as they remain in the supply system.

Did You Know? The Armed Forces Service Medal was originally intended to complement the Armed Forces Expeditionary Medal. The primary difference between the two is that the Armed Forces Service Medal is awarded for actions "through which no foreign armed opposition or imminent threat of hostile action was encountered". This definition separates the two medals in that the Armed Forces Expeditionary Medal is normally awarded for combat operations and other combat support missions.

❖ Humanitarian Service Medal

Bronze — Anodized or Gold-Plated

Regulation Ribbon Bar
Enamel Lapel Pin
Medal Reverse
Miniature Medals
Mini Ribbon (unofficial)
Enamel Hat Pin (unofficial)

Authorized on January 19, 1977 and awarded to Armed Forces personnel (including Reserve components) who, after April 1, 1975, distinguish themselves by meritorious direct participation in a DOD-approved significant military act or operation of a humanitarian nature. According to regulations, the participation must be "hands-on" at the site of the operation; personnel assigned to staff functions geographically separated from the operation are not eligible for this medal. Service members must be assigned and/or attached to participating units for specific operations by official orders. Members who were present for duty at specific qualifying locations for the medal but who did not make a direct contribution to the action or operation are specifically excluded from eligibility. It should be noted that some of the earliest recipients of the Humanitarian Service Medal, e.g., for the evacuations of Laos, Cambodia and Vietnam, would more likely be awarded the Armed Forces Service Medal in today's environment.

The medal was designed by Jim Hammond and sculptured by Jay Morris of the Institute of Heraldry. The front of the medal depicts a human right hand with open palm within a raised circle. At the top of the medal's reverse is the raised inscription, "FOR HUMANITARIAN SERVICE" set in three lines. In the center is an oak branch with three acorns and leaves and, below this, is the raised circular inscription, "UNITED STATES ARMED FORCES"

Note: All branches now use Coast Guard placement of stars.

Former Air Force Placement of Block Numeral Devices on the Humanitarian Service Medal

Service	All Services
Instituted	1977
Dates	1975 to Present
Criteria	Direct participation in specific operations of a humanitarian nature.
Devices	Bronze, Silver Star, Bronze Numeral

around the lower edge of the medal. The ribbon is medium blue with a wide center stripe of navy blue. It is edged by a wide stripe of purple which is separated from the light blue field by a narrow white stripe. Bronze and silver stars are authorized for additional awards.

The Secretary of the Air Force approved the Humanitarian Service Medal for more than 5,600 members of the 5th Bomb Wing and the 91st Missile Wing for humanitarian relief efforts to the civilian community in the wake of the severe flooding in the area of Minot, Burlington and Velva, N.D.

(USAF Photo)

❖ Outstanding Volunteer Service Medal

Bronze

Anodized or Gold-Plated

Regulation Ribbon Bar

Enamel Lapel Pin

Medal Reverse

Miniature Medals

Mini Ribbon (unofficial)

Enamel Hat Pin (unofficial)

The Outstanding Volunteer Service Medal was authorized in 1993 to members of the U.S. Armed Forces and reserve components and is awarded for outstanding and sustained voluntary service to the civilian community after December 31, 1992. It may be awarded to active duty and reserve members who perform outstanding volunteer service over time as opposed to a single event. The service performed must have been to the civilian community and must be strictly voluntary and not duty-related. The volunteerism must be of a sustained and direct nature and must be significant and produce tangible results while reflecting favorably on the Armed Forces and the Department of Defense. There are no specific time requirements as to how many hours must be spent on the volunteer activity, but the activity should consist of significant action and involvement rather than, for example, simply attending meetings as a member of a community service group. An individual would normally be considered for only one award during an assignment. Group level commanders, including commanders of provisional and composite groups, have approval authority for the medal.

Service	All Services
Instituted	1993
Dates	1993 to Present
Criteria	Awarded for outstanding and sustained voluntary service to the civilian community.
Devices	All Services: Bronze, Silver Star

The front of the bronze medal has a five-pointed star with a circular ring over each point; the star, a symbol of the military and representing outstanding service, is encircled by a laurel wreath which represents honor and achievement. The reverse has an oak leaf branch, symbolic of strength and potential, with three oak leaves and two acorns along with the inscriptions, "OUTSTANDING VOLUNTEER SERVICE," and "UNITED STATES ARMED FORCES." Bronze and silver stars are authorized to denote additional awards.

Master Sgt. Delmus Gillis is presented the Military Outstanding Volunteer Service Medal during the Annual Volunteer Recognition Ceremony at Kadena Air Base. (U.S. Air Force photo/Staff Sgt. Darnell Cannady)

❖ Air Force Air and Space Campaign Medal

Bronze

Regulation Ribbon Bar

Enamel Lapel Pin

Medal Reverse

Miniature Medals

Mini Ribbon (unofficial)

Enamel Hat Pin (unofficial)

The Air Force Air & Space Campaign Medal (ASCM) was authorized by the Secretary of the Air Force on April 24, 2002 to recognize personnel who are not eligible for other Department of Defense campaign medals but provide direct support of combat operations at home stations or from outside the geographical area of combat.

To qualify for the award, Air Force personnel must be assigned or attached to a unit engaged in the operation and have provided 30 consecutive or 60 nonconsecutive days of direct support as stated above. No individual may be eligible for both the ASCM and a DOD campaign/service medal awarded during a single tour in the same operation.

Subsequent support service in separate, approved operations are denoted by bronze and silver service stars on the ribbon.

U.S. Air Force F-16 return to Aviano Air Base in Italy after supporting Operation Odyssey Dawn.

Service	Air Force
Instituted	2002
Dates	1999 to Present
Criteria	Awarded for providing direct support of combat operations at home station or from outside the area of combat.
Devices	Bronze, Silver Star

Qualifying Operations

Operation Allied Force
  24 March 1999 – 10 June 1999[3]
Operation Joint Guardian
  11 June 1999 – Date to be Determined (DTBD)[3]
Operation Allied Harbour
  4 April 1999 – 1 September 1999[3]
Operation Sustain Hope/Shining Hope
  4 April 1999 – 10 July 1999[3]
Operation Noble Anvil
  24 March 1999 – 20 July 1999[3]
Kosovo Task Force Hawk
  5 April 1999 – 24 June 1999[3]
Kosovo Task Force Saber
  31 March 1999 – 8 July 1999[3]
Kosovo Task Force Falcon
  11 June 1999 – DTBD[3]
Kosovo Task Force Hunter
  1 April 1999 – 1 November 1999[3]
Operation Odyssey Dawn
  26 February 2011 – 31 October 2011[4]
Operation Unified Protector
  26 February 2011 – 31 October 2011[4]
Operations related to the Global War on Terrorism (to include Operation Iraqi Freedom and Operation Enduring Freedom) are not eligible for the ASCM.

❖ Air Force Nuclear Deterrence Operations Service Medal

Authorized by the Secretary of the Air Force May 27, 2014, for award to individuals for their direct support of nuclear deterrence operations.

"This service medal provides a clearly visible way to recognize the dedication and professionalism of our Airmen who are the guardians of our nation's nuclear deterrence. Because of our success, often times nuclear deterrence operations can be overlooked as a critical function," said Col. Zannis Pappas, the missile operations career field manager.

"The medal acknowledges the special challenges faced by those Airmen charged with supporting the nuclear enterprise and will be a point of pride by all who wear it."

The NDOSM may be awarded to Airmen who while assigned, attached, deployed or mobilized to a unit, provided support the Nuclear Enterprise for 120 consecutive or 179 non-consecutive days and were subject to a nuclear inspection or performed duties in nuclear operations to include nuclear weapon storage facilities; nuclear command, control and communication; cyber surety; security; safety; transportation; maintenance; facility management and maintenance; explosive ordnance disposal; aircrew certified for support to nuclear operations; weapons loaders; warning and attack assessment; personnel reliability program management; or research, development and acquisition of nuclear systems.

The medal will be worn with an "N" device for those who dispatched to a missile complex for 179 nonconsecutive days in direct support of intercontinental ballistic missile operations or are in direct support of nuclear laden aircraft. Only one "N" device will be worn, regardless of the number of qualifying assignments. An oak leaf cluster will be worn for subsequent awards, which will only be authorized when a PCS has occurred.

Eligibility for the medal is retroactive to Dec. 27, 1991. A member's current group commander is considered the awarding authority for the medal. Retired or separated Airmen can submit a request to the Air Force Personnel Center recognition section for validation. The award can be presented posthumously, as well, so family members of deceased Airmen can also contact AFPC for information.

The the front of the NDOSM has a laurel wreath surmounted by a nuclear symbol with a star bearing a disc in the center. The reverse has a circular inscription, "NUCLEAR DETERRENCE OPERATIONS SERVICE," a triangle between the first and last words, the U.S. Air Force "Hap Arnold" symbol and between its wings, the inscription "U.S. AIR FORCE."

The medal is gold in color to represent the legacy of the United States' strategic nuclear deterrence mission. The blue ribbon represents "nuclear dominance of the sky", the red represents "power and passion" in providing nuclear deterrence, green represents Earth and global capability, and gold represents the participating personnel, "the wealth of our nuclear enterprise."

❖ Air Force Overseas Ribbon *(Short Tour)*

The Air Force Overseas Ribbon (Short Tour) was created on October 12, 1980 by order of General Lew Allen, Air Force Chief of Staff and is awarded to Air Force personnel for less than two years of duty or as directed by Air Force policies. The Short Tour Ribbon is awarded for a permanent duty assignment of at least 181 consecutive days or, if stationed overseas, 300 days within an 18 month time span.

Airmen generally serve such assignments unaccompanied by family members, though a short assignment need not be unaccompanied. Additional awards are denoted by bronze and silver oak leaf clusters.

Service	Air Force
Instituted	1980
Criteria	Successful completion of an overseas tour designated as "short term" by appropriate authority.
Devices	Bronze, Silver Oak Leaf Cluster, Bronze Letter "A"

The "A" device is authorized on the Short Tour Ribbon to any service member who performs a tour of duty at an Arctic-based Air Force facility. Presently, Thule Air Force Base in Greenland is the only facility within the Arctic Circle boundary.

❖ Air Force Overseas Ribbon *(Long Tour)*

The Air Force Overseas Ribbon (Long Tour) was created on October 12, 1980 by order of General Lew Allen, Air Force Chief of Staff and is awarded to Air Force personnel for completing a standard overseas service assignment greater than two years in length.

Service	Air Force
Instituted	1980
Criteria	Successful completion of an overseas tour designated as "long term" by appropriate authority.
Devices	Bronze, Silver Oak Leaf Cluster

Long tour credit is awarded for completion of a prescribed overseas long tour (two years) by Air Force Instructions, or to any member assigned to a United States or overseas location who is subsequently sent under temporary duty orders (to include combat tours) for 365 or more days within a 3-year time frame. Additional awards are denoted by bronze and silver oak leaf clusters.

❖ Air Force Expeditionary Service Ribbon

The Air Force Expeditionary Service Ribbon was approved by the Secretary of the Air Force in October, 2003 to recognize service members who support air expeditionary force deployments subsequent to Oct. 1, 1999. For purposes of the award, "deployed status" is defined as either deployment on contingency, exercise, deployment orders or members sourced in direct support, in theater or out, of expeditionary operations with an overnight stay away from home station.

Service	Air Force
Instituted	2003
Dates	1999 to Present
Criteria	Awarded to recognize Air Force active duty, Reserve and Guard personnel who complete a contingency tour of duty in support of air expeditionary deployments.
Devices	Bronze, Silver Oak Leaf Cluster, Gold Frame

To qualify, members must have deployed for 45 consecutive or 90 nonconsecutive days with no time limit. Each 60/90 day deployment period counts towards an award of the ribbon or a bronze oak leaf cluster for each subsequent qualifying period. In Apr. 2004, the Secretary of the Air Force and Air Force Chief of Staff jointly approved the addition of a gold border to the Air Force Expeditionary Service Ribbon to signify satisfactory participation in combat operations, reflecting the global, expeditionary nature of airpower and the United States Air Force. The gold border is the same device as is used on the Air Force Presidential Unit Citation as well as many other U.S. unit awards.

❖ Air Force Longevity Service Award Ribbon

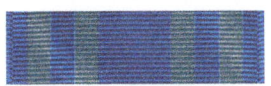

Awarded to U.S. Air Force personnel for 4 years honorable active federal military service with any branch of the U.S. Armed Forces or reserve components. Reserve and Guard require four years creditable service for retirement. An additional four years' of creditable service is denoted by a bronze oak leaf cluster. As an example, an individual who retires after 20 years service would wear 4 bronze oak leaf clusters on the ribbon. Individuals on active duty as of the institution date are authorized to wear the appropriate attachments to properly reflect their service both prior to and after that

Service	Air Force
Instituted	1957
Criteria	Successful completion of an aggregate total of four years of honorable active service.
Devices	Bronze, Silver Oak Leaf Cluster

date. Individuals who served both in the Army Air Force and continued their service into the U.S. Air Force until 1957 or later would be authorized to wear the Longevity Service Award with appropriate oak leaf clusters to properly represent their total service during both periods.

❖ Air Force Special Duty Ribbon

The Air Force Special Duty Ribbon recognized Airman who successfully complete a developmental special duty assignment. It replaces the Air Force Military Training Instructor Ribbon and the Air Force Recruiter Ribbon. Instructors and Recruiters are now eligible for the Air Force Special Duty award. The award is to recognize successful completion of a difficult and or

Service	Air Force
Instituted	September 4, 2014
Criteria	Successful completion of a special duty assignment.
Devices	Bronze, Silver Oak Leaf Cluster

highly responsible duty. Additional awards are noted by oak leaf clusters.

❖ Military Training Instructor Ribbon (Obsolete)

Established December 7, 1998 the Air Force Military Training Instructor Ribbon recognized past, present and future Military Training Instructors (MTI's) who display commitment and dedication to the training of Air Force personnel. This ribbon was for MTI's at Air Force Basic Military Training (BMT) and Officer Training School (OTS) (instructors at Technical Training Schools did not qualify) and was presented to Air Force active duty, Reserve and National Guard personnel upon graduation from Military Training Instructor School. Wear of the ribbon becomes permanent after successful completion of a 12 months MTI tour of duty. Each

Service	Air Force
Instituted	1998 Discontinued Sept. 2014
Criteria	Successful completion of at least 12 months tour of duty as a Military Training Instructor.
Devices	Bronze, Silver Oak Leaf Cluster

additional three years of MTI duty after the basic tour was noted by an oak leaf cluster. The ribbon was retroactive for any individual who has successfully completed 12 months duty as an MTI and was on active duty or in a reserve component as of Dec 7, 1998. The ribbon is replaced by the Air Force Special Duty Ribbon.

❖ Air Force Recruiter Ribbon (Obsolete)

The Secretary of the Air Force established the Air Force Recruiter Ribbon on June 21, 2000 to recognize officers and enlisted personnel who perform the challenging duties involved in Air Force recruiting. To qualify for the award, individuals must perform recruiting duty for a minimum period of three years. The award is retroactive to earlier recruiting assignments but only for persons who were on active duty status on the date of establishment, (June 21, 2000).

Service	Air Force
Instituted	2000 Discontinued Sept. 2014
Criteria	Successful completion of three year tour of duty as an Air Force Recruiter.
Devices	Bronze, Silver Oak Leaf Cluster 

Each additional three years of recruiting duty following the basic tour entitles the member to wear a bronze oak leaf cluster on the ribbon. The ribbon is replaced by the Air Force Special Duty Ribbon.

❖ Armed Forces Reserve Medal

Bronze

Anodized or Gold-Plated

Regulation Ribbon Bar

Enamel Lapel Pin

Medal Reverse

Mini Ribbon (unofficial)

Enamel Hat Pin (unofficial)

Miniature Medals

Authorized in 1950 for 10 years of honorable and satisfactory service within a 12 year period as a member of one or more of the Reserve Components of the Armed Forces of the United States.

An executive order of Aug. 8, 1996 authorized the award of a bronze letter "M" mobilization device to U.S. reserve component members who were called to active-duty service in support of designated operations on or after August 1, 1990 (the M device was not authorized for any operations prior to August 1, 1990 although it had been previously proposed). Units called up in support of Operations Desert Storm/Desert Shield were the first units to be authorized the "M" device. If an "M" is authorized, the medal is awarded even though service might be less than 10 years. Previous to this change, only bronze hourglasses were awarded at each successive 10 year point (first hourglass at the 20 year point).

The front of the medal depicts a flaming torch placed vertically between a crossed bugle and powder horn; thirteen stars and thirteen rays surround the design. The front of the medal is the same for all services; only the reverse design is different (see designs below). Bronze numerals beginning with "2" are worn to the right of the bronze "M" on the ribbon bar and below the "M" on the medal, indicating the total number of times the individual was mobilized. Bronze, silver and gold hourglasses are awarded for 10, 20 and 30 years service, respectively.

Service	All Services
Instituted	1950
Criteria	10 years of honorable service in any reserve component of the United States Armed Forces Reserve or award of "M" device.
Devices	Bronze, Silver and Gold Hourglass, Bronze Letter "M", Bronze Numeral

The different services medal reverses are shown here:

Army
has a Minuteman in front of a circle with 13 stars representing the original colonies.

Navy
has a sailing ship with an anchor on its front with an eagle with wings spread superimposed upon it.

Marine Corps
has the USMC emblem, eagle, globe and anchor.

Coast Guard
has the Coast Guard emblem, crossed anchor with the Coast Guard shield in the center.

National Guard
has the National Guard insignia on the reverse, an eagle with crossed fasces in its center.

160   Decorations, Medals, and Ribbons of the United States Air Force

❖ Air Force N.C.O. Professional Military Education Graduate Ribbon

The Air Force Non-Commissioned Officer Professional Military Education (PME) Graduate Ribbon was authorized by the Secretary of the Air Force on August 28, 1962 and is awarded to graduates of all Air Force-certified NCO PME schools, i.e., NCO Preparatory Course, Airman Leadership School, NCO Leadership School, NCO Academy and SRNCO Academy. Graduation from each successive level of PME entitles the member to wear an oak leaf cluster on the ribbon. The ribbon is not, however, awarded to members who only complete the correspondence courses or similar

Service	Air Force
Instituted	1962
Criteria	Successful completion of a certified NCO professional military education school.
Devices	Bronze, Silver Oak Leaf Cluster 

training conducted by other military services except for completion of the U.S. Army Sergeants Major Academy or the Navy Senior Enlisted Academy. This award also has the dubious distinction of bearing the longest name in United States award history.

❖ Air Force Basic Military Training (BMT) Honor Graduate Ribbon

The Basic Military Training Honor Graduate Ribbon was authorized by the Chief of Staff, U.S. Air Force on April 3, 1976, and is awarded to honor graduates of basic military training who, after July 29, 1976, have demonstrated excellence in all phases of academic and military training. It is limited to the top 10 percent of the training flight. The USAF BMT Honor Graduate Ribbon was designed by the Institute of Heraldry and is awarded to basic training graduates only. The ribbon has a wide center stripe of ultramarine

Service	Air Force
Instituted	1976
Criteria	Demonstration of excellence in all academic and military training phases of basic Air Force entry training.
Devices	None

blue flanked with equal stripes of yellow, brittany blue and white on either side. Since this is a "one-time only" award, no devices are authorized.

❖ Small Arms Expert Marksmanship Ribbon

Authorized on August 28, 1962. Awarded to Air Force personnel who, after Jan. 1, 1963, qualify as Expert with either the M16 rifle or issue handgun on the Air Force qualification course or on a prescribed course or who completes the Combat Rifle Program. The ribbon is only awarded once regardless of how many times an individual qualifies as "Expert." A bronze star device is added (only once)

Service	Air Force
Instituted	1962
Criteria	Qualification as expert with either the M-16 rifle or standard Air Force issue handgun.
Devices	Bronze Star

if the recipient meets the award criteria with both the rifle and handgun.

❖ Air Force Training Ribbon

The Air Force Training Ribbon was authorized on October 12, 1980 and awarded to Air Force members who complete an Air Force accession training program after August 14, 1974 such as Basic Military Training (BMT), Officer Training School (OTS), Reserve Officer Training Corps (ROTC), USAF Academy, Medical Services, Judge Advocate, Chaplain orientation etc. Also authorized for Guard and Reserve members who complete the appropriate training program. If a member completes two accession training programs, such as BMT and OTS,

Service	Air Force
Instituted	1980
Criteria	Successful completion of an Air Force accession training program.
Devices	Bronze, Silver Oak Leaf Cluster

a bronze oak leaf cluster is worn on the ribbon. The award is retroactive for those personnel on active duty as of the authorization date.

❖ Philippine Defense Medal

Country	Republic of the Philippines
Instituted	1945 (Army)
Dates	8 December 1941 and 15 June 1942.
Criteria	Service in defense of the Philippines between 8 December 1941 and 15 June 1942.
Devices	Bronze Star

The Philippine Defense Ribbon was instituted by the Philippine Commonwealth (now The Philippine Republic) in 1944 and authorized for wear on the U.S. uniform by the United States Government in 1945. It is awarded for service in the defense of the Philippine Islands from December 8, 1941 to June 15, 1942.

To qualify, the recipient must: (a) have been assigned or stationed in Philippine territory or in Philippine waters for not less than 30 days during the above period and/or (b) have participated in any engagement against the enemy on Philippine territory, in Philippine waters or in the air over the Philippines or Philippine waters during the above period.

Participation includes members of the defense garrison of the Bataan Peninsula, or of the fortified islands at the entrance to Manila Bay or members of and present with a unit actually under enemy fire or air attack, or crew members or passengers in an airplane which was under enemy aerial or ground fire. Individuals eligible under both (a) and (b) above are entitled to wear a bronze star on the ribbon bar.

The Philippine Defense Ribbon is classified as a foreign service award. The medal was designed and struck for the Philippine Government by the Manila firm of El Oro and is a circular gold disc with an outer edge of ten scallops. The medal's center depicts a female figure with a sword and shield representing the Philippines. Above the figure are three stars and surrounding it is a green enamel wreath. At the bottom right of the medal is a map of Corregidor and Bataan. The reverse of the medal has the raised inscription, "FOR THE DEFENSE OF THE PHILIPPINES" in English set in four lines. The ribbon is red with a white stripe near each edge and, repeating the starred motif of the medal, three white five-pointed stars in the form of a triangle base down in the center.

❖ Philippine Liberation Medal

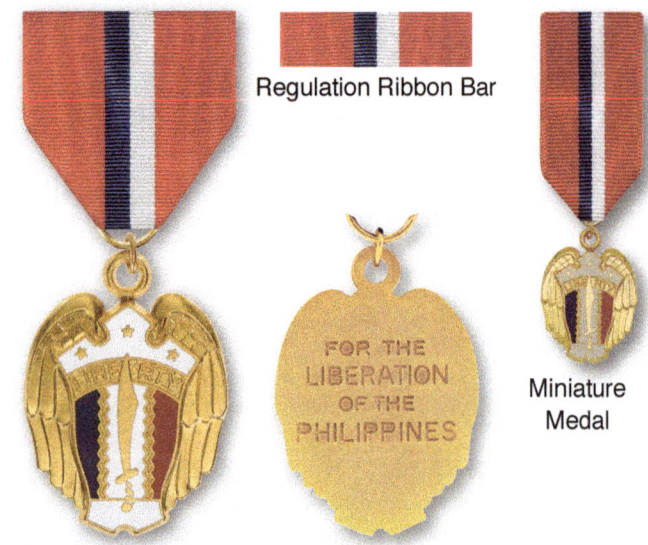

Country	Republic of the Philippines
Instituted	1945 (Army)
Dates	17 October 1944 and 3 September 1945.
Criteria	Service in the liberation of the Philippines between 17 October 1944 and 3 September 1945.
Devices	Bronze Star

Awarded by the Philippine Commonwealth (now The Philippine Republic) for service in the liberation of the Philippine Islands from October 17, 1944 to September 3, 1945. In order to qualify, one of the following provisions must be met:
a. Participation in the initial landing operation on Leyte and adjoining islands from 17-20 October 1944.
b. Participation in any engagement against the enemy during the Philippine Liberation Campaign.
c. Service in the Philippine Islands or in ships in Philippine Waters for not less than 30 days during the period from October 17, 1944, to September 2, 1945.

Individuals eligible under any two of the foregoing provisions are authorized to wear one bronze star on the ribbon bar. Personnel eligible under all three provisions are authorized to wear two bronze stars on the ribbon bar.

The Philippine Liberation Ribbon is classified as a foreign service award. The medal was designed and struck by the Manila firm of El Oro for the Philippine Government. The medal is gold with a Philippine sword, point up, superimposed over a white native shield having three gold stars at the top and the word, "LIBERTY" below. Below are vertical stripes of blue, white and red enamel with the sword being in the center of the white stripe. At the sides of the medal and below the shield are gold arched wings. The reverse of the medal has the raised inscription, "FOR THE LIBERATION OF THE PHILIPPINES" set in four lines (all inscriptions are in English). The ribbon is red with a narrow blue stripe and a narrow white stripe in the center.

❖ Philippine Independence Medal

Country	Republic of the Philippines
Instituted	1946 (Army)
Dates	4 July 1946
Criteria	Receipt of both the Philippine Defense and Liberation Medals/Ribbons. Originally presented to those present for duty in the Philippines on 4 July 1946.
Devices	None

Awarded by the Philippine Commonwealth to those members of the Armed Forces who received both the Philippine Defense Ribbon and the Philippine Liberation Ribbon. The Philippine Independence Ribbon was authorized in 1946 by the United States and the Philippine Commonwealth. It is one of the more unusual awards presented to U.S. Service personnel since it has two independent and totally applicable sets of award criteria. As originally promulgated, the ribbon was presented to those members of the United States Armed Forces who were actually serving in the Philippine Islands or in Philippine territorial waters on 4 July 1946. In 1954, the criteria was changed to grant the ribbon to all those who were previously awarded both the Philippine Defense Ribbon and the Philippine Liberation Ribbon.

Although the award qualifications established in 1946 were removed from applicable regulations, no attempt was made to rescind the previous awards made under those earlier criteria. The Philippine Independence Ribbon is classified as a foreign service award. The medal was designed and struck for the Philippine Government by the Manila firm of El Oro. The medal is a circular gold disc with a female figure in the center, dressed in native garb and holding the Philippine flag. There are flags on either side of the figure and she is surrounded by a circular border. Inside the border is a raised inscription, "PHILIPPINE INDEPENDENCE" (in English) around the top and July 4, 1946 at the bottom. The reverse contains the inscription, "GRANTED PHILIPPINE INDEPENDENCE BY THE UNITED STATES OF AMERICA" set in six lines (also in English). The ribbon is derived from the colors of the Philippine flag and consists of a medium blue base with a narrow white center stripe bordered by thin red stripes. There are thin, golden yellow stripes at each edge.

❖ Distinguished Flying Cross (United Kingdom)

Country	United Kingdom
Instituted	3 June 1918
Dates	1918 to present
Criteria	Acts of valor or devotion to duty in air operations against an enemy.
Devices	bar as shown above for additional awards

The Distinguished Flying Cross is a military decoration awarded to the United Kingdom's Royal Air Force and other services, and formerly to officers of other Commonwealth countries, instituted for "an act or acts of valor, courage or devotion to duty while flying in active operations against the enemy". Honorary awards were made to about a thousand aircrew from other non-Commonwealth countries during World War II. The medal is a cross flory and is 2⅛ inches wide. The horizontal and bottom bars are terminated with bumps, the upper bar with a rose. The medal's face features aeroplane propellers superimposed on the vertical arms of the cross and wings on the horizontal arms. In the centre is a laurel wreath around the RAF monogram surmounted by an Imperial Crown.

The reverse features the Royal Cypher in the center and the year of issue engraved on the lower arm. The medal is issued named and dated.

The ribbon was originally white with broad purple horizontal stripes, but changed in 1919 to the current white with purple broad diagonal stripes.

❖ Croix De Guerre (France)

Country	France
Instituted	1939
Criteria	Individual feats of arms as recognized by mention in dispatches.
Devices	Bronze, Silver, Gold Stars and Bronze Palm

The French Croix de Guerre was instituted in 1915 and was awarded to soldiers and sailors of all ranks in the French and Allied forces for individual feats of arms mentioned in despatches by the commanding officer of any unit from an Army down to a regiment. The medal designed by sculptor Paul-Albert Bartholomé is a bronze, straight-armed cross patte with crossed swords in the angles. At the center of the cross is the head of the figure of La Republique crested by a Phrygian cap, the traditional figure of France, around which is the raised, circular inscription, "REPUBLIQUE FRANCAISE." The reverse contains the dates, "1939–1940, 1939–1945, or simply 1940."

Emblems on the ribbon denote the level at which the medal was achieved. For an Army Despatch: a bronze palm or laurel branch (known as Croix de Guerre avec Palme); for an Army Corps Despatch: a gilt star; for a Divisional Despatch: a silver star; for a Brigade, Regimental or Unit Despatch: a bronze star. There are no limits on the number of devices which may be worn on the ribbon. The World War I Croix de Guerre was reinstituted on September 26, 1939 at the outset of World War II. The new version was identical to the 1915 model with the exception of the date: 1939 on the reverse and a new ribbon 37 mm wide, predominantly green with three central 1.5 mm red stripes, 4 mm apart and 8 mm red edges. The Free French Government awarded the Croix de Guerre to allies in Middle East and European theater; generally to officers or to especially valorous service men and women.

❖ Croix de Guerre (Belgium)

Country	Belgium
Instituted	1915
Criteria	Individual feats of arms as recognized by mention in dispatches.
Devices	Bronze, Silver, Gold Stars and Bronze Palm

The World War II Croix de Guerre was established on 20 July 1940 by the Belgian government in exile. It differed from the World War I version in its statute and slight changes to the reverse of the central medallion and the ribbon.

It was still mainly awarded to individuals, but was also authorized as a unit award. The Belgian fourragère was awarded by the Belgian Government to a unit that was cited twice. The Belgian fourragère was only worn by those who were members of the unit at the time of the award. The World War II Croix de Guerre only differs from the WW I award in the royal cypher of King Leopold III on the back of the medal and the Palm (if awarded) having the monogram "L" (for Leopold III) on it.

❖ RVN Air Force Distinguished Service Order *June 4, 1964*

Bronze
First Class
Second Class
First Class Miniature

The Vietnam Distinguished Service Order was also awarded to allied officers, and in the United States forces the decoration was considered the equivalent of the Legion of Merit. The 2nd class of the order was also presented to allied officers as well as NCOs. The RVN DSO ranked just below the National Order of Vietnam and the Vietnam Military Merit Medal. It was not a commonly presented medal, compared to such medals as the Vietnam Gallantry Cross and Vietnam Campaign Medal.

Purpose: Presented by the Republic of Vietnam for citations and wounds in combat or line of duty, or exceptional achievements that reflect great credit or benefit to the Air Force in any field.

The first class was for officers and the second class for enlisted personnel. The first class of the order had a rosette device centered on the medal and ribbon.

Description: Front: a gold four-pointed star with stylized jet planes in silver in each angle, space between in black, 50mm across (or smaller depending on manufacturer); Suspension is by a pair of gold wings. The ribbon is red 5mm, blue 27mm, red 5mm.

First Class Description: There is a rosette on the suspension ribbon and service bar.

Second Class Description: The ribbon is without a rosette.

Background: These Air Force DSO's come in large and small sizes, the stars being respectively 50mm or 35mm from horizontal tip to tip, but with no significance in the different sizes. Usually only awarded to very senior U.S. Air Force Officers with at least 12 months service in Vietnam or for exceptional valor.

❖ Air Force Meritorious Service Medal *June 5, 1964*

Bronze
Regulation Ribbon Bar

Purpose: For Vietnamese NCO's and enlisted men of the Air Force for citations and wounds in combat or line of duty, or exceptional achievements that reflect great credit on or benefit to the Air Force in any field.

Description: Front: silver four-pointed star with stylized jet planes in gold in each angle, with the space between in black, 40mm across (depending on manufacturer); Suspension is by a pair of gold wings. The ribbon is blue 3mm, white 2˚mm, blue 7mm, light blue 11mm, blue 7mm, white 2˚mm, blue 3mm.

For foreign military personnel the medal was intended to recognize significant military achievement, both in combat and non-combat service, which exceeded that required for the Vietnam Gallantry Cross but did not warrant receipt of the higher decorations such as the National Order of Vietnam or the Vietnam Military Merit Medal.

❖ RVN Air Gallantry Cross June 5, 1964

Bronze

Purpose: Presented by the Republic of Vietnam for display of heroism and exceptional bravery in flight or in extremely dangerous situations. Awarded to RVN Air Force personnel, civilian flying personnel serving in the Air Force and allied flying personnel.

Description: Front: Maltese cross in silver with the center of the arms indented and with stylized gold jet planes in the corners of the arms, and in the center a blue disk with a silver star within two thin silver circles, 40mm; Suspension is by a pair of gold wings. The ribbon is grey 12mm, blue 12mm, grey 12mm.

Gold Wing Purpose: For citation at Air Force level.
Description: The device is gold stylized wings and star.

Silver Wing Purpose: For citation at Tactical Wing level.
Description: The device is silver stylized wings and star.

Bronze Wing Purpose: For citation at Squadron level.
Description: The device is bronze stylized wings and star.

❖ RVN Armed Forces Honor Medal January 7, 1953

First Class   Second Class   Medal Reverse

Purpose: Presented by the Republic of Vietnam for contributions to the formation and organization of the Armed Forces and the training of troops and technical cadres of the various branches. It was intended for non-combat achievements.

Description: Front: a cross formee couped with additional points reflected down the arms and with thin blade points coming between the arms, and in the central disk, a coiled dragon with a ribbon around inscribed, with a wreath of oak leaves around the design of the cross arms, 38mm. Back: plain. Suspension is by a laurel wreath.

First Class  **Purpose: For officers.**

Description: Gold. The ribbon is yellow 1˚mm, red 6mm, yellow 3mm, light blue 3mm, yellow 3mm, light blue 3mm, yellow 3mm, light blue 3mm, yellow 3mm, red 6mm, yellow 1˚mm. Device on the service bar is a gold eagle with shield on breast and holding swords.

Second Class

Purpose: For NCO's and enlisted men.

Description: Silver. The ribbon is 7˚mm, yellow 3mm, light blue 3mm, yellow 3mm, light blue 3mm, yellow 3mm, light blue 3mm, yellow 3mm, red 7˚mm. Device on the service bar is a silver eagle with shield on its breast and holding swords. This medal without the ribbon devices was widely presented to U.S. officers and men after six months staff service in combat or non combat units. The award was orginally entitled in French as *La Medaille du Merite Vietnamien* and was intended for "French or foreign military men who participate in the capacity of advisors or contribute to organization of the National Army. There are French made verisons and American made verisons which most closely follow the orginal Vietnamese design. Large images of the medals are Vietnamese while miniature medals are American made.

❖ RVN Wound Medal

The Vietnam Wound Medal was a military decoration of South Vietnam established in 1950 and patterned after a French medal wound medal. The decoration was the South Vietnamese equivalent of the United States Purple Heart, and was awarded to any South Vietnamese military personnel who, were either killed or wounded in action against enemies of the Republic of Vietnam.

United States Air Force personnel are not authorized to wear the Vietnam Wound Medal on a military uniform since it duplicates the award of the the Purple Heart medal.

Many believed it was an authorized foreign award from the Republic of South Vietnam. **It is not.**

❖ RVN Staff Service Medal   *Two classes — May 12, 1964*

Purpose: Presented by the Republic of Vietnam for staff service to the Armed Forces evidencing outstanding initiative and devotion to duty.

Description: Front: A square fortress design, with bastions at each point, suspended from one point, with a sword and writing brush crossing underneath, and in the center a blue diamond with gold crossed rifles, wings and anchor symbol of the Armed Forces, 40mm.

First Class Purpose: For officers.
Description: The ribbon is green 3mm, diagonal red 7mm and white 3mm stripes 30mm, green 3mm.

Second Class Purpose: For NCO's and enlisted men.
Description: The ribbon is blue 3mm, diagonal red 7mm and white 3mm stripes 30mm, blue 3mm.

First Class   Second Class

Background: This was widely given to American advisors. The U.S. made version closely resembles the Vietnamese-made ones; one small detail of difference is that the sword and pen of the U.S. made one has a more squarish shape in contrast to the more sculptured shape of the Vietnamese-made one. It normally required at least six months duty with a Vietnamese unit for award to allied personnel. It is also occasionally referred to as the Staff Service Honor Medal.

❖ RVN Technical Service Medal *Two classes — June 5, 1964*

Anodized or Gold-Plated / Miniature Medal

Description: Front: gold, four aircraft propeller blades, 50mm across, interspersed with four ship's propeller blades, and between those eight white enameled rays, inside a planchet shaped as a gear, and in the center on a blue-green background—the Armed Forces insignia of wings, crossed rifles, and an anchor.

First Class Purpose: For officers.

Description: The ribbon is silver grey 5mm, red 2mm, silver grey 20mm, red 2mm, silver grey 5mm, and in the center two thread-like red stripes 1mm apart.

Second Class Purpose: For NCO's and enlisted men.

Description: The ribbon is the same except without the two thread-like red stripes in the center.

Purpose: Presented by the Republic of Vietnam for military servicemen and civilians working as military technicians who have shown outstanding professional capacity, initiative, and devotion to duty.

Background: This was also frequently awarded to American advisors. It is occasionally called the Technical Service Honor Medal.

❖ RVN Training Service Medal *Two classes — May 12, 1964*

First Class / Second Class

Description: Gold rectangle, 20mm wide and 50mm high. Front: sword surmounted with open book and with inscription at bottom.

First Class Purpose: For officers.

Description: The ribbon is white 3mm, pink 9mm, white 11mm with two thread-like pink stripes 1mm apart in center, pink 9mm, white 3mm.

Second Class Purpose: For NCO's and enlisted men.

Description: The ribbon is the same as the First Class, but without the two thread-like pink stripes in the center.

Purpose: Presented by the Republic of Vietnam for instructors and cadres at military schools and training centers and civilians and foreigners who contribute significantly to training.

Background: It is occasionally called the Training Service Honor Medal.

❖ RVN Civil Actions Medal Two classes — May 12 1964

Purpose: Presented by the Republic of Vietnam for outstanding achievements in the field of civil affairs.

Description: Front: eight-pointed gold star, with the points on the diagonal being smooth and long and the points on the horizontal and vertical being a little shorter and with cut lines, and in the center a brown disk with the figure of a soldier, a child, and a farmer with a shovel, surrounded with a white ribbon inscribed above with many short lines between, 30mm. Back: plain.

First Class Purpose: For officers.
Description: The ribbon is green 2mm, red 5mm, green 22mm with two thin thread-like red stripes in center 1mm apart, red 5mm, green 2mm.

Second Class Purpose: For NCO's and enlisted men.
Description: The ribbon is the same but without the two thread-like red stripes in center.
Unit Award Description: The ribbon is the same as for the First Class. It is in a gold frame with a leaf pattern.

Background: Particularly as a unit award, this was widely bestowed on the American forces in Vietnam. One US-made version closely resembles the Vietnamese-made ones except that the central disk is higher, the enamel neater, the gold brighter, and the reverse plain. It is occasionally called the Civic Actions Honor Medal.

❖ RVN Air Service Medal Four grades — May 12, 1964

Purpose: Presented by the Republic of Vietnam for a prescribed number of flight hours.
Description: Front: a six pointed gold star with cut lines on the points, and in the center a light blue globe surmounted with a gold jet plane, 36 mm. Suspension is by a gold pair of wings.
First Grade Purpose: For 1,000 flying hours.
Description: There is a small gold jet plane device on the suspension ribbon and service bar.
Second Grade Purpose: For 600 flying hours.
Description: There is a small silver jet plane device.
Third Grade Purpose: For 300 flying hours.
Description: There is a small bronze jet plane device.
Honor Grade
Purpose: For honorary bestowal on a member of another service or a foreign serviceman for a worthy mission involving 10 flights on a RVNAF or allied aircraft.
Description: There was a large wreath in gold, silver, or bronze. Or it is possible these may simply be for the above grades in a way done earlier, and the Honor Grade is simply without a device. Unfortunately, information on this is lacking.

Background: The categorization of the grades and devices is according to JGS/RVNAF Directive HT-655-425. The wreath devices for the suspension ribbon are quite large, about 22mm, but the jet plane devices are the same tiny ones used on the service bars.

Philippine Republic Presidential Unit Citation

Service All Services
Instituted 1948
Devices None
Criteria Awarded to units of the U.S. Armed Forces for service in the war against Japan and/or for 1970 and 1972 disaster relief.

Korean Republic Presidential Unit Citation

Service All Services
Instituted 1951
Devices None
Criteria Awarded to certain units of the U.S. Armed Forces for services rendered during the Korean War.

Republic of Vietnam Presidential Unit Citation

Service Army/Navy/Marine Corps/Coast Guard
Instituted 1954
Devices None
Criteria Awarded to certain units of the U.S. Armed Forces for humanitarian service in the evacuation of civilians from North and Central Vietnam.

Republic of Vietnam Gallantry Cross Unit Citation

Service All Services
Instituted 1966
Devices
Criteria Awarded to certain units of the U.S. Armed Forces for valorous combat achievement during the Vietnam War, 1 March 1961 to 28 March 1974.

Republic of Vietnam Civil Actions Unit Citation

Service All Services
Instituted 1966
Devices
Criteria Awarded to certain units of the U.S. Armed Forces for meritorious service during the Vietnam War, 1 March 1961 to 28 March 1974.

❖ United Nations Service Medal (Korea)

For service on behalf of the United Nations in Korea during the Korean Conflict. The United Nations Service Medal is classified as a foreign service award. It was authorized by the United Nations General Assembly on December 12, 1950 and the Department of Defense approved it for United States Armed Forces on November 27, 1951. The medal was awarded to any member of the United States Armed Forces for service in support of the United Nations Command during the period from June 27, 1950 to July 27, 1954. Individuals who were awarded the Korean Service Medal automatically established eligibility for this decoration.

Designed by the United Nations, the medal is a circular bronze disc containing the United Nations emblem (a polar projection of the world taken from the North Pole, encircled by two olive branches). The reverse of the medal has the raised inscription, "FOR SERVICE IN DEFENCE OF THE PRINCIPLES OF THE CHARTER OF THE UNITED NATIONS" set in five lines. The medal is suspended permanently from a bar, similar to British medals, with the raised inscription "KOREA." The ribbon passes through the bar and has narrow stripes of alternating light blue ("United Nations Blue") and white. For further information on United Nations medals, see *United Nations Medals and Missions by Lawrence H. Borts*, Medals of America Press, 1998.

Service	All Services
Instituted	1951
Devices	None
Criteria	Service on behalf of the United Nations in Korea between 27 June 1950 and 27 July 1954.
Notes	Above date denotes when award was authorized for wear by U.S. Armed Forces personnel.

❖ United Nations Medal

For six months service on behalf of the United Nations in one of twenty-seven missions.

The United Nations Medal is designated as a foreign service award. It was authorized by the United Nations General Assembly on July 30, 1959 and approved for wear on the U.S. military uniform by Executive Order on March 11, 1964. The medal is awarded to any member of the United States Armed Forces for not less than six months service in support of a United Nations mission.

Designed by the United Nations the medal is a bronze disc with the United Nations emblem (a polar projection of the world taken from the North Pole, encircled by two olive branches). Centered above this are the bold letters, "UN." The reverse of the medal contains the raised inscription, "IN THE SERVICE OF PEACE". The medallion for all UN operations is the same for all authorized operations. Originally the only UN ribbon authorized on the uniform but U.S. policy changed to permit the unique ribbon authorized for each United Nations operation to be worn. Individuals who participate in more than one UN operation wear only the first ribbon/medal for which they qualify but add a three-sixteenth inch bronze star for each subsequent award.

Service	All Services
Instituted	1964
Criteria	Six months service with any U.N. peacekeeping mission.
Devices	Bronze Star
Notes	Above date denotes when award was authorized for wear by U.S. Armed Forces personnel.

Participation in United Nations Missions by U.S. Armed Forces Personnel

Originally, U.S. military personnel serving with United Nations Missions were permitted to wear only two UN medals, the United Nations Korean Service Medal and the United Nations Medal (Item 1 and 2 below). However, changes in Department of Defense policy in 1996 authorized the wear of the ribbons of 11 missions on the US military uniform.

This was followed, in 2011, by the addition of 16 more to the list, which, along with the United Nations Special Service Medal, brought the total to 28. However, only one ribbon may be worn on the US military uniform and awards for any subsequent missions are denoted by the three-sixteenth inch bronze stars.

KOREA
United Nations Korean Service
Country/Location: Korea
Dates: 1950 - 1953

UNTSO
United Nations Truce Supervision Organization
Country/Location: Israel, Egypt
Dates: 1948 - Present

UNMOGIP
United Nations Military Observer Group in India/Pakistan
Country/Location: India, Pakistan
Dates: 1949 - Present

UNOGIL
United Nations Observer Group in Lebanon
Country/Location: Lebanon
Dates: 1958

UNSF/UNTEA
United Nations Security Force in West Guinea (West Irian)
Country/Location: West New Guinea (West Irian)
Dates: 1962 - 1963

UNIKOM
United Nations Iraq/Kuwait Observation Mission
Country/Location: Iraq/Kuwait
Dates: 1991 - 2003

MINURSO
United Nations Mission for the Referendum in Western Sahara
Country/Location: Morocco
Dates: 1991 to Present

UNAMIC
United Nations Advance Mission in Cambodia
Country/Location: Cambodia
Dates: 1991 -1992

UNPROFOR
United Nations Protection Force
Country/Location: Former Yoguslavia (Bosnia, Herzegovina, Croatia, Serbia, Montenegro, Macedonia
Dates: 1992 - 1995

UNTAC
United Nations Transitional Authority in Cambodia
Country/Location: Cambodia
Dates: 1992 - 1993

ONUMOZ
United Nations Operation in Mozambique
Country/Location: Mozambique
Dates: 1992 - 1994

UNOSOM II
United Nations Operation in Somalia II
Country/Location: Somalia
Dates: 1993 - 1995

UNOMIG
United Nations Observer Mission in Georgia
Country/Location: Georgia (Russia)
Dates: 1993 - 2009

UNMIH
United Nations Mission in Haiti
Country/Location: Haiti
Dates: 1993 - 1996

UNPREDEP
United Nations Prevention Deployment Force
Country/Location: Former Yugoslavia; Republic of Macedonia
Dates: 1995 - 1999

172 Decorations, Medals, and Ribbons of the United States Air Force

Participation in United Nations Missions by U.S. Armed Forces Personnel

UNTAES
United Nations Transitional Administration for Eastern Slavonia, Baranja and Western Sirmium
Country/Location: Croatia
Dates: 1996 - 1998

UNSMIH
United Nations Support Mission in Haiti
Country/Location: Haiti
Dates: 1996 - 1997

MINUGUA
United Nations Verification Mission in Guatemala
Country/Location: Guatemala
Dates: 1997-1997

UNMIK
United Nations Interim Administration Mission in Kosovo
Country/Location: Kosovo
Dates: 1999 - Present

UNTAET
United Nations Transitional Administration in East Timor
Country/Location: Timor (New Guinea)
Dates: 1999 - 2002

MONUC
United Nations Organization Mission in the Democratic Republic of the Congo
Country/Location: Congo
Dates: 1999 - 2010

UNMEE
United Nations Mission to Ethiopia and Eritrea
Country/Location: Ethiopia, Eritrea
Dates: 2000 - 2008

UNMISET
United Nations Mission of Support in East Timor
Country/Location: Timor (New Guinea)
Dates: 2000 - 2005

UNMIL
United Nations Mission in Liberia
Country/Location: Liberia (West Africa)
Dates: 2003 - Present

MINUSTAH
United Nations Stabilization Mission in Haiti
Country/Location: Haiti
Dates: 2004 - Present

UNAMID
United Nations / African Union Hybrid Operation in Darfur
Country/Location: Darfur (East Africa)
Dates: 2007 - Present

MINURCAT
United Nations Mission in the Central African Republic and Chad
Country/Location: Central African Republic, Chad (Central Africa)
Dates: 2007 - 2010

MONUSCO
United Nations Organization Stabilization Mission in the Democratic Republic of the Congo
Country/Location: Congo
Dates: 2010 - Present

UNSSM United Nations

UNAMI

Background: Established in 1994 by the Secretary General of the United Nations, the UNSSM is awarded to military and civilian personnel service in capacities other than established peace-keeping missions or those permanently assigned to UN Headquarters. The UNSSM may be awarded to eligible personnel service for a minimum of ninety (90) consecutive days under the control of the UN in operations or offices for which no other United Nations award is authorized. Posthumous awards may be granted to personnel otherwise eligible for the medal who died while serving under the United Nations before completing the required 90 days of service.

Clasps: Clasps engraved with the name of the country or United Nations organization (e.g.: UNHCR, UNSCOM, UNAMI, etc.) may be added to the medal suspension ribbon and ribbon bar.

❖ NATO Medals

Silver Bronze

The NATO Meritorious Service Medal was established in 2003 for military and civilian personnel commended for providing exceptional or remarkable service to NATO. The Medal is the personal Award of The Secretary General of NATO, who signs each citation. Generally fewer than 50 medals are awarded each year and it is the only significant award for individual effort on the NATO staff. It can be awarded to both Military and Civilian staff. The criteria for the award reflects: the performance of acts of courage in difficult or dangerous circumstances; showing exceptional leadership or personal example; making an outstanding individual contribution to a NATO sponsored programme or activity; or enduring particular hardship or deprivation in the interest of NATO.

Medal and Ribbon Descriptions

The ribbon and medal fabric is NATO Blue with white edges, with silver and gold threads centered on the white. The medal disc is of silver color, occassional you will see copies being sold with the regular brass medallion. The NATO Meritorious Service Medal is now authorised for wear on U.S. Military uniforms.

Former Yugoslavia NATO Medal (Kosovo) Medal Reverse

Miniature Medals

Service	All Services
Instituted	1992
Criteria	30 days service in or 90 days outside the former Republic of Yugoslavia and the Adriatic Sea under NATO command in direct support of NATO operations.
Devices	Bronze Star
Notes	Above date denotes when award was authorized for wear by U.S. military personnel. "Former Yugoslavia" and "Kosovo" Bars not authorized for wear by U.S. Military personnel.

Awarded to U.S. military personnel for service under the NATO command and in direct support of NATO operations. Recipients, as of this writing, may qualify for two NATO operations:

(1) Former Yugoslavia: 30 days service inside or 90 days outside the former Republic of Yugoslavia after July 1, 1992 to a date to be determined.

(2) Kosovo: 30 continuous/accumulated days in or around the former Yugoslavian province of Kosovo from October 13, 1998 to a date to be determined.

Multiple rotations or tours in either operational area will only qualify for a single award of that medal.

The NATO Medal, like the United Nations Medal, has a common planchet/pendant but comes with unique ribbons for each operation. As in the case of the United Nations, U.S. Service personnel who qualify for both NATO Medals will wear the first medal/ribbon awarded and a bronze service star on the ribbon bar and suspension ribbon to denote the second award. As before however, the two medal clasps which may accompany the medal. i.e., "FORMER YUGOSLAVIA and KOSOVO" may not be worn on the US military uniform.

The medal is a bronze disk featuring the NATO symbol in the center surrounded by olive branches around the periphery. The reverse contains the inscription, "NORTH ATLANTIC TREATY ORGANIZATION" in English around the top edge and the same wording in French along the lower edge. A horizontal olive branch separates the central area into two areas. Atop this, set in three lines, is the inscription, "IN SERVICE OF PEACE AND FREEDOM" in English. The same text in French on four lines is inscribed in the lower half.

❖ Article 5 NATO Medal

Eagle Assist (1) Active Endeavor (2)   Medal Reverse

Regulation Ribbon Bar

Service	All Services
Instituted	2002
Criteria	30 days service as part of Operation "Eagle Assist" (Medal 1) or Operation Active Endeavor (Medal 2).
Devices	None for Air Force Personnel
Notes	As per a memorandum issued by the Deputy Secretary of Defense dated 2 March 2006, the above medals are now authorized for wear on the uniform by U.S. military personnel.

❖ Non-Article 5 NATO Medal

Balkans Medal (3)   ISAF Medal (4)   Medal Reverse

Regulation Ribbon Bars

Service	All Services
Instituted	2002
Criteria	30 days service as part of NATO operations in the Balkans (Medal 3) of Afghanistan (Medal 4).
Devices	None for Air Force Personnel
Notes	As per a memorandum issued by the Deputy Secretary of Defense dated 2 March 2006, the above medals are now authorized for wear on the uniform by U.S. military personnel.

In November, 2002, the NATO Military Committee issued a new NATO Medal Policy in which two classes of service awards will now be issued, namely "Article 5" and "Non-Article 5". The reference is to Article 5 of the original NATO Charter Treaty in which the member nations agreed that an armed attack against any one of them in Europe or North America shall be considered an attack against them all and if such an armed attack occurs, each of them will take such action, including the use of armed force, to restore and maintain the security of the North Atlantic area. Non-Article 5 operations are those conducted as a peace support or crisis operation authorized by the North Atlantic Council.

To date, two Article 5 Medals have been issued by NATO, the first being for Operation "Eagle Assist" (Medal 1 above). Following the 9-11 attacks, NATO Early Warning (NAEW&C) aircraft were deployed from October 12, 2001 to May 16, 2002, to monitor the airspace over the United States to protect against further airborne attack by terrorists. The second award (Medal 2 above), is awarded to personnel who took part in Operation "Active Endeavor", the deployment of a NATO Standing Naval Force to patrol the Eastern Mediterranean against hostile forces.

That effort began on October 26, 2001 and will be terminated at a date to be announced in the future. In addition, two Non-Article 5 NATO have been authorized for U.S. military personnel.

The qualification period for the NATO Balkans Medal (Medal 3) is thirty days of continuous or accumulated service from January 1, 2003 to a date to be determined. The NATO medals for Afghanistan and Iraq (Medal 4) are also awarded for 30 days of service in country.

The medal designs are the same as all previous NATO Medals. As in the past, only one NATO Medal may be worn on the uniform with subsequent operations and/or tours indicated by bronze stars affixed to the center of the ribbon bar or suspension ribbons. Also as before, the mission bars depicted above may not be worn on the U.S. military uniform.

❖ Multinational Force and Observers Medal

Service	All Services
Instituted	1982
Criteria	6 months service with the Multinational Force & Observers peacekeeping force in the Sinai Desert.
Devices	Bronze numerals

The international peacekeeping force known as The Multinational Force and Observers (MFO) was established following the ratification of the Camp David Accords and the 1979 peace treaty between Israel and Egypt. Its sole purpose was to monitor the withdrawal of Israeli forces from the occupied portions of the Sinai Peninsula and the return of that territory to the sovereignty of Egypt.

The MFO Medal was established by the Director General on March 24, 1982 to recognize those personnel who served at least 90 days with the Multinational Force and Observers after August 3, 1981 (the requirement was changed to 170 days after March 15, 1985). Periods of service on behalf of the MFO outside the Sinai are also counted towards medal eligibility.

The medal is a bronze disk depicting a stylized dove of peace surrounded by olive branches in its center. Around the edge of the medallion are the raised inscriptions, "MULTINATIONAL FORCE" at the top and, "& OBSERVERS" on the lower half. The reverse is plain with the inscription, "UNITED IN SERVICE FOR PEACE" set on 5 lines (all inscriptions are in English).

The second and subsequent tours with the MFO are indicated by appropriate bronze numerals affixed to the center of the ribbon bar or suspension ribbon starting with the numeral "2"- the ribbon/medal itself representing the first award.

❖ Inter-American Defense Board Medal

Service	All Services
Instituted	1981
Criteria	Service with the Inter-American Defense Board for at least 1 year.
Devices	Gold Star

The medal and ribbon were authorized on December 11, 1945 by the Inter-American Defense Board, (IADB) and were approved by the U.S. Department of Defense for wear by U.S. military personnel on May 12, 1981. The IADB Medal is classified as a foreign service award and is awarded for permanent wear to military personnel who have served on the Inter-American Defense Board for at least one year, either as chairman of the board, delegates, advisors, officers of the staff, as officers of the secretariat or officers of the Inter-American Defense College. The medal is a golden-bronze circular disk with a representation of the globe of the world in the center depicting the Western Hemisphere. Around the periphery of the globe are the arrayed the flags of the member nations of the IADB. The reverse of the medal is plain. A five-sixteenth inch diameter gold star device is worn on the ribbon bar and the suspension ribbon for each five years of service to the IADB.

In the United States, the Inter-American Defense Board Medal was only recognized as a military award in May 1981. Since that time, the Inter-American Defense Board Medal had been approved for wear on United States military uniforms, ranking below United States decorations and before the military awards of individual foreign countries.

USAF F-4Ds over Vietnam

❖ Republic of Vietnam Campaign Medal

Regulation Ribbon Bar

Miniature Medals

Anodized or Gold-Plated Medal Reverse

Service	All Services
Instituted	1966
Devices	Bar inscribed "1960-"
Criteria	6 months service in the Republic of Vietnam between 1965 and 1973 or if wounded, captured or killed in action during the above period.
Notes	Bar inscribed "1960-" is the only authorized version.

The Republic of Vietnam Campaign Medal was established by the Government of the Republic of Vietnam on May 12, 1964 and authorized for award to members of the United States Armed Forces by the Department of Defense on June 20, 1966. To qualify for award, personnel must meet one of the following requirements:

(1) Have served in the Republic of Vietnam for 6 months during the period from March 1, 1961 to March 28, 1973.

(2) Have served outside the geographical limits of the Republic of Vietnam and contributed direct combat support to the Republic of Vietnam and Armed Forces for six months. Such individuals must meet the criteria established for the Armed Forces Expeditionary Medal (Vietnam) or the Vietnam Service Medal, during the period of service required to qualify for the Republic of Vietnam Campaign Medal.

(3) Have served for less than six months and have been wounded by hostile forces, captured by hostile forces, but later escaped, was rescued or released or killed in action.

Special eligibility rules were established for personnel assigned in the Republic of Vietnam on January 28, 1973. To be eligible for the medal, an individual must have served a minimum of 60 days in the Republic of Vietnam as of that date or have completed a minimum of 60 days service in the Republic of Vietnam during the period from January 28, 1973 to March 28, 1973, inclusive.

The Republic of Vietnam Campaign Medal is a white six-pointed star with cut lined, broad gold star points between and a central green disk with a map of Vietnam in silver surmounted with three painted flames in red, signifying the three regions of Vietnam. The reverse contains the inscription, "VIET-NAM" in a lined circle in the center with the name of the medal inscribed in Vietnamese text at the upper and lower edges separated by many short lines. The device, an integral part of the award, is a silver ribbon 28mm long on the suspension ribbon and 15mm long on the service bar inscribed, "1960- " and was evidently intended to include a terminal date for the hostilities. Many examples of this medal are found with devices inscribed with other dates but this is only version authorized for U.S. personnel.

❖ Saudi Arabian Medal for the Liberation of Kuwait

Anodized or Gold-Plated

Regulation Ribbon Bar

Medal Reverse

Miniature Medals

Established in 1991 by the Government of Saudi Arabia for members of the Coalition Forces who participated in Operation DESERT STORM and the liberation of Kuwait. In the same year, the U.S. Defense Department authorized the acceptance and wearing of the Kuwait Liberation Medal by members of the Armed Forces of the United States.

Service	All Services
Instituted	1991
Criteria	Participation in, or support of, Operation Desert Storm. (Jan. - Feb. 1991)
Devices	Gold Palm with crossed swords

To be eligible, U.S. military personnel must have served for at least one day in support of Operation DESERT STORM between January 17 and February 28, 1991 in The Persian Gulf, Red Sea, Gulf of Oman, portions of the Arabian Sea, The Gulf of Aden or the total land areas of Iraq, Kuwait, Saudi Arabia, Oman, Bahrain, Qatar and the United Arab Emirates. The recipient must have been attached to or regularly serving for one or more days with an organization participating in ground and/or shore operations, aboard a naval vessel directly supporting military operations, actually participating as a crew member in one or more aerial flights supporting military operations in the areas designated above or serving on temporary duty for 30 consecutive days during this period. That time limitation may be waived for people participating in actual combat operations.

The medal depicts the map of Kuwait in the center with a crown at its top between two encircling palm branches, all of which is fashioned in gold. Above this is a gold palm tree surmounted by two crossed swords. Surrounding the entire design is a representation of an exploding bomb in silver. The reverse is plain. The ribbon bar is issued with a replica of the palm tree with crossed swords found on the medal and is the only authorized attachment.

178 Decorations, Medals, and Ribbons of the United States Air Force

An F-16C Fighting Falcon fighter aircraft from the 388th Tactical Fighter Wing, Hill Air Force Base, Utah, is prepared for a strike against targets in Iraq and Kuwait during Operation Desert Storm.

(USAF Photo)

❖ Kuwait Liberation Medal (Emirate of Kuwait)

Regulation Ribbon Bar

Bronze   Medal Reverse   Miniature Medals

Service	All Services
Instituted	1995
Devices	None
Criteria	Participation in, or support of, Operations Desert Shield and/or Desert Storm (1990-93).
Notes	Above date denotes when award was authorized for wear by U.S. military personnel.

Established in July, 1994 by the Government of Kuwait for members of the United States military who participated in Operations DESERT SHIELD and DESERT STORM. On March 16, 1995, the Secretary of Defense authorized the acceptance and wearing of the Kuwait Liberation Medal (Kuwait) by members of the Armed Forces of the United States. To be eligible, U.S. military personnel must have served in support of Operations DESERT SHIELD and DESERT STORM between August 2, 1990 and August 31, 1993, in The Arabian Gulf, Red Sea, Gulf of Oman, portions of the Arabian Sea , The Gulf of Aden or the total land areas of Iraq, Kuwait, Saudi Arabia, Oman, Bahrain, Qatar and the United Arab Emirates. The recipient must have been attached to or regularly serving for one or more days with an organization participating in ground and/or shore operations, aboard a naval vessel directly supporting military operations, actually participating as a crew member in one or more aerial flights directly supporting military operations in the areas designated above or serving on temporary duty for 30 consecutive days or 60 nonconsecutive days during this period. That time limitation may be waived for people participating in actual combat operations. The Kuwait Liberation Medal (Kuwait) follows the Kuwait Liberation Medal from the government of Saudi Arabia in the order of precedence. The medal is a bronze disk which depicts the Kuwaiti Coat of Arms with the Arabic inscription, "1991 - Liberation Medal." The reverse contains a map of Kuwait with a series of rays emanating from the center out to the edge of the medal - all in bas-relief. The ribbon bar may be one of the most unusual ever displayed on the American military uniform. It consists of three equal stripes of red, white and green with a black, trapezoidal-shaped section silk-screened across the entire upper half. No attachments are authorized for the medal or ribbon.

(USAF Photo)

USAF Photo

❖ Republic of Korea War Service Medal

Regulation Ribbon Bar

Miniature Medals

Bronze   Anodized or Gold-Plated   Medal Reverse

The Republic of Korea War Service Medal was established in 1951 by the Government of the Republic of Korea for presentation to the foreign military personnel who served on or over the Korean Peninsula or in its territorial waters between June 27, 1950 and July 27, 1953. However, it was not approved for acceptance and wear until 1999. To be eligible for this award, U.S. military personnel must have been on permanent assignment or on temporary duty for 30 consecutive days or 60 non-consecutive days. The duty must have been performed within the territorial limits of Korea, in the waters immediately adjacent thereto or in aerial flight over Korea participating in actual combat operations or in support of combat operations. The 48 year interval between establishment and its formal acceptance represents the second longest period of time in U.S. history between an event of significant national and military importance and the establishment of an appropriate commemorative medal.

Service	All Services
Instituted	1953
Devices	Taeguk disk on ribbon
Criteria	Service on the Korean Peninsula between 1950 and 1953.
Notes	Not accepted by the United States Government for wear on the military uniform until 1999. *Some original 1953 medals had a taeguk in the center of the drape like the ribbon bar.

The medal is a bronze disk containing a map of the Korean Peninsula at top center over a grid of the world and olive branches on either side of the design. Below the map are two crossed bullets. In the center of the ribbon and earlier medal drapes (1950's), is an ancient oriental symbol called a taeguk (the top half is red and the bottom half is blue). The reverse contains the inscription, "FOR SERVICE IN KOREA" in English embossed on two lines with two small blank plaques on which the recipient's name may be engraved.

180   Decorations, Medals, and Ribbons of the United States Air Force

Examples of Air Force Korean War Medal Displays

Medals of America 181

Commemorative Medals

Long an American tradition dating back to the Revolution, today many veterans use Commemorative Medals to fill out their displays and highlight special events which they participated in. Commemoratives are not authorized for wear on the uniform but for personal display by veterans and families. The Commemoratives shown on this page and the next are just a few that are available for veterans and their families. These examples are of high quality and use the same military specification as official ribbons.

USAF Service Commemorative Medal

Air Force Service Commemorative Medal

Instituted: 1999

Qualifying Dates: 1947 - Present
Criteria: Struck to honor all who honorably served in the U.S. Air Force between 1947 and the present.

Combat Service Commemorative Medal

Combat Service Commemorative Medal

Qualifying Dates: 1941 to Present

Criteria: Struck to honor all Soldiers, Sailors, Marines and Airmen who served in an overseas combat theater or expeditionary combat operation.

Cold War Victory Commemorative Medal

Cold War Victory Commemorative Military Medal

Qualifying Dates: 1945 - 1991

Criteria: Struck to recognize any honorable military service between 2 Sept 1945 and 26 December 1991.

Victory over Japan VJ Commemorative Medal

Asiatic Pacific Victory Commemorative Medal

Qualifying Dates: 1941-1946

Criteria: Struck to honor all soldiers, sailors, marines and airmen who served in or supported the Pacific Theater.

World War II Commemorative Medal

World War II Victory Commemorative Medal

Qualifying Dates: 1941 - 1946

Criteria: Struck to honor all who served in the United States Armed Forces During WWII and those who worked in essential war industry.

Victory in Europe Commemorative Medal

WWII Europe-Africa-Middle East Commemorative Medal

Qualifying Dates: 1941-1946

Criteria: Struck to honor all soldiers, sailors, marines and airmen who served in the European, African and Middle Eastern Theaters during WWII.

Korean Defense Commemorative Medal

Korean Defense 50th Anniv Commemorative Medal

Qualifying Dates: 1950 - Present

Criteria: Commemorates 50 years in defense of South Korea and is for all military personnel who have served in South Korea or in direct support anytime between 1950 and Present.

USAF Outstanding Unit Award Commemorative Medal

Air Force Outstanding Unit Award Comm Medal

Criteria: Honors all airmen awarded the USAF Outstanding Unit Award Ribbon.

Guard and Reserve Mobilization Commemorative Medal

National Guard and Reserve Mobilization Comm Medal

Criteria: Honors all US Armed Forces who have been mobilized for active service since September 8, 1939 to present.

Foreign Expeditionary Service Commemorative Medal

Foreign Expeditionary Commeemorative Medal

Criteria: Honors all U.S. Armed Forces personnel who have been have deployed overseas as part of an expeditionary forces.

Air Guard and Reserve Commemorative Medal

National Guard and Reserve Service Commemorative Medal

Qualifying Dates: 1801-Present

Criteria: Designed to honor the devotion, loyalty and achievement of all who served in the United States Guard and Reserve Forces over the past 200 years.

American Defense Commemorative Medal

American Defense Service Commemorative Medal

Qualifying Dates: 1775 to Present

Criteria: To honor those who served at least 30 days in the United States Armed Forces during any period of service.

Air Combat Action Commemorative Medal

Air Combat Action Commemorative Medal

Instituted: 2004

Qualifying Dates: All Periods

Criteria: To honor all USAF aircrew members who served in air combat operations to include refueling operations.

Overseas Service Commemorative Medal

Overseas Service Commemorative Medal -

Qualifying Dates: 1918 to present.

Criteria: Struck to honor all Soldiers, Sailors, Marines and Airmen who served in an overseas theater or expeditionary operation outside the United States for 30 days or more.

Honorable Discharge Commemorative Medal

Honorable Discharge Commemorative Medal

Qualifying Dates: 1918 to ppresent.

Criteria: Struck to honor all Soldiers, Sailors, Marines,Airmen and Coast Guardmen who recieved an Honorable Discharge for service in Armed Forces of the United States.

Notes and Comments

An artist once told me it took two people to do a painting. One to paint and one to tell the artist when to stop. This book is like that. Where do you stop? It may be a little heavy on Vietnamese Air Force awards but maybe not. Commemorative Medals have come into such wide spread use for displays that to not mention them would be an emission. I may have missed some foreign awards that have been presented lately and if you notice that please let me know. A book like this is always a work in progress.

Bibliography

Borts, Lawrence. United Nations Medals and Missions, 1997.

Campbell, J. Duncan. Aviation Badges and Insignia of the United States Army, 1913-1946, 1977.

Dept. of Defense Manual DOD 1348.33M. Manual of Military Decorations and Awards, 1993.

Foster, Frank and Borts, Lawrence. U.S. Military Medals 1939 To Present, 9th ed.

Foster, Frank and Sylvester, John. The Decorations and Medals of the Republic of Vietnam and Her Allies,
1950-1975, 1995.

Kerrigan, E. American Medals and Decorations, 1990.

Maguire, Jon A. Silver Wings, Pinks and Greens, 1994.

Morgan, J.L. Pete American Military Patch Guide, 2014.

Official Guide to the Army Air Forces. Simon and Schuster, 1944.

Ogletree, Maj Larry. "The Missile Badge," 1996.

Oliver, Ray. "What's In A Name?," 1983.

Rosignoli, Guido. Badges and Insignia of World War II, 1980.

Smith, Richard W. Shoulder Sleeve Insignia of the U.S. Armed Forces, 1981.

Spink, Barry L. "A Chronology of the Enlisted Rank Chevron of the United Statess Air Force," 1992.

Strandberg, J.E. and Bender, R.J. The Call to Duty, 1994.

Strobaugh, Donald R. "U.S. Air Force Parachutist Insignia, 1956 - 1963." 1980.

U.S. Air Force Instruction 11-402 - Aviation Service, Aerocal Ratings and Badges, 2014.

U.S. Air Force Instruction 36-2803 - The Air Force Awards and Decorations Program, 2014.

U.S. Air Force Instruction 36-2903 - Dress and Personal Appearance of Air Force Personnel, 2014.

U.S. Air Force Instruction 36-2923 - Aeronautical, Duty, and Occupational Badges, 1994.

U.S. Air Force Regulation 35-5 - Missile Badges, 1966.

U.S. Air Force Regulation 50-43 - USAF Small Arms Marksmanship Badge, 2014.

U.S. Air Force Regulation 125-3. Security Police, 1975.

U.S. Air Force Regulation 900-21 - Air Weapons Controller Badge, 1985.

U.S. Air Force Regulation 900-39 - Explosive Ordnance Disposal Badge, 1978.

U.S. Air Force Regulation 900-48 - Awards, Ceremonies and Honors, 1982 & 1989.

U.S. Army Regulation 600-35, 1944.

U.S. Army Regulation 672-5 - Military Awards, 2010.

Warnock, A. Timothy. USAF Combat Medals, Streamers, and Campaigns, 1990.

Adjutant General of the Army - American Decorations 1862-1926, 1927

Belden, B.L. - United States War Medals, 1916

Borts, L.H. - United Nations Medals and Missions, 1998

Committee on Veterans' Affairs, U.S. Senate - Medal of Honor Recipients 1863-1978, 1979

Dept. of Defense Manual DOD 1348.33M - Manual of Military Decorations & Awards, 1996, Change 1 (2006)

Dorling, H.T. - Ribbons and Medals, 1983

Foster, F.C. - Complete Guide to United States Army Medals, Badges and Insignia, 2004

Gleim, A.F. - United States Medals of Honor 1862-1989, 1989

Gleim, A.F. - War Department Gallantry Citations for Pre W W I Service, 1986

Inter-American Defense Board- Norms for Protocol, Symbols, Insignia and Gifts, 1984

Kerrigan, E. - American Badges and Insignia, 1967

Kerrigan, E. - American Medals and Decorations, 1990

Kerrigan, E. - American War Medals and Decorations, 1971

Lelle, John E. - The Brevet Medal, 1988

Mayo, J.H. - Medals and Decorations of the British Army & Navy, 1897

National Geographic Magazine, December, 1919

National Geographic Society - Insignia and Decorations of the U.S. Armed Forces, 1944

Uniforms, Flags and Insignia of South Vietnam 1971 translated by Duong Tam Chi

U.S. Air Force Instruction 36-2903 - Dress and Personal Appearance of U.S.A.F. Personnel, 18 July 2011

U.S. Air Force Instruction 36-2803 - The Air Force Awards andDecorations Program, June, 2001

U.S. Army Regulation 670 -1- Wear and Appearance of Army Uniforms and Insignia, 2005

U.S. Army Regulation 600-8-22- Military Awards, 2006

Vietnam Council on Foreign Relations - Awards & Decorations of Vietnam, 1972

Wilkins, P.A. - The History of the Victoria Cross, 1904

Wyllie, Col. R.E. - Orders, Decorations and Insignia, 1921

Wikipedia® is a registered trademark of the Wikimedia Foundation, Inc.

INDEX

Achievement Medal:
    Aerial 54,57,58, 102
    Air Force 54,57,58, 102
    Army 58
    Army Reserve Components 58
    Coast Guard 58
    Joint Service 54,57,58, 107
    Navy and Marine Corps 58
Active Endeavor Medal (NATO) 54,57,58, 174
Actual Size Military Medal Variations 27
Additional Award and Campaign Devices (text) 62,65
Aerial Achievement Medal 102
World War II Occupation Medals 54,58, 133
Afghanistan Campaign Medal (U.S.) 54,57,58, 146
Afghanistan Medal (NATO) 58,174
Air and Space Campaign Medal, Air Force 57, 156
Air Force Achievement Medal 54,57,58, 108
Air Force Air and Space Campaign Medal 57, 156
Air Force Basic Military Training Honor Graduate Ribbon ... 57,161
Air Force Combat Readiness Medal 57,116
Air Force Combat Action Medal 57,109
Air Force Commendation Medal 57,101
Air Force Cross 57,76
Air Force Distinguished Service Medal 57,80
Air Force Expeditionary Service Ribbon 57,158
Air Force Gallant Unit Citation 57, 112
Air Force Good Conduct Medal 57, 119
Air Force Longevity Service Award Ribbon 57, 159
Air Force Medal of Honor 57, 68
Air Force Meritorious Unit Award 57, 113
Air Force Military Training Instructor Ribbon 57, 160
Air Force N.C.O. Professional Military Education
    Graduate Ribbon 57, 161
Air Force Organizational Excellence Award 57, 113
Air Force Outstanding Airman of the Year Ribbon .. 57, 121
Air Force Outstanding Unit Award 57, 113
Air Force Overseas Ribbon (Long Tour) 57, 158
Air Force Overseas Ribbon (Short Tour) 57, 158
Air Force Presidential Unit Citation 57, 111
Air Force Recognition Ribbon 57, 121
Air Force Recruiter Ribbon 57, 160
Air Force Ribbons and Devices (Precedence chart) 57
Air Force Small Arms Expert Marksmanship Ribbon 57, 162
Air Force Special Duty Ribbon 57, 159
Air Force Training Ribbon 57, 162
Air Medal 57, 100
Air Medal Devices (text) 100
Air Reserve Forces Meritorious Service Medal 57, 120
Airman's Medal 57, 91
American Campaign Medal 57,125
American Defense Service Medal 57,124
American Defense Service Medal (clasps/devices) 124
Andre Medal 4
Antarctic Expedition Medal, U.S., (1939-1941) 58
Antarctica Service Medal 57, 137
Antarctica Service Medal (bars/devices) 137
Arctic Service Medal (Coast Guard) 58
Arctic Service Ribbon (Navy, Marine Corps) 58
Armed Forces Expeditionary Medal 57, 138
Armed Forces Honor Medal, Republic of Vietnam 168
Armed Forces Reserve Medal 57, 155
Armed Forces Ribbon Devices 65

Armed Forces Service Medal 57,153
Army Achievement Medal 58
Army Commendation Medal 58,104
Army Distinguished Service Cross 54,74
Army Distinguished Service Medal 54,79
Army Good Conduct Medal 54, 117
Army Good Conduct Medal (clasps/bars) 117
Army Medal of Honor 69
Army Meritorious Unit Commendation 54,110
Army N.C.O. Professional Development Ribbon 58
Army of Occupation of Germany Medal (World War I) ... 54,122
Army of Occupation Medal (World War II) 57, 133
Army of Occupation Medal (World War II) (clasps/bars) ... 130, 184
Army Overseas Service Ribbon 58
Army Presidential Unit Citation 58, 110
Army Reserve Components Achievement Medal 58
Army Reserve Components Overseas Training Ribbon ... 58
Army Sea Duty Ribbon 58
Army Service Ribbon 58
Army Superior Unit Award 58
Army Valorous Unit Award 58
Asiatic-Pacific Campaign Medal 57, 128
Background of United States Air Force Military Awards 1
Badge of Military Merit (Purple Heart) 4,94
Balkans Medal (NATO) 174
Basic Military Training Honor Graduate Ribbon,
    Air Force 57,161
Basic Training Honor Graduate Ribbon, Coast Guard 58
Bicentennial Unit Commendation, Coast Guard 58
Bosnia (Former Yugoslavia) Medal (NATO) 174
Bronze Star Medal 57,93
Bronze Letter "V" (text) 63
Bronze Letter "V", Usage Variations (table) 65
Campaign Medal, Republic of Vietnam 57,177
Ceremonial Guard Ribbon, Navy 58
China Service Medal 58
Civil Actions Medal, Republic of Vietnam 171
Civil Actions Unit Citation, Republic of Vietnam ... 54,170
Civil War, (1861-65) (text) 7
Civil War Campaign Medal (Army) 8,54
Claiming or Replacing Medals 40
Classic U.S. Armed Forces Displays 32
Coast Guard Achievement Medal 58
Coast Guard Arctic Service Medal 58
Coast Guard Basic Training Honor Graduate Ribbon 58
Coast Guard Bicentennial Unit Commendation 58
Coast Guard Combat Action Ribbon 58
Coast Guard Commandant's Letter of
    Commendation Ribbon 58
Coast Guard Commendation Medal 58
Coast Guard Distinguished Service Medal 58
Coast Guard "E" Ribbon 58
Coast Guard Enlisted Person of the Year Ribbon 58
Coast Guard Expert Pistol Shot Medal 58
Coast Guard Expert Rifleman Medal 58
Coast Guard Good Conduct Medal 58
Coast Guard Medal 58
Coast Guard Meritorious Team Commendation 58
Coast Guard Meritorious Unit Commendation 58
Coast Guard Overseas Service Ribbon 58
Coast Guard Pistol Marksmanship Ribbon 58

Coast Guard Presidential Unit Citation	58
Coast Guard Reserve Good Conduct Medal	58
Coast Guard Recruiting Service Ribbon	58
Coast Guard Restricted Duty Ribbon	58
Coast Guard Rifle Marksmanship Ribbon	58
Coast Guard Sea Service Ribbon	58
Coast Guard Special Operations Service Ribbon	58
Coast Guard Unit Commendation	58
Cold War (1945-1991) (text)	17
Cold War Recognition Certificate	41
Combat Action Medal (Air Force)	57, 109
Combat Action Ribbon (Coast Guard)	58
Combat Action Ribbon (Navy & Marine Corps)	58
Combat Readiness Medal (Air Force)	45, 116
Commandant's Letter of Commendation Ribbon, Coast Guard	58
Commemorative Medals - 225 Years of American Tradition	184
Commemorative Medals (Unofficial)	184
Commendation Medal:	
Air Force	57, 105
Congressional Medal of Honor: see: "Medal of Honor"	
Correct Wear of Multi-Service Awards on the Uniform	58
Croix de Guerre (France)	166
Croix de Guerre (Belgium)	166
Defense Board Medal, Inter-American	57, 178
Defense Distinguished Service Medal	57, 78
Defense Meritorious Service Medal	57, 97
Defense Ribbon/Medal, Philippine Republic	57, 164
Defense Service Medal, Korea	57, 152
Defense Superior Service Medal	57, 84
Different Forms of a Military Medal	26
Display of Appurtenances	62, 64
Display Case Tells the Story	32
Display Cases	32
Distinguished Flying Cross	57, 88
Distinguished Flying Cross, United Kingdom	165
Distinguished Service Cross, Army	72, 75
Distinguished Service Medal:	
Air Force	57, 80
Army	54, 79
"E" Ribbon, Coast Guard	58
"E" Ribbon, Navy	58
Eagle Assist Medal (NATO)	57, 174
Early United States Military Medals	4
European-African-Middle Eastern Campaign Medal	57, 130
Expeditionary Medal:	
Armed Forces	57, 138
Global War on Terrorism	57, 150
Expeditionary Service Ribbon, Air Force	57, 158
Expert Marksmanship Ribbon, Air Force Small Arms	57, 162
Expert Pistol Shot Medal, Coast Guard	58
Expert Pistol Shot Medal, Navy	58
Expert Rifleman Medal, Coast Guard	58
Expert Rifleman Medal, Navy	58
Fidelity Medallion ("Andre" Medal)	4
French Croix de Guerre (World War II)	166
Gallant Unit Citation, Air Force	57, 112
Gallantry Cross Air, Republic of Vietnam	168
Gallantry Cross Unit Citation, Republic of Vietnam	57, 170
GlobalWar on Terrorism (2001- present) (text)	25

Global War on Terrorism Expeditionary Medal	57, 150
Global War on Terrorism Service Medal	57, 151
Gold Lifesaving Medal (Coast Guard)	58
Good Conduct Medal:	
Air Force	57, 119
Army	54, 117
Army (clasps/bars)	117
Coast Guard	58
Coast Guard Reserve	58
Marine Corps	58
Navy	58
Gulf War (1991-1995) (text)	22
History of U.S. Armed Forces Decorations, Unit Awards and Service Ribbons (chart)	54
Honor Graduate Ribbon, Air Force Basic Military Training	57, 161
Honor Graduate Ribbon, Coast Guard, Basic Training	58
How Medals are Worn and Displayed:	
U.S. Air Force	28, 32, 44
How Medals are Worn and Displayed by Veterans	50
How to Determine a Veteran's Military Medals	28
Humane Action, Medal for	57, 154
Humanitarian Service Medal	57, 154
Independence Ribbon/Medal, Philippine	57, 162
Institute of Heraldry, The	192
Inter-American Defense Board Medal	176
Iraq Campaign Medal	57, 148
Issue of U.S. Medals to Veterans, Retirees & Families	40
"Japan" Clasp (Army)	117
Joint Meritorious Unit Award	57, 112
Joint Service Achievement Medal	57, 107
Joint Service Commendation Medal	57, 103
Knotted Bar/Clasp, Army Good Conduct Medal	117
Korea Defense Service Medal	57, 152
Korean Presidential Unit Citation	57, 170
Korean Service Medal, United Nations	57, 171
Korean Service Medal (U.S.)	57, 136
Korean War (1950-1953) (text)	18
Korean War Service Medal (Republic of Korea)	57, 180
Kosovo Campaign Medal (U.S.)	57, 144
Kosovo Medal (NATO)	174
Kuwaiti Medal for the Liberation of Kuwait	57, 179
Legion of Merit	57, 85
Legion of Merit for Foreign Armed Forces	86, 87
Letter of Commendation Ribbon Coast Guard Commandant's	58
Liberation of Afghanistan, Iraq & War on Terrorism	22
Liberation of Kuwait, Medal for:	
Emirate of Kuwait	57, 179
Saudi Arabia	57, 178
Liberation Ribbon/Medal, Philippine	57, 162
Lifesaving Medal, Gold	59
Lifesaving Medal, Silver	59
Longevity Service Award Ribbon, Air Force	57, 159
Marine Corps Expeditionary Medal	58
Marine Corps Drill Instructor Ribbon	58
Marine Corps Good Conduct Medal	58
Marine Corps Recruiting Ribbon	58
Marine Security Guard Ribbon	58
Medal for Humane Action	57, 154

Medal for the Liberation of Kuwait:	
Emirate of Kuwait	57, 179
Saudi Arabia	57, 178
Medal of Honor, The	68
Medal of Honor, Air Force	57, 70
Medal of Honor, Army	7, 69
Medal of Honor, Navy	68
Meritorious Service Medal	57, 98
Meritorious Service Medal:	
Defense	57, 97
Air Reserve Forces	57, 120
Meritorious Unit Award:	
Air Force	57, 113
Joint	57, 112
Meritorious Unit Commendation:	
Army	54, 58, 112
Coast Guard	58
Navy	58
Mexican Border Service Medal (Army)	54, 122
Mexican Service Medal (Army)	54, 122
Military Medal Variations, Actual Size	27, 43
Military Society Medals (1865-1913) (text)	5, 6
Military Training Instructor Ribbon, Air Force	57, 159
Multinational Force and Observers Medal	57, 176
Multi-Service Awards, Correct Wear on the Uniform	58
N.C.O. Professional Development Ribbon, Army	58
N.C.O. Professional Military Education	
Graduate Ribbon, Air Force	57, 161
National Defense Service Medal	57, 135
NATO Medals (1998-present) (text)	18
NATO Medals:	
Article 5 Medal for Active Endeavor	57, 175
Article 5 Medal for Eagle Assist	57, 175
Medal for Former Yugoslavia (Bosnia)	57, 174
Medal for Kosovo	57, 174
Medal Meritorious Service	57, 174
Non-Article 5 Medal for Afghanistan & Iraq	57, 175
Non-Article 5 Medal for the Balkans	57, 175
Navy and Marine Corps Achievement Medal	58
Navy and Marine Corps Commendation Medal	58
Navy and Marine Corps Medal	58
Navy and Marine Corps Overseas Service Ribbon	58
Navy Arctic Service Ribbon	58
Navy Ceremonial Guard Ribbon	58
Navy Combat Action Ribbon	58
Navy Cross	58
Navy "E" Ribbon	58
Navy Expeditionary Medal	58
Navy Expert Pistol Shot Medal	58
Navy Expert Rifleman Medal	58
Navy Fleet Marine Force Ribbon	58
Navy Good Conduct Medal	58
Navy Meritorious Unit Commendation	58
Navy Presidential Unit Citation	58
Navy Recruit Training Service Ribbon	58
Navy Recruiting Service Ribbon	58
Navy Rifle Marksmanship Ribbon	58
Navy Sea Service Deployment Ribbon	58
Navy Unit Commendation	58
North Atlantic Treaty Organization: see: "NATO"	
Occupation Medal, World War I	54, 123
Occupation Medals, World War II	57, 133

Occupation Medals, World War II (claps/bars)	133
Order of Precedence (text)	56
Order of Precedence (chart):	
Air Force	57
Organizational Excellence Award, Air Force	57, 113
Outstanding Airman of the Year Ribbon, Air Force	57, 121
Outstanding Unit Award, Air Force	57, 113
Outstanding Volunteer Service Medal	57, 155
Overseas Ribbon, Air Force (Long Tour)	57, 158
Overseas Ribbon, Air Force (Short Tour)	57, 158
Overseas Service Ribbon, Army	58
Overseas Service Ribbon, Coast Guard	58
Overseas Service Ribbon, Navy & Marine Corps	58
Overseas Training Ribbon, Army Reserve Components	58
Philippine Defense Ribbon	57, 162
Philippine Independence Ribbon	57, 163
Philippine Liberation Ribbon	57, 162
Philippine Presidential Unit Citation	57, 170
Pistol Marksmanship Ribbon. Coast Guard	58
Pistol Marksmanship Ribbon, Navy	58
Placement of Devices on the Ribbon	62, 63, 64, 65
Precedence Charts:	
Air Force	57
Presidential Unit Citation:	
Air Force	57, 110
Army	54, 109
Coast Guard	58
Navy	58
Republic of Korea	57, 170
Republic of the Philippines	57, 170
Republic of Vietnam	57, 170
Prisoner of War Medal	57, 114
Proper Wear of U.S. Ribbons and Medals	40, 42
Purple Heart	4, 5, 54, 57, 94-96
Pyramid of Honor	42
Recognition Ribbon, Air Force	57, 122
Recruiter Ribbon, Air Force	57, 160
Replacing U.S. Medals	40
Republic of Korea Presidential Unit Citation	57, 170
Republic of Korea War Service Medal	57, 180
Republic of the Philippines Awards:	
Defense Ribbon/Medal	57, 162
Independence Ribbon/Medal	57, 163
Liberation Ribbon/Medal	57, 162
Presidential Unit Citation	57, 170
Republic of Vietnam Awards:	
Distinguished Service Order	165
Meritorious Service Medal	165
Air Gallantry Cross	166
Armed Forces Honor Medal	166
Wound Medal	167
Staff Service Medal	167
Technical Service Medal	168
Training Service Medal	168
Air Service Medal	171
Campaign Medal	177
Civil Actions Medal	171
Civil Actions Unit Citation	172
Gallantry Cross Unit Citation	172
Presidential Unit Citation	172
Reserve Medal, Armed Forces	57, 160
Ribbon Chest Display (Precedence Charts):	

Air Force	57
Ribbon Devices, Armed Forces	62-65
Saudi Arabian Medal for the Liberation of Kuwait	57, 178
Silver Lifesaving Medal (Coast Guard)	58
Silver Star (Medal)	57, 82-83
Small Arms Expert Marksmanship Ribbon, Air Force	57, 161
Soldier's Medal	54, 90
Southwest Asia Service Medal	57, 142
Stolen Valor Act	66
Superior Service Medal, Defense	57, 84
Superior Unit Award, Army	58
Training Ribbon, Air Force	57, 161
Types of Military Medals, Ribbons and Devices	26
U.S. Air Force Awards: see listings under: "Air Force"	
Unclaimed U.S. Medals, Obtaining	40-41
Unit Award:	
Air Force Meritorious	57, 113
Air Force Outstanding	57, 113
Joint Meritorious	57, 112
Unit Citation, Air Force Gallant	57, 112
Republic of Korea	57, 170
Republic of the Philippines	57, 170
Republic of Vietnam	57, 170
Unit Citation, Republic of Vietnam:	
Civil Actions	57, 170
Gallantry Cross	57, 170
United Nations Medal	57, 58, 171-173
United Nations Medals Currently Authorized for U.S. Personnel	57, 58, 171-173
United Nations Missions Participated in by United States Military Personnel	171-173
United Nations Service Medal ("Korea")	57, 58, 171
Usage Variations of the Bronze Letter "V" (table)	65
Veterans' Military Medals	28
Veterans Pride Initiative	192
Victory Medal, World War I	54, 123
Victory Medal, World War I (clasps/bars)	123
Victory Medal, World War II	57, 58, 132
Vietnam Republic Awards: See Republic of Vietnam	
Vietnam Service Medal (U.S.)	57, 140-141
Vietnam War (1961-1973) (text)	20
War on Terrorism, Global, Expeditionary Medal	57, 58, 150
War on Terrorism, Global, Service Medal	57, 58, 151
War Service Medal, Republic of Korea	57, 180
Wear of Devices on Ribbons (charts)	62-65
Wear of Medals, Insignia and the Uniform by Veterans, Retirees and Former Service Members	50
Wearing of Medals, Miniatures and Ribbons on Uniforms	42
Women's Army Corps Service Medal	54, 125
World War I (1917-1918) (text)	10
World War I Victory Medal	54, 123
World War I Victory Medal (clasps/bars)	123
World War II (1941-1945)	12
World War II Occupation Medals	57, 58, 132
World War II Occupation Medals (clasps/bars)	57, 58, 133
World War II Victory Medal	57, 58, 132
Yugoslavia (Bosnia) Medal (NATO)	58, 174

Medals of America 189

Bringing Order to U.S. Awards Design with the Institute of Heraldry

Heraldry Defined. Heraldry is a simple yet practical art and science that dates back to the 12th century. In simple terms, heraldry is the use of symbols, metals (gold & silver) and tinctures (colors) to identify a position, organization, or individual. It consists of the application of design techniques, using forms, symbols and colors within a framework of fixed terms, rules and principles to create a meaningful composition which is distinctive. The art is concerned with the combination of design elements and style of rendering; the science governs the selection and arrangement of words for description, the principles pertaining to the propriety of various elements of design, and rules or laws to be followed in the interest of maintaining the universal system.

Background. Although heraldic symbols have been used by the United States military since the late 18th century, its origin as a European custom discouraged widespread use. Heraldry was associated with royalty—the spirit of democracy that dominated this period of our history rejected such symbols. Consequently, there was no formal use or acceptance of heraldry in the early history of the United States.

On 17 June 1918, however, President Woodrow Wilson wrote to the Secretary of War, the Honorable Newton Baker, suggesting that the design of military medals be "artistically reconsidered by the official art commission." As a result of this correspondence, a Heraldic Program Office was created within the War Department General Staff to take responsibility for the coordination and approval of coats of arms, decorations and other insignia for Army organizations. In 1924, formal staff responsibility for specific military designs was delegated to the Quartermaster General.

As the need for symbolism expanded, the scope of heraldic services evolved into a sizable program. The expansion of the Army brought about by World War II significantly contributed to the growth of the program. In 1949, the Munitions Board—acting for the Army, Navy and Air Force—directed the Army to provide heraldic services to all military departments. The Army's heraldic responsibility expanded in 1957 through the enactment of Public Law 85-263, authorizing the Secretary of the Army to furnish heraldic services to the military departments and other branches of the federal government.

On 10 August 1960, Army General Order Number 29 established "The Institute of Heraldry" under the control of the Quartermaster General. The Institute is the only organization within the federal government devoted to the art and science of military heraldry and official symbolism. Upon reorganization of the Army in 1962, responsibility for the Heraldic Program was assigned to the Adjutant General's Office. In a continued effort to streamline organizational processes and increase efficiency, responsibility for the heraldic program moved from the Adjutant General to the Administrative Assistant to the Secretary of the Army in October 2004. The Institute celebrated its 50th anniversary in August 2010.

The mission of The Institute of Heraldry is to furnish heraldic services to the Executive Office of the President, the Department of Defense, and all other Federal agencies. The work of The Institute of Heraldry encompasses research, design, development, standardization, quality control, and other services which are fundamental to the creation and custody of official heraldic items. Such items include coats of arms, decorations, flags, streamers, agency seals, badges, and other types of insignia that are approved for use and/or display. The Institute of Heraldry also provides the general public with limited research and information services concerning heraldic insignia.

The Institute of Heraldry and the Commission of Fine Arts share a long and illustrious relationship in the design of official government insignia. This relationship was codified in law on 2 September 1957 when the 85th Congress passed an Act to amend title 10, United States Code, to authorize the Secretary of the Army to furnish heraldic services. Under provisions of the Act, the Commission of Fine Arts, upon request of the Institute of Heraldry, advises upon the merits of proposed designs for medals, insignia, seals and other significant emblems for the United States Government.

Special thanks to the Director of The Institute of Heraldry for providing the information on this page. The Institute of Heraldry is a national treasure. Their web site is an amazing source of information on military awards and insignia for all Americans.

America's Best Books on Military Medals

Best Selling Medals Book in the World!

Military Medals of the United States

Over 200,000 copies sold!

- Criteria for every medal listed in full detail with dates and campaigns.
- Color pictures of all U.S. Military Decorations, Service Medals, Marksmanship Medals and Ribbons, plus commonly presented foreign medals.
- Separate color ribbon displays in order of precedence for Army, Navy, Marines, Air Force, Coast Guard and Merchant Marine awards since 1939.
- Complete chapter on devices for awards and ribbons (cross indexed with medals).
- Complete section on wear and display of U.S. Military Medals for all Branches.
- Section on How To Claim Your Medals From the Government.

NEW Edition! 64 more pages! more color, more detail

192 pages

The Decorations, Medals, Badges and Insignia of the United States Army

Best Seller!

The most complete guide to United States Army Medals, ribbons, badges, rank, insignia, and patches from WW II to the present. Each medal, insignia and major combat patch shown in full color. All medals and ribbons described in detail to include campaigns. The most impressive and complete reference on US Army awards and insignia ever produced.

- Criteria and color pictures of all U. S. Army Decorations, Service Medals, and Ribbons, plus many foreign medals
- Complete order of precedence display for Army awards since 1939
- Details on devices of ribbons (cross indexed with medals) • Section on wear and display of Army Medals plus How To Claim Your Medals From the Government. 8 1/2 x 11, 184 pages, Order Today!

In e book, print on demand, softback or hardcover

The Decorations, Medals, Badges and Insignia of the United States Navy

The most complete guide to Navy Medals, ribbons, rank, ratings, and insignia from WW II to the present. Every medal, badge and insignia shown in full color with complete details to include campaigns. • Criteria and color pictures of all U.S. Navy Decorations, Service Medals, Ribbons, Insignia, Badges and Ratings • Complete color order of precedence for Navy awards since 1939 • Devices for awards and ribbons • Details on wear, display and claiming of U.S. Military Medals • 8 1/2" x 11" • 124 pages

All Books available on Amazon!

Medals of America 191

Veterans Pride Initiative

The Department of Veterans Affairs has issued a call to all veterans to express their patriotism and pride when observing Veterans Day and other major patriotic holidays by wearing the medals earned in their military service.

To show their pride in military service, former Secretary of Veterans Affairs Jim Nicholson urged veterans to wear their military medals on civilian clothes on national patriotic holidays.

The Secretary of Veterans' Affairs called it a great way to show our communities the spirit of American veterans and to remind neighbors of the service and sacrifice of those who guard democracy.

As we all joined to salute America's veterans and Armed Forces on Veterans Day, Memorial Day and the 4th of July, veterans are urged to wear their medals and show their pride while participating in public observations or just being with friends and family. Individuals' veteran medals tell a story of service in the cause of freedom that all Americans need to hear.

Q. What is the Veterans Pride Initiative?
A. The Veterans Pride Initiative encourages America's veterans to wear their medals or miniature replicas on civilian attire on patriotic national holidays. It is derived from an Australia and New Zealand tradition of wearing medals at ceremonies and marches on April 25, ANZAC (Australian and New Zealand Army Corps) Day.

Q. On what holidays does this initiative recommend veterans wear their medals?
A. It encourages veterans to wear decorations on Veterans Day, Memorial Day and the Fourth of July.

Q. How should the medals be worn?
A. Veterans wearing their decorations on their civilian clothing should place them over the left breast. Links to information - such as the correct placement of individual awards - are included on http://www.va.gov/veteranspride.

www.ingramcontent.com/pod-product-compliance
Lightning Source LLC
Chambersburg PA
CBHW042024100526
44587CB00029B/4287